THOMAS WRIGHT

NARRATIVES

OF

SORCERY AND MAGIC,

FROM THE MOST AUTHENTIC SOURCES

Volume 2

Elibron Classics
www.elibron.com

Elibron Classics series.

ISBN 1-4021-9401-3 (paperback)
ISBN 1-4021-1042-1 (hardcover)

This Elibron Classics Replica Edition is an unabridged facsimile of the edition published in 1851 by Richard Bentley, London.

NARRATIVES

OF

SORCERY AND MAGIC,

FROM THE MOST AUTHENTIC SOURCES.

BY

THOMAS WRIGHT, ESQ., M.A., F.S.A., &c.

CORRESPONDING MEMBER OF THE NATIONAL INSTITUTE OF FRANCE,
(ACADEMIE DES INSCRIPTIONS ET BELLES LETTRES.)

SECOND EDITION.

IN TWO VOLUMES.

VOL. II.

LONDON:
RICHARD BENTLEY, NEW BURLINGTON STREET.
1851.

CONTENTS

OF VOLUME THE SECOND.

SORCERY AND MAGIC.

CHAPTER XVIII.

ADVENTURES OF DOCTOR TORRALVA.

SPAIN had not in the sixteenth century ceased to be celebrated for its magicians, as we learn from a variety of allusions in writers of that and the subsequent periods. We have seen that it was then the country from which magical rings were procured, and that it was equally with other lands the scene of treasure-hunting and of witchcraft. Nor was it wanting in great magicians. One of these gave considerable celebrity to the village of Bargota, near Viana, in the diocese of Calahorra. The curé of Bargota, who is wèll known to every reader of the glorious romance of Cervantes, astonished the territories of Rioja and Navarre by his extraordinary feats. Among other exploits he was in the habit of transporting himself to distant countries, and returning in an incredibly short space of time. In this way he witnessed most of the remarkable occurrences of the wars in Italy at the commencement of the sixteenth century, in which Spain had a special interest, and he announced his intelligence the same day at Viana and Logroño. He was forewarned of each event by the demon, his familiar. The latter told him one day that the pope would that night die a violent death. It appears that his holiness had an intrigue with a lady whose husband held a high office in the papal court. The latter was afraid to complain openly, but he was none the less eager for revenge, and he joined with some desperate ruffians in a plot to take away the pope's life. The demon was of course rejoiced at the prospect of evil, but his friend the curé determined to cheat him and save the head of the church from the danger which threatened him. He pretended to be seized with an eager desire to proceed to Rome, that he might hear the rumours to which such a remarkable occurrence must give rise, and to witness the pope's funeral. The desire was no sooner expressed than it was gratified. On his arrival at the eternal city, the cure hastened to the papal palace, forced his way into the presence of the sovereign pontiff, and told him the whole particulars of the plot against his life, and thus defeated the designs of the conspirators. After having thus outwitted him, the curé wished to have no further intercourse with Satan; he made a voluntary confession to the pope, and in return for the signal service he had performed, his holiness gave him a full absolution. On his return, he was delivered, as a matter of form, into the custody of the inquisitors of Logrono, but he was acquitted, and restored to his liberty.

There lived at the same time a magician who gained far greater celebrity than the curé of Bargota, and who adopted the same extraordinary mode of travelling. This was doctor Eugenio Torralva, a physician in the family of the admiral of Castille.* Torralva was born at Cuença, but at the age of fifteen he was sent to Rome, where he became attached to the bishop of Volterra, Francesco Soderini, in the quality of a page. He now pursued with great earnestness the study of philosophy and medicine, under dom Cipion and the masters Mariana, Avanselo, and Maguera, until he obtained the degree of doctor in medicine. Under these teachers, Torralva learnt to have doubts of the immortality of the soul and the divinity of Christ, and made great advances in scepticism. About the year 1501, when he was already a practitioner in medicine at Rome, he formed a very intimate acquaintance with one master Alfonso, a man who had first quitted the Jewish faith for Mahomedanism, from which he had been converted to Christianity, and he had then finally adopted natural reli-

* Torralva, un grande hombre, y nigromante,
Medico, y familiar del almirante.
LUIS ÇAPATA, CARLO FAMOSO, canto xxviii.

The authority for the details of the history of this extraordinary personage is Llorente, who derived his information from the original papers relating to his trial, preserved in the archives of the inquisition. Part of the story is told rather differently in the metrical history of Capata.

gion or deism. This man's discourses overthrew the little faith that still remained in Torralva's mind, and he became a confirmed sceptic, although he appears to have concealed his opinions from the world, and perhaps he subsequently renounced them.

Among Torralva's friends at Rome was a dominican monk, called brother Pietro, who told him one day that he had in his service "an angel of the order of good spirits," named Zequiel, who was so powerful in the knowledge of the future and of hidden things that he was without his equal in the spiritual world, and of such a peculiar temper that, while other spirits made bargains with their employers before they would give them their services, Zequiel was so disinterested that he despised all considerations of this kind, and served only in friendship those who placed their confidence in him and deserved his attachment. The least attempt at restraint, brother Pietro said, would drive him away for ever.

Torralva's curiosity was excited, and when brother Pietro generously proposed to resign the familiar spirit to his friend, the offer was eagerly accepted. It appears that the person most concerned in this transaction made no objection to the change of masters, and at the summons of brother Pietro, Zequiel made his appearance, in the form of a fair young man, with light hair, and dressed in a flesh-coloured habit and black surtout. He addressed himself to Torralva, and said, "I will be yours as long as you live, and will follow you wherever you are obliged to go." From this time Zequiel appeared to Torralva at every change of the moon, and as often as the physician wanted his services, which was generally for the purpose of transporting him in a short space of time to distant places. In these interviews, the spirit took sometimes the semblance of a traveller, and sometimes that of a hermit. In his intercourse with Torralva, he said nothing contrary to Christianity, but accompanied him to church, and never counselled him to evil; from which circumstances the physician concluded that his familiar was a good angel. He always conversed in the Latin or Italian languages.

Rome had now become to Torralva a second country; but about the year 1502 he went to Spain, and subsequently he travelled through most parts of Italy, until he again fixed himself at Rome, under the protection of his old patron the bishop of Volterra, who had been made a cardinal on the 31st of May, 1503. With this introduction he soon obtained the favour of others of the cardinals, and rose to high repute for his skill in medicine. Having met at this time with some books on chiromancy, he became an eager student in that art, in the knowledge of which he subsequently surpassed most of his contemporaries. Torralva owed his medical knowledge partly to his familiar, who taught him the secret virtues of many plants, with which other physicians were not acquainted; and when the practitioner took exorbitant fees, Zequiel rebuked him, telling him that, since he had received his knowledge for nothing, he ought to impart it gratuitously. And when on several occasions Torralva was in want of money, he found a supply in his chamber, which he believed was furnished him by the good spirit, who, however, would never acknowledge that he was the secret benefactor who had relieved him from his embarrasment.

Torralva returned to Spain in 1510, and lived for some time at the court of Ferdinand the Catholic. One day Zequiel, whose informations were usually of a political character, told him that the king would soon receive disagreeable news. Torralva immediately communicated this piece of information to Ximenes de Cisneros, archbishop of Toledo, (who was subsequently raised to the dignity of cardinal, and made inquisitor general of Spain,) and the grand captain Gonzalo Fernandez de Cordova. The same day a courier arrived with dispatches from Africa, containing intelligence of the ill success of the expedition against the Moors, and of the death of don Garcia de Toledo, son of the duke of Alva, who commanded it.

Torralva seems to have made no secret of his intercourse with Zequiel. He had received his familiar from a monk, and the spirit is said to have shown himself to the cardinal of Volterra at the physician's wish; the latter now did not hesitate to acquaint the archbishop of Toledo and the grand captain how he came by his early intelligence. The archbishop earnestly desired to be permitted to have the same privilege as the Italian cardinal, and Torralva wished to gratify him, but Zequiel refused, though he softened his refusal by telling him to inform the archbishop that he would one day be a king, a prophecy which was believed to be fulfilled when he was made absolute governor of Spain and the Indies.

The physician was frequently favoured with revelations of this kind. On one occasion, when Torralva was at Rome, Zequiel told him that his friend, Pietro Margano, would lose his life if he went out of the city that day. He was not able to see him in order to warn him of his danger, and Pietro went out of Rome and was assassinated. Zequiel told him on another occasion that the cardinal of Sienna would end his life in a tragical manner, which was verified in 1517, after the judgment of pope Leo X. against him. Torralva re-established himself in Rome in 1513, and soon after his arrival he had a great desire to see his intimate friend Thomas de Becara, who was then at Venice; upon which Zequiel took him thither and back in so short a space of time that his absence was not perceived by his friends in Rome.

It was not long before he again returned to Spain, where, about the year 1516, the cardinal of Santa Cruz, don Bernardino de Carbajal, consulted him on a subject of some importance. A Spanish lady named Rosales had complained to don Bernardino that her nights were disturbed by a phantom which appeared in the form of a murdered man. The cardinal had sent his physician, Dr. Morales, who watched at night with the lady, but saw no apparition, although she gave him notice of its appearance, and pointed out the place where it stood. Don Bernardino hoped to know more of the matter by the means of Torralva, and he requested him to go with the physician Morales to pass the night in the lady's house. They went together, and an hour after midnight they heard the lady's cry of alarm, and went into her room, where, as before, Morales saw nothing. But Torralva, who was better acquainted with the spiritual world, perceived a figure resembling a dead man, behind which appeared another apparition in the form of a woman. He asked with a firm voice, "What dost thou seek here?" to which the apparition replied, "A treasure," and immediately disappeared. Torralva consulted Zequiel on this subject, and was informed that there was buried under the house the corpse of a man who had been stabbed to death with a poignard.

Torralva was soon at Rome again, and among his more intimate friends there was don Diego de Zuniga, a relative of the duke of Bejar, and brother to don Antonio, grand prior of the order of St. John in Castile. In 1519, the two friends returned to Spain together. On their way, at Barcelonetta near Turin, while they were walking and conversing with the secretary, Azevedo, (who had been adjutant-general of the Spanish armies in Italy and Savoy,) Azevedo and Zuñiga thought they saw something indefinable pass by Torralva's side He told them it was his angel Zequiel, who had approached him to whisper in his ear. Zuñiga had a great desire to see Zequiel, but Torralva could not prevail with the latter to show himself. At Barcelona, Torralva saw in the house of the canon. Juan Garcia, a book of chiromancy, and in the margin of one of the leaves was written a magical process to enable a person to gain money at play. Zuniga, who appears to have been a man of no very exalted morality, wished to make himself master of this art, and Torralva copied the characters, and told his friend that he must write them with his own hand on paper, using for ink the blood of a bat, and that the writing must be performed on a Wednesday, because that day was dedicated to Mercury. This charm he was to wear on his person when at play.

In 1520, Torralva went again to Rome. Being at Valladolid, he told Diego de Zuñiga of his intentions, informing him that he had the means of travelling there with extraordinary rapidity, that he had but to place himself astride on a stick, and he was carried through the air, guided by a cloud of fire. On his arrival at Rome, he saw the cardinal of Volterra and the grand prior of the order of St. John, who were very earnest with him that he should give them his familiar spirit. Torralva entreated Zequiel to comply with their wish, but in vain. In 1525, Zequiel recommended him to return to Spain, assuring him that he would obtain the place of physician to the infanta Eleanora, queen dowager of Portugal, and subsequently consort of François I. of France. Torralva obeyed the suggestion of his monitor, and obtained the promised appointment.

It was after his return to Spain, and before he obtained this appointment, that a circumstance occurred which added greatly to Torralva's celebrity. On the evening of the fifth of May, of the year last-mentioned, (1525,) the physician received a visit from Zequiel, who told him that Rome would be taken next day by the troops of the emperor,* and

* Capata, who gives an account of this voyage according to the popular tradition, makes Torralva leave the admiral's town

Torralva desired to be taken to Rome to see this important event. They left Valladolid together at eleven o'clock at night, on foot, as if to take a walk; but at a short distance from the town Zequiel gave his companion a stick full of knots, and said, "Shut your eyes, and fear nothing; take this in your hand, and no harm will happen to you." After a little time, at Zequiel's bidding, Torralva opened his eyes, and he found himself so near the sea that he could have touched the water with his hand; and the black cloud which had previously enveloped him gave place immediately to so bright a light, that he was afraid

of Medina de Rioseco instead of Valladolid. He says that Torralva was sitting pensive and sad in his chamber contemplating the sky, when Zequiel appeared to him, who is described thus:—

> " Zaqueil un familiar, qu'en la figura
> De un viejo sano ant'el se aparescia,
> Con un bordon, y en cuerpo en vestidura
> Blanca que hasta el suelo le cubria:
> Y con la barba blanca a la cinturá,
> Como assi tan pensoso estar le via,
> En la cerrada pieca en este instante
> Se aparescio a Torralva nigromante."
>
> CARLO FAMOSO, cant. XXX.

Zequiel asked him why he was pensive, to which he replied that he was puzzled with the stars. The familiar then informed him that the constable of Bourbon was before Rome, which would be taken next day.

> " Havra sangre y crueldad en abundancia,
> De que yo espero haver muy grand ganancia."

Çapata imagined that the familiar might be a demon, and that he would naturally delight in the horrors which attended the sack of Rome.

of being burnt. Zequiel saw his alarm, and rebuked him for it in a familiar phrase, "*No temas, bestia fiera!*" (fear nothing, stupid fellow.) Torralva then shut his eyes again, and after awhile felt himself on the solid ground, and heard his companion bid him open his eyes, and see if he knew where he was. He recognised the city of Rome spread out before him, and knew that he was standing on the tower of Nona. The clock of the castle of St. Angelo was just striking the hour of midnight, so that they had been exactly one hour on their journey. The city was then shrouded in night, and they waited till daybreak, when they passed through the different parts of the city, and witnessed the events of that terrible day, the attack of the besiegers, the death of the constable of Bourbon, the flight of the pope into the castle of St. Angelo, the terror and slaughter of the citizens, the pollution of the churches, and the wild riot of the conquerors. It took them an hour and a half to return to Valladolid, and when Zequiel left the doctor there, he said to him, "In future you will believe all I tell you." Torralva immediately made public all he had seen during this extraordinary excursion, and when in due course of time news arrived of the capture and sack of Rome, the court of Spain was filled with astonishment.

Torralva's fame as a magician was now in everybody's mouth, and it seems that men of high rank, both in church and state, had been cognizant of, if not accomplices in, his practices of forbidden arts. It was at length by one of his intimate friends that he was denounced to the inquisitors, who would perhaps have taken no notice of him had they not been urged to the pursuit. Diego de Zuñiga, the same who had been so long a confidant in his intercourse with the familiar, and who had even benefited by his arts to profit at the gambling-table, had suddenly become fanatical and superstitious. Not satisfied with repentance for his own sins, Zuñiga denounced Torralva to the inquisition of Cuença, and when the doctor visited that city at the beginning of the year 1528, he was arrested and thrown into prison. He immediately confessed all his dealings with Zequiel, whom he persisted in regarding as a good angel, and made no less than eight several written declarations, the same in effect, but contradicting each other in some of the particulars. As these seem to have been thought not to be entirely satisfactory, Torralva was put to the torture, the result of which was that he declared himself convinced that Zequiel was a demon. He said that his familiar had warned him that a danger hung over him if he went to Cuença at that time, but that he had disregarded the admonition.

The inquisitors now changed their severity to indulgence, and on the 6th of March, 1529, they suspended Torralva's process for a year. But before the expiration of that period, a new accuser presented himself, and deposed to his disputes at Rome in his younger days on the immortality of the soul and the divinity of Jesus Christ. This placed the question in a new light, and Torralva underwent examination again on the 29th of January, 1530, when he made a new declaration on the subject of his early education and opinions. The case now assumed a still more serious character, and the inquisitors of Cuença having communicated with the supreme council of the inquisition in Spain, received directions to appoint some pious and learned persons to labour for the conversion of the accused, and to persuade him to renounce, sincerely and absolutely, the science of chiromancy, his intercourse with Zequiel, and all treaties he might have entered into with the evil one, for the unburthening of his conscience and the salvation of his soul. The inquisitors intrusted this task to brother Augustino Barragan, prior of the convent of Dominicans at Cuença, and Diego Manriques, a canon of the cathedral, and these men laboured with so much zeal and effect, that Torralva agreed to do everything they wished, except that he would not undertake to see Zequiel no more. For it appears that the familiar remained so far faithful to his original promise, that he continued to visit Torralva in the prison of the inquisition, and the doctor represented to his converters that he was obliged to see him whether he would or not. The inquisitors themselves were so credulous, that they requested their prisoner to inquire of Zequiel what was his opinion of the doctrines of Luther and Erasmus; and they were gratified beyond measure when they learnt that he condemned the two reformers, with this difference only, that he considered Luther to be a bad man, while he represented Erasmus as his superior in cunning and cleverness. Perhaps this piece of information brought Torralva a little into favour, and his treatment was not so rigorous as that experienced by many at the hands of the same prosecutors.

On the 6th of March, 1531, he was condemned to make the general ordinary abjuration of heresies, to undergo the punishment of imprisonment and the *san benito* as long as it might please the inquisitor-general, to undertake to have no further communication with the spirit Zequiel, and never to lend an ear to any of his proposals.

Although Torralva had been betrayed by one friend, he had others who remained faithful to him. Before his celebrated journey to Rome in 1525, he had been appointed to the office of physician to the family of the admiral of Castile, don Frederico Enriquez, which he still held at the time of his arrest. The admiral had always proved himself a warm friend and a staunch protector; he did not desert him in his trials, and it was no doubt to his influential interference that Torralva owed what indulgence was shown to him during his imprisonment. We have every reason to believe that it was through his protection also that soon after the process was ended, the inquisitor-general gave Torralva his pardon, and set him at liberty, in consequence, as it was pretended, of his sincere repentance. The admiral received the magician again as his physician, and continued his favour and protection to him.

Such is the history, taken entirely from his own declarations and confessions, of a magician whose fame has been immortalised in Don Quixote.

CHAPTER XIX.

TRIAL OF THE EARL AND COUNTESS OF SOMERSET.

The story of doctor Torralva has drawn us a little from the chronological order of our chapters. The wholesale persecution of the witches of Labourd in the French Basque territory, and the trial of those of Zugarramurdi, on the Spanish side of the frontier, give us a fair picture of the prevalence and intensity of the belief in sorcery among all the nations of Europe during the earlier years of the seventeenth century. We cannot be surprised if, under these circumstances, the charge was often made a weapon of resentment and revenge, not only in the lowest, but sometimes even in the highest class of society, and if even people of rank and education were credulous enough to have recourse to the assistance of the sorcerer and witch. We will proceed to take a few examples of each of these cases, and our own country at this period furnishes us with one of the most extraordinary, and at the same time mysterious, tragedies that are to be found in our annals.

No period of English history offers us so much that is dark and repugnant as the reign of James I. The private history of that monarch's court is very imperfectly known, and the few revelations that have been made are calculated to convince us that in this case "ignorance is bliss." Perhaps of all the mysterious affairs of this reign, none present more difficulties than the history of James's first great favourite, Robert Carr.

This man was of a respectable Scottish family, but he had received a mean education, and the merits which gained him the royal favour were a "comely personage" and a taste in dress. The king's fondness for him was shown openly in an undignified manner; for, to use the words of a nobleman who was in constant attendance at king James's court, the monarch "would lean on his arm, pinch his cheek, smooth his ruffled garment, and, when directing discourse to others, nevertheless gaze on him." Such was one of the principal heroes of the tragedy now to be related, but the person who appears most active in it was a lady.

The lady Frances Howard, daughter of Thomas, earl of Suffolk, and great niece of Henry Howard, earl of Northampton and lord high treasurer of England, had been married in 1606 to Robert, earl of Essex, who was in after life distinguished as the parliamentary leader. It was a marriage of family policy, and at the time it took place the bride was thirteen years of age and the bridegroom only fourteen. The lady grew up to be one of the most dissolute of the ladies of James's court—which was not remarkable for its morality—and according to the court scandal of the day, she had intrigued with prince Henry, and had "been cast off by him" on account of her notorious infidelity. At length the countess of Essex became passionately enamoured of the king's favourite, who was raised to the peerage in the spring of 1611, under the title of viscount Rochester.

It appears that there were at the same time two separate intrigues in progress to bring together lord Rochester and the countess of Essex; one had its foundation in interest alone, and the other was the offspring of ambition and love.

The old courtiers were alarmed at the power of the young favourite, and were anxious to secure themselves by obtaining his favour, and none more so than the aged treasurer Henry earl of Northampton. At a time when the commons of England were preparing to assert their dignity and rights, a great part of the nobility seem to have sunk into a degree of baseness which it is not easy to imagine, and there appears but too much reason for believing that the earl of Northampton did not shrink from using the prostitution of his kinswoman to secure his influence at court. It was probably in that ancient and sad-looking mansion which still looks over the commencement of the Strand, and was then the earl's residence, and known as Northampton (now Northumberland) house, that the plot was managed which eventually led to the ill-fated marriage of which I am going to tell the consequences. The plotters are said to have employed in this intrigue a follower of the new favourite, named Copinger, at whose house the meetings between lord Rochester and lady Essex sometimes took place.

The lady, however, was too ardent in her passion to wait the effect of this intrigue, or perhaps she was not fully acquainted with the designs of her relatives. She made her confidante of Mrs. Anne Turner, the widow of a physician of respectability, a woman not deficient in beauty, and who was at this time the mistress of sir Arthur Mainwaring, an attendant on the prince. With this worthy companion in her evil doings, the countess repaired to Dr. Simon Foreman, the magician who, as has been stated, was living at Lambeth, and with whom Mrs. Turner appears to have been already acquainted. It was soon agreed between them that Foreman should by his magic bewitch the lord Rochester, and so turn his affections that they should be irrevocably fixed on lady Essex, and he was in the same way to influence sir Arthur Mainwaring towards Mrs. Turner The intercourse between the ladies and the conjurer became now frequent, and he used all his skill in charms and images to effect their desire. At a subsequent period Foreman's wife deposed in court " that Mrs. Turner and her husband would sometimes be locked upp in his studye for three or four howres together;" and the countess became so intimate that she spoke of Foreman as her " sweet father."

The result of all these intrigues was that lord Rochester became violently enamoured of the countess, and they formed an intimacy which soon assumed a criminal character. Their stolen meetings were held at Mrs. Turner's house in Paternoster-row, at Copinger's, and elsewhere, and became a matter of public scandal. But in the meanwhile a new obstacle had risen in the way of their criminal enjoyments. The young earl of Essex, who had been separated from his wife immediately after their premature marriage, returned from the wars abroad to claim his rights at home. The lady Essex had scarcely known her husband, she could have no love towards him, and she was unwilling to relinquish her attachments and courtly tastes to live in private with a nobleman who never seems to have been much of a courtier. It required the earnest expostulations of her father to bring the young couple together, and when the earl of Essex, disturbed at the reports which soon reached him of her recent mode of life, took her to his house at Chartley, her coldness towards her lord was turned into intense hatred.

Mrs. Turner was again sent to Foreman, who undertook to bewitch the earl of Essex in the contrary sense to that in which he had enchanted the viscount Rochester. New images were made, and new charms invented, and the doctor furnished powders to be administered, and washes to bathe his linen, which were to render the earl of Essex incapable of loving his lady. The latter had been convinced that Foreman's charms had procured her the affection of her lover, and she was now disappointed at finding them ineffectual against her husband. Letters addressed by her at this time to Mrs. Turner and Dr. Foreman were produced at a later period, in which she complained that "my lord is very well as ever he was," and expressed her aversion to him and her wish to be rid of him.

In the midst of these dark transactions a new circumstance happened which threatened to impede their intrigues. This was the sudden death of their grand agent, doctor Foreman, who, to use the words of a manuscript report of the subsequent trial, " a little before his death desired he might be buryed very deepe in the ground, or else (saith hee) I shall feare you all." * Foreman himself appears to have been apprehensive of the consequences of his dealings in this affair, for Lilly, who was acquainted with his widow, tells us that " he professed to her there would be much trouble about Carr and the countess of Essex, who frequently resorted unto him, and from whose company he would sometimes lock himself in his study a whole day." Mrs. Fore-

* Lilly received from Foreman's widow the following singular account of his sudden death. " The Sunday night before he died, his wife and he being at supper in their garden-house, she being pleasant, told him, that she had been informed he could resolve whether man or wife should die first; ' Whether shall I,' quoth she, 'bury you or no?' ' Oh, Trunco,' for so he called her, ' thou shalt bury me, but thou wilt much repent it.' ' Yea, but how long first?' ' I shall die,' said he, ' ere Thursday night.' Monday came, all was well. Tuesday came, he not sick. Wednesday came, and still he was well; with which his impertinent wife did much twit him in his teeth. Thursday came, and dinner was ended, he very well: he went down to the water side, and took a pair of oars to go to some buildings he was in hand with in Puddle-dock. Being in the middle of the Thames, he presently fell down, only saying, ' An impost, an impost,' and so died. *A most sad storm of wind immediately following.*"

man, when afterwards examined in court, deposed, "that Mrs. Turner came to her house immediatelye after her husband's death, and did demaund certaine pictures, which were in her husband's studdy, namely, one picture in waxe, very sumptuously apparrelled in silke and sattin, as alsoe another sitting in forme of a naked woman, spreading and layinge forthe her haire in a glasse, which Mrs. Turner did confidentlye affirme to be in a boxe, and that she knewe in what part of the roome in the studye they were." Foreman is reported to have said, in reply to the expostulations of the countess, that the devil, as he had learnt, had no power over the person of the earl of Essex; yet she persisted in her designs, and after Foreman's death, another conjurer was employed, one doctor Lavoire or Savory, as the name is differently written in different manuscripts.

But a more powerful agent than the conjurers was now brought in. We have no means of ascertaining at what time king James was first made acquainted with the amourous intrigues of his favourite, but, as the latter was as anxious to get the lady Essex away from her husband as she was to leave him, the English Solomon resolved that both should be gratified. The countess was instructed to bring against the earl of Essex a charge of conjugal incapacity, a commission of reverend prelates of the church was appointed to sit in judgment, over whom the king presided in person, and a jury of matrons was found to give their opinion that the lady Essex was a maiden. James seems to have gloated over this revolting process with the same degree of pleasure which he had derived from the examination of the witches in Edinborough; the earl of Essex appears to have made no opposition, and the king pressed with indecent eagerness a judgment of divorce. This being effected, the king, with no less indecency, hastened a marriage between his favourite and the lady, with whose character he could not have been unacquainted, and heaped new honours upon the former for this occasion. On the third of November, 1613, Robert Carr, viscount Rochester, was elevated to the rank and title of earl of Somerset; and on St. Stephen's day, (December 26,) king James gave the lady to his minion at the altar, and the marriage was celebrated by the court with unusual splendour.

There was one circumstance connected with this guilty marriage, or at least contemporaneous with the intrigues which have just been described, that became in the sequel the foundation of events still more extraordinary.

Sir Thomas Overbury, who is known by literary compositions of some merit, was almost as much the favourite of Carr in the earlier period of his fortunes, as Carr was of the king; and although represented in the common published accounts as a man of honourable character, there appears to be not wanting grounds for suspecting that he was a fit companion for the monarch and his favourite. It appears from documents afterwards brought forward, that sir Thomas Overbury exercised for several years the extraordinary vocation of imparting ideas and language to the earl of Somerset, as to a puppet, who, by means of his secret suggestions, moved the inclinations of king James which way he would, governed councils, and fascinated the beauties of the court; and that he crowned his various achievements by writing love-letters in his patron's name, through which lady Essex was led to indulge a guilty passion. Yet strangely enough, when his patron resolved to marry his mistress, and was supported in that resolution by the open approval and encouragement of his sovereign, Overbury is represented as putting himself forward indiscreetly to oppose the marriage, and as thus drawing upon himself the hatred of the favourite and his mistress. It was determined by some means or other to get Overbury out of the way; the king, at the instigation (as it is said) of Somerset and the earl of Northampton, offered to send him ambassador to Russia, and when (also, it is said, at Somerset's suggestion) he refused the employment, James, in a fit of anger, ordered him to be committed close prisoner to the tower. Here Overbury lingered in a sickly state of body till the 19th of October, 1613, when he died.

For a while after the marriage, the king's attachment to the earl of Somerset seemed to increase from day to day, and honours and riches were showered thick upon him, but at length it was perceived that James began to be tired of his favourite, and his enemies seized the opportunity to conspire his ruin. Among these, the archbishop of Canterbury, Abbot, with whom Somerset had quarrelled, was one of the most active, and he has left us an account of the way in which these intrigues were carried on. "We could have no way so good," says the archbishop, "to effectuate that which was the common desire, as to bring in another in his room; one nail, the proverb is, being to be driven out by another. It was now observed that the king began to cast his eye upon George Villiers, who was then cup-bearer, and seemed a modest and courteous youth. But king James had a fashion, that he would never admit any to nearness about himself, but such a one as the queen should commend to him, and make some suit in that behalf, in order that, if the queen afterwards, being ill-treated, should complain of this *dear one*, he might make his answer, 'It is come of yourself, for you were the party that commended him unto me.' Our old master took delight in things of this nature." The queen hated Somerset, and after a good deal of communications and intriguing, she consented to act the part required; and Villiers was appointed a gentleman of the chamber, in spite of the opposition of the old favourite, who was made to feel more and more that he was losing favour with the king. Still the king continued outwardly to show him the same attention as before, and even increased his honours, by which he was lulled into security, while a deep plot was laid for his final overthrow, in which James, daily more attached to the new object, appears to have concurred.

All who looked forward for advancement through the new favourite were zealous in persecuting the old one, and among these were sir Ralph Winwood, one of the secretaries of state and a creature of

Villiers, and sir Francis Bacon, to whom Villiers held out the prospect of the chancellorship of England. The first of these got up the accusation on which Somerset was tried, and the second was employed to conduct the prosecution. It was stated that sir Thomas Overbury had been poisoned in the tower by agents of the countess and earl of Somerset, that his body had been hastily and privately buried without having been shown even to his friends, and that Somerset's power over the king had been used to hush up and conceal the crime. Several inferior agents were committed to prison, and by the king's orders a warrant was made to arrest the earl of Somerset, which is said to have been executed after he left the king's presence at Royston. In the last scene of this court drama, the king exhibited the most heartless duplicity. The following account is given by an eye-witness, sir Anthony Weldon.

" The king with this took his farewell for a time of London, and was accompanied with Somerset to Royston, where no sooner he brought him, but the earl instantly took his leave, little imagining what viper lay among the herbs. Nor must I forget to let you know how perfect the king was in the art of dissimulation, or, to give it his own phrase, kingcraft. The earle of Somerset never parted from him with more seeming affection than at this time, when he knew Somerset should never see him more; and had you seen that seeming affection, (as the author himselfe did,) you would rather have believed he was in his rising than setting. The earle, when he kissed his hand, the king hung about his neck, slabbering his cheeks, saying,

"'For God's sake, when shall I see thee againe? On my soule, I shall neither eat nor sleep until you come again?'

"The earle told him on Monday, (this being on the Friday)—

"'For God's sake, let me,' said the king, 'shall I, shall I?' then lolled about his neck. 'Then for God's sake, give thy lady this kiss for me.'

"In the same manner, at the stayres' head, at the middle of the stayres, and at the stayres' foot. The earl was now in his coach when the king used these very words, (in the hearing of four servants, of whom one was Somerset's great creature, and of the bed-chamber, who reported it instantly to the author of this history), 'I shall never see his face more.'"

The earl was placed under arrest on his return to London, but instead of proceeding to an examination of the two principal offenders, the minor actors in the tragedy were first brought to trial. The object in view from the beginning appears to have been to bring forward as little evidence as possible, but to use every means of inducing the various persons accused to confess themselves guilty and accuse their supposed employers. Although at first some of them obstinately denied any knowledge of the crime imputed to them, they all ended by confessing whatever was required, influenced either by hope or fear, and when their confessions had been obtained, they were hurried to the gallows with as little delay as possible. We can hardly doubt, from the evidence, that the countess of Somerset had been anxious for Overbury's death, and that she had suborned persons to poison him, but it certainly did not appear by the evidence that he had been poisoned by them.

During these trials the public excitement was so great that Westminster-hall was intensely crowded, and immense sums were given for places on the scaffolding erected for the occasion. This was especially the case on the 7th of November, 1615,the day when Mrs. Turner was arraigned, and a feeling of superstitious fear seized upon the assemblage when on that occasion the instruments of Foreman's conjurations were exposed to view. It appears that when Mrs. Turner was arrested, she sent her maid in haste to Foreman's widow, to warn her that the privy council would probably give orders to search her house, and to urge her to burn any of her husband's papers that were calculated to compromise her. Mrs. Foreman saw that the trouble which her husband foretold had arrived, and she followed the suggestion thus conveyed to her, but a few documents were preserved that were now brought into court, and among these were the two guilty letters addressed by lady Essex from Chartley to Mrs. Turner and Foreman, which, according to some accounts, had been found in the conjuror's pockets after his sudden death. The various articles which were seized in Foreman's house related to the attempts to enchant the earls of Somerset and Essex, and not to the murder of Overbury. "There was shewed in court certeine pictures of a man and a woman made in lead, and also a mould of brasse wherein they were cast, a blacke scarfe alsoe full of white crosses, which Mrs. Turner had in her custodie ;" in addition to which there were " inchanted paps and other pictures." These might be innocent enough, if they had not been followed by a parcel of Foreman's written charms and conjurations. " In some of these parchments," says the contemporary report of the trial in the manuscript from which we are quoting, " the devill had particular names, who were conjured to torment the lord Somersett and sir Arthur Mannering, if theire loves should not contynue, the one to the countesse, the other to Mrs. Turner." The horror caused by these revelations was so great, that the multitude assembled in the hall were involuntarily led into the delusion that the demons were present among them, witnessing the exposure of their victims, and suddenly in the midst of this sensation, " there was heard a crack from the scaffold which carryed a great feare, tumult, and commotion, amongst the spectators and through the hall, every one feareing hurt, as if the devill had bine present and growen angry to have his workemanshipp knowne by such as were not his owne schollars." The reporter adds, " There was alsoe a note showed in courte, made by doctor Foreman, and written in parchment, signifying what ladyes loved what lords in the court, but the lord chiefe justice would not suffer it to be read openly in courte." This " note," or book, is understood to have been a diary of Foreman's dealings with the persons implicated; and, according to the scandal of the time, the reason why my lord chief justice objected to reading it was, that his own wife's name was the first which caught his eye on opening it.* Mrs. Turner had been a favourite with the court ladies on account of her skill in inventing new fashions; fully aware that it was useless to make any defence, she sought to move compassion by representing that she was a mere servant to the will of people of higher rank, on whom she had to depend for the support of herself and children. Her fate is said to have excited much commiseration.

Several months were allowed to elapse after the execution of the minor agents, on whose confessions these charges rested, before the great offenders were proceeded against. The countess of Somerset was brought to her trial on the 24th of May, 1616, and she at once pleaded guilty, under the evident impression that this plea was to merit a pardon. This had no doubt been arranged before-hand. There remained nothing now but to condemn the earl, whose trial was fixed for the day following, the 25th of May; but he, it appears, was more difficult to deal with than the other prisoners. The conduct of the king and the earl on this occasion was calculated to excite extraordinary suspicions; for the reports of the trial and the version of the story which came before the public were evidently drawn up for the purpose of deceiving. An attempt has been made to throw some light on these mysterious transactions

* Had we Foreman's private diaries for this period, they would no doubt throw much light on contemporary history. The immorality of the conjuror's private character is sufficiently evinced by that portion of his secret diaries privately printed by Mr. Halliwell.

by Mr. Amos, who has examined the documents relating to this trial preserved in the State Paper-office, and has collected the materials which we are now to use.*

The letters of Bacon, whose conduct throughout these trials was, to say the least, most unmanly, show us that the king looked forward to the trial of Somerset with the greatest uneasiness, and that every effort was made to induce him to admit the justice of the prosecution, even by the promise of the king's pardon. Bacon writes to sir George Villiers, on the second of May, "That same little charm, which may be secretly infused into Somerset's ear some few hours before his trial, was excellently well thought of by his majesty, and I do approve it both for matter and time; only, if it seems good to his majesty . . . . I could wish it were made a little stronger, by giving him some hopes that his majesty will be good to his lady and child, &c. . . . For the person that should deliver this message, I am not so well seen in the region of his friends, as to be able to make choice of a particular; my lord treasurer, the lord Knollys, or any of his nearest friends, should not be trusted with it, for they may go too far, and perhaps work contrary to his majesty's ends. Those which occur to me are my lord Hay, my lord Burleigh, of England I mean, and sir Robert Carre." On the fifth of May, Bacon writes to Villiers, after stating his opinion

* The Grand Oyer of Poisoning: the Trial of the Earl of Somerset for the poisoning of Sir Thomas Overbury in the Tower of London. By Andrew Amos, Esq. London, Bentley, 1846.

that the "resuscitation of Somerset's fortune" would be impolitic: "But yet the glimmering of that which the king hath done to others, by way of talk to him, cannot hurt, as I conceive; but I would not have that part of the message as from the king, but added by the messenger, as from himself . . . The time I wish to be the Tuesday, being the even of his lady's arraignment; for, as his majesty first conceived, I would not have it stay in his stomach too long, lest it sour in the digestion." He was, in fact, to be taken by surprise, and not left time for calm reflection. Several other letters and papers of Bacon contain similar intimations; and it appears from one, that while the countess and her husband were kept perfectly in the secret as to what course the other was pursuing, or what evidence existed against the other, they were still played off against each other. Bacon says, on the 10th of May, "It is thought that at the day of her trial the lady will confess the indictment; which, if she do, no evidence ought to be given. But because it shall not be a dumb show, and for his majesty's honour in so solemn an assembly, I purpose to make a declaration of the proceedings of this great work of justice, from the beginning to the end, wherein, nevertheless, I will be careful no ways to prevent or discover the evidence of the next day. In this my lord chancellor and I have likewise used a point of providence; for I did forecast, that if in that narrative, by the connection of things, *anything should be spoken that should show him guilty*, she might break forth into passionate protestations *for his clearing*: which, though it may be justly made light of, yet it is better avoided; therefore, my lord chancellor and I have devised, that upon the entrance into that declaration she shall, *in respect of her weakness,* and *not to add further affliction, be withdrawn.*" In a paper of questions for the management of the earl's trial, in Bacon's handwriting, it is suggested, "Whether, if my lord of Somerset should *break forth into any speech of taxing the king,* he be not presently by the lord steward to be interrupted and silenced; and, if he persist, he be not to be told, that if he take that course, *he is to be withdrawn, and evidence to be given in his absence.*" It must be observed, that there is no intimation that Somerset had ever threatened to save himself by accusing the king, so that the fear on that head must have arisen from some great misgiving on the part of the latter.

Sir George Moore had been appointed lieutenant of the Tower when Somerset was committed, and in his family have been preserved the autograph letters which the king addressed to him during the preparations for the trial.* From these, we see how anxiously James was acting in the views expressed in the above extracts from Bacon's letters. In the first of the king's letters, dated on the 9th of May, James says to sir George Moore, "As the only confidence I had in your honesty made me, without the knowledge of any, put you in that place of trust which you now possess, so must I now use your trust and secresy in a thing greatly concerning my honour and service;" and he then desires him to admit, in the greatest secresy, to his prisoner, a private messenger, who was to persuade him to confess. On the 13th of May, the king writes again, "Al-

* They are now at Losely, in Surrey, and were printed in Kemp's "Losely Papers."

though I fear that the last message I sent to your unfortunate prisoner shall not take the effect that I wish it should, yet I cannot leave off to use all means possible to move him to do that which is most honourable for me, and his own best. You shall, therefore, give him assurance in my name, that if he will yet before his trial confess clearly unto the commissioners his guiltiness of this fact, I will not only perform what I promised by my last messenger, both towards him and his wife, but I will enlarge it . . . Assure him that I protest upon my honour, my end in this is for his and his wife's good; you will do well likewise, of yourself to cast out unto him, that you fear *his wife shall plead weakly for his innocence,* and that you find the commissioners have, you know not how, some secret assurance that, in the end, *she will confess of him;* but this must only be as from yourself, and therefore you must not let him know that I have written to you . . . . if he remain obstinate, I desire not that you should trouble me with an answer; for it is to no end, and no news is better than *evil news.*" In another letter, undated, the king speaks in the same strain, and adds, "It is easy to be seen that he would threaten me, with laying an aspersion upon me of being in some sort accessory to his crime;" and in a fourth, which appears to have been written early on the morning of the trial, James gives some curious directions what should be done with the earl, in case he refused to go to the trial. It appears that Somerset did not believe that the king would allow him to be brought to a public trial.

These letters to sir George Moore furnish a striking confirmation of sir Anthony Weldon's narrative of what took place on the eve of the trial, which will be best given in his own words:—"And now, for the last act, enters Somerset himselfe on the stage, who (being told, as the manner is, by the lieutenant, that he must provyde to goe next day to his tryal) did absolutely refuse it, and said they should carry him in his bed—that the king had assured him he should not come to any tryal, neither durst the king bring him to tryal. This was in an high strain, and in a language not well understood by sir George Moore, (then lieutenant in Elwaies his room) that made Moore quiver and shake; and however he was accounted a wise man, yet he was neare at his wits' end. Yet away goes Moore to Greenewich, as late as it was, (being twelve at night), bounseth at the back stayres as if mad, to whom came Jo. Loveston, one of the grooms, out of his bed, inquires the reason of that distemper at so late a season. Moore tells him he must speak with the king. Loveston replyes, 'He is quiet,' (which in the Scottish dialect, is fast asleep.) Moore says, 'You must awake him.' Moore was called in, (the chamber left to the king and Moore.) He tells the king those passages, and desired to be directed by the king, for he was gone beyond his owne reason, to heare such bold and undutiful expressions from a faulty subject against a just sovereigne. The king falls into a passion of tears: 'On my soule, Moore, I wot not what to do! Thou art a wise man; help me in this great strait, and thou shalt finde thou dost it for a thankful master;' with other sad expressions. Moore leaves the king in that passion, but assures him he will prove the utmost of his wit to serve his majesty; and was really rewarded with a suit, worth to him £1,500 (although Annandale, his great friend, did cheat him of one half; so was there falsehood in friendship). Sir George Moore returns to Somerset about three next morning of that day he was to come to triall, enters Somerset's chamber, tells him he had been with the king, found him a most affectionate master unto him, and full of grace in his intentions towards him. 'But,' said he, 'to satisfie justice you must appeare, although returne instantly againe, without any further proceedings; only you shall know your enemies and their malice, though they shall have no power over you.' With this trick of wit he allayed his fury, and got him quietly, about eight in the morning, to the hall; yet feared his former bold language might revert againe, and being brought by this trick into the toile, might have more enraged him to fly out into some strange discovery; for prevention whereof he had two servants placed on each side of him, with a cloak on their arms, giving them withall a peremptory order, if that Somerset did any way fly out on the king, they should instantly hoodwink him with their cloaks, take him violently from the bar, and carry him away; for which he would secure them from any danger, and they should not want also a bountiful reward. But the earle, finding himself over-reached, recollected a better temper, and went on calmly in his tryall, where he held the company untill seven at night. But who had seen the king's restlesse motion all that day, sending to every boat he saw landing at the bridge, cursing all that came without tidings, would have easily judged all was not right, and there had been some grounds for his feares of Somerset's boldnesse; but at last one bringing him word he was condemned and the passages, all was quiet. This is the very relation from Moore's owne mouth, and this told *verbatim* in Wanstead Parke, to two gentlemen, (of which the author was one,) who were both left by him to their own freedome, without engaging them, even in those times of high distemperatures, unto a faithful secresie in concealing it, yet, though he failed in his wisdome, they failed not in that worth inherent in every noble spirit, never speaking of it till after the king's death."

Somerset's trial was, in every respect, a mere mockery of justice. He was tried, not by his peers in parliament, but by a select number of peers chosen for the occasion, who were his personal enemies or creatures of the court. His judges again urged him to plead guilty, intimating that his wife had made a confession that implicated him, and holding out the prospect of a full pardon as the reward of his confession. When he still insisted upon his innocence, they brought against him no witnesses, but merely adduced as evidence the confessions of the persons who had already been hanged, and who had never been confronted with the man they accused. On the contrary, one gentleman, sir John Lidcot, no friend of Somerset's, having presumed, on the scaffold, to ask Weston, who it was pretended had delivered the poison, whether he had poisoned Overbury or not, was thrown into the Tower and treated harshly. Late in the afternoon the earl began an able and eloquent defence, in which he explained away or denied every circumstance adduced to show that he knew of the murder; and he insisted that his assertions ought to have greater weight with the court than those of condemned felons, proved by their own confessions to be persons of base character, and whom he had no opportunity of cross examining. The peers found him guilty.

When we look even at the report of Somerset's trial which was published to the world by those who were far from being friends to him, we are struck with the unsatisfactory character of the evidence upon which he was condemned But our astonishment is increased when we read the original depositions of the pretended agents, many of which are fortunately preserved in the State Paper Office, and are now, for the first time, published by Mr. Amos. We there find these witnesses, in statements drawn from them, it would appear, by the most unworthy means, contradicting one another, and contradicting themselves; so much so that these papers would lead us almost necessarily to the conclusion that there was no poisoning at all. They are mostly in the handwriting of Coke, who directed the examination of the persons accused, and are covered with notes and erasures by Bacon, who conducted, under the immediate direction of the king, the prosecution; and we discover from these notes, and from a comparison of the extracts read in court at the trial, that Bacon not only suppressed carefully everything that would tell in favour of the earl of Somerset, but that he altered phrases and falsified the original in order to make a direct accusation of what in that original was little better than a supposition.

It is clear from the original depositions that sir Thomas Overbury was either not poisoned, or that he must have been poisoned by the king's own physician, who constantly attended upon him in the Tower. This is a very important circumstance, and was entirely concealed from the public. In fact, during the whole course of proceedings in this strange affair, no attempt was made to prove that Overbury did die of poison, but that was taken as an acknowledged fact The king and the public prosecutors seem to have acted on the mere personal conviction that such was the case. The king's physician, Mayerne, who, as we have said, had attended on the deceased, and prescribed constantly for him, was not examined at all, nor were any medical men brought forward to give an opinion on the cause which had produced, death. It is proved by the depositions in the State Paper Office, that an inquest was held on the body, that his friends were permitted to visit it, and that no particular secresy was observed; yet not only were no physicians brought forward on the trial to state if any marks of the presence of poison had been observed on the body, but the depositions on this subject were concealed, and it was represented falsely that the body had been buried hastily and privately, and that Overbury's friends had not been allowed access to it. Several persons who might have given important evidence on the trial, had mere truth been sought, were certainly kept out of the way.

Mr. Amos points out the improbability of the whole story of the poisoning, as it was made the groundwork of the trial, and we may fairly doubt if it were not a fiction to cover circumstances which could not safely be revealed. We learn from the narrative of sir Anthony Weldon, that Franklin, one of the minor agents, confessed that Sir Thomas Overbury was *smothered* by him and Weston, and was not poisoned. "The suspicious circumstance that none of Franklin's examinations taken before his trial are forthcoming, gives some countenance to this report." Mr. Amos's book contains a mass of evidence on this and other points which my space will not allow me to transfer to this review of the subject.

It must be confessed that, even with the important additional evidence thus brought to light, the history of sir Thomas Overbury's murder is still clouded in mystery. The conclusion to which we are naturally led by the foregoing facts is, that any satisfactory evidence which could have been brought forward would have involved other accomplices, whose names it was necessary to keep carefully from public suspicion, and that the real object of the prosecution was the ruin and disgrace of the favourite, whom at last James, actuated by fear or some other motive, did not sacrifice to the utmost extent of the wishes of his enemies. The presumption is indeed strong that the murder was authorised by king James himself. This supposition, at least, explains various circumstances which are otherwise totally inexplicable. We thus understand why the minor agents in the plot, and especially the unfortunate lieutenant of the Tower, (sir Gervais Helwysse,) and Overbury's jailor, Weston, were so summarily despatched out of the world. We thus understand the tampering with their depositions, which, with all the arrangements for the trial, were made according to the king's own directions. And still more, we understand James's anxiety to prevent Somerset's anticipated revelations.

With this new view of the subject, we are led further to ask for a reason for this extraordinary state murder, and here at present we are left entirely to conjecture. The common story that Overbury's murder was a mere act of revenge for his opposition to the marriage of Somerset with the countess of Essex, has always appeared to me to be in the highest degree improbable, when we consider the part he appears to have previously acted in promoting Somerset's amours, and the part which he knew the king was acting in promoting the marriage. It now appears in the light of a cover for some other transactions, invented probably by the king, but in which Somerset acquiesced in the trial, because it did not necessarily involve his own guilt, (as he only acknowledged to having been the means of sending Overbury to the Tower,) and because he could not confute it without making revelations which he had then determined not to make. It is certain from passages of contemporary letters and papers, that, at the time when sir Thomas Overbury was committed to the Tower, no such excuse for his committal was talked of, but that, on the contrary, it was looked upon generally as a mysterious transaction in which the favourite had no direct share, except that some persons imagined that the anger of the king towards his friend portended a diminution in the influence of the favourite himself. A Mr. Packer, in a letter from the court to sir Ralph Winwood, dated April 22, 1613, mentions that the king sent the lord chancellor and lord Pembroke to offer an "embassage" to sir Thomas Overbury, which sir Thomas immediately refused, and that, some said, "he added some other speech which was very ill taken," and that thereupon the king sent for the council, and after making an angry speech, gave orders to them to send Overbury to prison. Other reasons were also suggested. A courtier, in a letter dated the 6th of May, 1613, writes, "Some say, lord Rochester took sir T. Overbury's committing to heart. Others talk as if it were a great diminution of his favour and credit, which the king doubting, would not have it so construed; but the next day told the council that he meant him more grace and favour, as should be seen in a short time, and that he took more delight and contentment in his company and conversation than in any man's living." On the 27th of May, 1613, sir H. Weston writes, "Sir Thomas Overbury is still where he was, (in the Tower,) and as he was, without any alteration; the viscount Rochester no way sinking in point of favour, which are two strange consistents." The earl of Southampton, writing to sir Ralph Winwood, on the 4th of August, 1613, says, "And much ado there hath been to keep sir Thomas Overbury from a public censure of banishment and loss of office, *such a rooted hatred lyeth in the king's heart towards him.*"

The most probable supposition that we can make is, that Overbury was possessed of important royal secrets, which the king had reasons for fearing he might disclose, or that he had been a participator in crimes or vices which made him a dangerous person. According to hints thrown out by Mr. Amos, the discovery of the secret would, perhaps, reveal scenes of royal depravity which it were as well should remain unknown. It is certain that there was at the time an opinion abroad, that sir Thomas Overbury had been an agent in evil deeds. He was even very commonly suspected of having had some hand in procuring the death of prince Henry, who was far from being a favourite with his father, who hated the favourite, and who was popularly believed to have been poisoned. There are a few very remarkable passages in the papers of the time, relating to this event, which certainly, when put together, tend to raise suspicion, and sir Edward Coke excited the king's anger to the highest degree, and was the cause of sir Thomas Monson's trial being abruptly put a stop to, by an unguarded expression in court, which alluded to those suspicions against Overbury, and which it is said that James never forgave.

CHAPTER XX.

LA MARECHALE D'ANCRE.

While this tragedy was acting in England, a somewhat similar one, though under different circumstances, was in progress in France.

On the death of Henri IV., slain by the assassin Ravaillac in 1610, his son, Louis XIII. being but a child, the royal power fell into the hands of the queen mother, Marie de Medicis. Among the servants attached to Marie before her marriage, was a woman of extraordinary address and talent, the daughter of Marie's nurse, named Eleonora Dori, or, a name she adopted afterwards, Eleonora Galigai. She soon became a great favourite with her mistress, whom she accompanied into France as a confidential attendant, and she gradually gained an unbounded influence over Henri's queen. One of the gentlemen followers of the queen was a Florentine, named Concino Concini, whose grandfather was secretary to the grand duke Cosmo, but the property he had scraped together was dissipated by his children, and Conchino, who had passed his youth so wildly that it is said to have become almost proverbial for parents to warn their children of his example, was in indigent circumstances. In consequence of this, he went to seek his fortune at Rome, where he entered the service of the cardinal of Lorraine, who was then there, but he did not return with him to France. On the marriage of Marie de Medicis, he obtained, as has just been stated, a place in her household, and seeing the influence of Eleonora Galigai, he paid his court to her, and with the queen's approbation, married her. The king is said to have looked on Concini with disfavour, and to have been opposed to the marriage.

When Marie de Medicis became ruler of France, the influence of Concini and his wife was immediately apparent. She was a woman of intelligence and prudence, but her husband was bold and hardy of temper, ambitious and overbearing, and was never at rest till he made his influence apparent to every one. His insolence increased with the queen's power, and he exhibited it in an offensive manner towards the old French nobles of the court of the great Henri. These frequently leagued together against him, and had recourse to arms, but having the power of the state at his command, he proceeded against them as rebels, and forced them to submission. Thus the period while the Concini were in power was for France a time of turbulence and distress.

Immediately after the king's death, Concini was made first gentleman of the chamber, and was rewarded with other lucrative posts. He was thus enabled to purchase the marquisate of Ancre, in Picardy, which title he now assumed. In 1613, the marquis d'Ancre was for a short time in disfavour, but he was soon restored, and then he was created maréchal of France. With all these dignities, he also held the important office of governor of Normandy.

In 1615, the nobles, irritated at the manner in which they were treated by one whom they looked on as a mere upstart, and who had no talents to support his influence, which he owed only to his wife and to his own devotion to the service of the queen, were already plotting his overthrow; and although they then failed, they were indefatigable in their efforts to aggravate the populace and men of all ranks against him. During this and the following years his unpopularity increased daily. In 1616, he offered an unnecessary and unwise provocation to the Parisians. A citizen named Picard had the command of the watch, at the gate of Bussy, one night when the queen's Italian minister was passing that way with his carriage. Picard, urged probably by the general dislike which the people of Paris bore to the maréchal d'Ancre, refused to open the gate till the latter had shown his passport. The maréchal ordered two of his valets to seize Picard, and administer a severe beating to him, as a punishment for the affront. The populace rose, seized the two valets, and hanged them on two gallows at the door of Picard's house, who from this moment became a hero among the Parisians.

Although the maréchal's wife was more cautious of giving personal offence, her manners and character were equally unpopular. She was eccentric, loved to live apart from the world, and was of a suspicious and unsociable temper. She was, moreover, superstitious, and attributed her constant state of ill-health to the effects of sorcery. She caused herself frequently to be exorcised by Italian priests, and always had her face veiled in public to screen her from the gaze of *i guardatori*, as she expressed it,—against the influence of the evil eye. These peculiarities, joined with the belief that she principally ruled the queen-mother, made her equally with her husband an object of popular odium. People accused her of practising the very sorcery which she suspected in others, and it was widely believed that she had bewitched the queen.

The maréchal had two children by his wife, a son and a daughter. The latter died in 1616, to the great grief of her parents; her father is said to have looked upon this blow to his affections as a warning from above that his own fall was approaching, and his apprehensions were so great, that he proposed to his wife to retire from political life, and take refuge in Italy. But she was confident in her influence with the queen, and persuaded him to stay.

As the period of the favourite's downfall approached, people became bolder in their attacks upon both, and less reserved in their speech. Scandalous anecdotes were sent abroad, and bitter and angry epigrams were published in abundance. People assailed them in coarse puns on the words *ancre* and *encre*, and these were even uttered in the queen's presence. It is reported, that when one day the queen-mother said to one of her attendants, "*Apportez-moi mon voile*," the comte du Lude, who was standing by, remarked, with a smile, "*Un navire qui est* à l'Ancre *n'a pas autrement besoin de voiles.*"

It was to one who had risen into importance at court partly by his favour, Charles d'Albert duc de Luynes, that the maréchal d'Ancre eventually owed his fall. This nobleman saw that his own power would be the immediate consequence of the destruction of his rival. He nourished in every possible way the popular feeling against him, and he instilled all sorts of suspicions into the mind of the young king. The latter was getting tired of his mother's rule, and the restraint in which he was held by her minister, and though still not much more than a child, he was anxious to assume the reins of government. He therefore entered eagerly into the conspiracy; and when the duke and the other conspirators saw their time was come, they strengthened the king's resolution by dark insinuations that the minister was meditating the destruction of his royal person as a means of rendering his own influence perpetual.

Even with the king's authority, the enemies of the maréchal d'Ancre did not dare to attack their victim in a fair and open way, but it was resolved to effect their object by assassination. For this purpose they took into their confidence the baron de Vitry, d'Ancre's bitterest personal enemy, and his brother Du Hallier, and the kiug not only authorised them to commit the murder, but promised to reward Vitry with the maréchal's staff. Some other desperate characters were joined with them.

On the morning of the 24th of April, 1617, the

king rose early in the morning and announced a *parti de chasse.* Preparations were immediately made, and the horses and carriages brought out. Under cover of this announcement, Vitry, Du Hallier, and their fellow-assassins, were collected within the gateway of the palace. The maréchal d'Ancre had not himself apartments in the Louvre, but he lodged in a house which formed what was called the *capitainerie* of the Louvre, at the end of the garden towards the present Rue du Coq, where this garden was entered by a little bridge which was called popularly the Pont d'Amour. A person was placed to watch this bridge, while the conspirators waited for the signal to inform them that the maréchal was in view. This signal was given about ten o'clock in the forenoon, and the conspirators overtook their victim as he was entering upon the Pont du Louvre. The baron de Vitry was so fierce and eager that he passed the maréchal before he was aware of him, and was called back by his brother Du Hallier. One or two pistols were then discharged at him, on which he fell wounded, and they instantly dispatched him with their swords.

The young king, in the utmost anxiety, had seized his arquebuse, and he now came forward to the window to encourage the assassins, shouting out publicly, "I thank you, gentlemen: now I am king indeed!" The persons to whom these words were addressed had the baseness not only to share the plunder of the maréchal's person, but they afterwards disputed the merit of having struck the first blow, for the sake of the reward. When the maréchale heard of her husband's fate, she hurried to her chamber, undressed herself, and went to bed, hiding under her her own jewels, and the jewels of the crown, which were entrusted to her care, to save them. But the assassins came and, dragging her roughly out of her bed, carried off all the jewellery and whatever they found in the room of value, as lawful plunder. The same day the king gave d'Ancre's staff of maréchal to the baron de Vitry, and the others were all largely recompensed. The estates of the Concinis were granted to the duc de Luynes. The queen-mother saw that her government was at an end, and she quietly resigned herself to her fate; she was exiled from court, and sent to reside at Blois.

The maréchal's enemies at court had now had their triumph, and it remained only for the populace to take theirs. The body of the murdered favourite had been carried off by some of his followers, and was buried secretly and by night in the church of St. Germain l'Auxerrois. Next morning some traitor gave information to the Parisians, and pointed out the place where he was interred. The populace rose tumultuously, hurried to the church, and, in spite of the remonstrances of the guardians of the church, who appealed to their respect for the dead, they forced their way in, broke up the floor, and tearing open the grave—it was said, with their finger-nails—broke the coffin, and drew the body naked into the street. There they dragged it along ferociously through mud and dirt, till they reached the head of the Pont Neuf, where stood a gallows, which had been erected by the maréchal's orders. They suspended the corpse on this gallows, and let it hang there a short time, during which they cut off the nose and ears, and otherwise mutilated it, with horrible curses and vociferations, obliging everybody they met to join in shouting *vive le roi!* Then they took it down, and dragged it to the bronze statue of Henri IV., where it was passed through a fire, which had been hastily made for the purpose. Thence the mob, continually increasing in numbers and ferocity, dragged the body to the place before the hotel of the maréchal, in the Faubourg St. Germain, where they repeated their outrages, beating the corpse with stones and sticks, amid the most horrible yells and screams. The same scene was repeated in front of the maréchal's lodgings at the Louvre. It is said that the king, who was looking on from the balcony of the Louvre, encouraged the mob. After similar exhibitions in all the public places of Paris, the mutilated and disfigured body was at last carried to the place of the Grève, where a large fire was ready to receive it. The populace had become savage with drink, and before the remains of the maréchal were committed to the flames, the flesh was torn in shreds from the bones in the struggles of individuals to obtain a portion to carry home and burn at their own houses. It was reported that people had obtained high prices for sheep's kidneys, under the pretence that they were the kidneys of the maréchal de l'Ancre.

The duc de Luynes was now at the head of the government, and he determined to complete his work by the destruction of the maréchale. On the 29th of April she was committed to the Bastile, where she was treated with cruelty and insult. Her son, a mere child, was also thrown into prison, after having been stripped naked, and it is said he was left a whole day without clothes or food. When at length inquiries were made after him, so great was the inhumanity of the enemies of the late favourite, that some of the principal ladies of the court had the boy brought before them to dance a sarabande, a dance in which he was said to excel.

Meanwhile no means were neglected to vilify the name of the favourite, and prejudice people against his widow. Writers were employed to traduce them both; numerous pamphlets were published, detailing the insolence of the maréchal, and the sorceries of the maréchale; they were both made the subject of indecent raillerie; brutal and licentious songs and epigrams were composed,* in many

* The following is one of the more temperate of these effusions.

A LA MEMOIRE DE LA MARQUISE ET DU MARQUIS.

L'on parle d'une marquise
Et du coyon Florentin,
Qui eut pour son entreprise
Le royaume de Pantin.
S'elle estoit bonne sorciere,
Ainsi que chacun croyoit,
Au lieu d'estre prisonniere,
Maintenant elle riroit.
Mais sa finesse et ses charmes
Que deux monstres de l'enfer
N'ont peu empescher les armes
Vengeresse des coyons.
Aussi n'est-il pas propice,
Que deux monstres de l'enfer

of which the Parisians were invited to treat the widow as they had treated her husband.*

The only accusations brought against the maréchale d'Ancre at her trial, were those of being a witch, of holding communication with witches, and of having bewitched the queen-mother. The proofs were her familiar intercourse with Montalto, the Jew physician who had accompanied Marie de Medicis from Italy, the exorcisms to which she had subjected herself as a defence against the witchcraft to which she believed herself exposed, and which were performed by Italian priests in the church of the Augustins, and the extraordinary influence she had always exerted over the queen. It appears that at times, when suffering from dreadful pains in the head, the fancy or the superstition of her medical attendants had ordered the application of a newly-killed cock, or other bird, and this was now represented as a sacrifice to the demons. Her retired and in many cases strange manners were also cited against her. She often sat alone, strangely pensive and abstracted, and at such times it was her habit to continue rolling bits of wax

S'opposent à la justice
Tant des flames que du fer.

* As in the following sample.

SUR LA SORCIERE DE CONCHINE.

C'est assez, c'est assez, execrable Megere,
Infernalle furie, engence de vipere,
D'avoir desus la France vomy tant de venin!
Peuple, dressés un feu, pour brusler la sorciere;
Jettés la cendre au vent, escartés la poussiere,
Qu'on luy fasse de mesme qu'on a faict au faquin.

between her fingers until they assumed the form of little bullets, which she threw into a coffer that lay by her. When her room was searched, after her arrest, a number of coffers filled with these bullets of wax were found, and these were taken for corroborative evidence that she was a sorcerer. It was looked upon as a circumstance of more importance that the astrological nativities of the queen and her children, carefully drawn up, were found in her possession; these, which in truth only showed the interest the favourite took in the fate of the royal family, were looked upon as instruments of sorcery. It was further reported abroad, to increase the popular hatred, that they found in her cabinet a quantity of books of magic, with virgin parchment, and a great number of magical characters.*

On several occasions between the end of April and the beginning of July, the maréchale was put to the torture for the purpose of compelling her to confess that she had bewitched the queen-mother, but she bore it all with firmness. It is said, that when asked what were the charms she used to gain possession of the queen's affections, she replied proudly, that it was but the power of a weak mind over a strong one. The proofs against her were, however, pronounced to be sufficient to convict her

* One of the scurrilous pamphlets published after the assassination of the maréchal d'Ancre, under the title of "*La Medée de la France, dépeinte en la personne de la marquise d'Ancre*," tells us, "Ils ont trouvé dans son cabinet quantité de livres de magie, du parchemin vierge, et grand nombre de caracteres."

of the crime of high treason, and she was condemned to be beheaded and then burnt, her house to be razed to the ground, and all her blood struck with incapacity.

The maréchale d'Ancre expected that the utmost severity she had to expect was banishment and confiscation of her property, and when she heard her sentence, she was struck with the utmost astonishment, cried out repeatedly in her distress, "*Oimé povretta!*" and declared in arrest of judgment that she was with child. This plea, however, she immediately retracted, and when she was led to execution on the 8th of July, she submitted to her fate with firmness and resignation. The fury of the Parisian mob had itself abated, and the hated Italian favourite became on the scaffold an object of general commiseration.

CHAPTER XXI.

LOUIS GAUFRIDI.

THE belief in witchcraft was at this time turned to a new purpose by the Romish priesthood. They had long claimed exclusively for the church of Rome a transcendental authority and power which they were fain, in their present contest with the Protestant reformers, to support with pretended miracles; and the belief which gained ground in the latter half of the sixteenth century, that people under the influence of witchcraft were possessed with demons in the same manner as the demoniacs of the New Testament, was too favourable to their plans to be neglected. Perhaps a great number of the Catholic clergy believed conscientiously in the reality of these possessions, but in the more remarkable cases which have been chronicled, the patients were evidently persons tutored for the occasion; and upon the evidence of such people men of character were hurried to the gallows or the stake.

There were many of these pretended cases of obsession in England, but they were generally discouraged by the church, and were in most cases detected and exposed. In 1575, a woman of Westwell, in Kent, named Mildred Nerrington, pretended to be possessed, and accused a poor old woman of the neighbourhood of having sent a devil into her. The affair went so far, that the vicar of the parish, with a neighbouring clergyman, believed that they had expelled the demon by their prayers, and printed a relation of it. The civil power in this case was more effectual in establishing truth than the ecclesiastical, for the pretended demoniac confessed before two justices of the peace that it was an imposture, and she explained the way in which she had deceived the two clergymen. In 1579, a Welch girl, named Elizabeth Orton, pretended to fall into trances, and see visions, which were published with great solemnity by some Roman Catholic priests; but she also was detected, and made a public confession in Chester cathedral. Two years afterwards, another case of pretended demoniacs, in which some Jesuits were implicated, was similarly exposed. In 1598, a Protestant clergyman, named William Darrell, made a great noise by his pretended dispossessing of demoniacs in Nottinghamshire; but his practice also ended in exposure. With a view to such cases, which were multiplying alarmingly, the convocation of the clergy, in the first year of king James, made a canon, "that no minister or ministers, without license and direction of the bishop, under his hand and seal obtained, attempt, upon any pretence whatsoever, either of possession or obsession, by fasting and prayer, to cast out any devil or devils, under pain of the imputation of imposture or cozenage, or deposition from the ministry."

Such cases were differently treated by the church in countries where the Romish faith was established, and where, though many of the more honest and better informed of the popish clergy regarded them at least with suspicion, they were encouraged by the teaching and example of those who were looked upon as the greatest authorities. Solemn forms of invocation were composed for the purpose of exorcising the demons, and driving them away from their victims; and these were as various and as superstitious as the charms of the magicians. The grand authority on this subject was an Italian ecclesiastic of the sixteenth century, named Geronimo Mengi, who published two collections of these exorcisms, which in the Latin edition are entitled *Flagellum Dœmonum*, the whip or scourge of demons, and *Fustis Dœmonum*, a club for the demons. In the introductory chapters of these books, the author describes the manner in which the exorcist was to prepare for his important office, treats of the nature of the evil beings with whom he was to deal, and warns him against their cunning and tergiversation. Among other things, he discusses the question whether it be lawful to make use of insulting language to the demons, and he resolves it in the affirmative. Another recommendation of this author shows the spirit of the whole—the demons were to be compelled to give some open testimony to the truth of the Romish faith. Sometimes, he says, the demons are very obstinate, but the exorciser was to persevere day after day with great patience, and, above all, he was to endeavour to obtain possession of the instruments of sorcery, which, being burnt, would greatly weaken the power of the evil one. Finally, he directs that the demoniacs should, if possible, be exorcised in an open church, before as large a congregation of people as possible.

These doctrines became in France and other countries, the groundwork for extraordinary cases of individual persecution, of which the one I am now going to relate was not the least remarkable.

At Aix, in Provence, there was a convent of Ursuline nuns. It was one of the poorest of the monastic orders of females, for which reason they were allowed several ways of gaining a livelihood; and they seem to have been easily made the tools of the priests. Among the Ursulines of Aix there was, in the year 1610, a young lady named Magdalen de la Palude, who appears then to have been a new convert. She was the daughter of the sieur de la Palude, a Provençal gentleman, who lived in the neighbourhood of Marseilles. Magdalen had not been long among the sisters of St. Ursula before she was seized with trances, and these soon communicated themselves to one of the nuns named Louise Capeau, whom she had chosen to be her intimate friend, and subsequently to some of their companions. It was evident they were possessed, and the superior of the priests proceeded to exorcise them in a little chapel, but to no purpose, and for a full year the demons continued obstinate.

Among the mountains, about three leagues from Aix, is the cave of La Sainte Baume, or "the holy cavern," in which Mary Magdalen, according to the popish tradition, was said to have passed her latter days, and which was now looked upon as a very holy place of pilgrimage. A convent had been founded on the spot, dedicated to the two patron saints of Provence, St. Magdalen and St. Maximin, the prior of which, at the time these events occurred, was Sebastian Michaelis, who was of sufficient importance to hold the office of an inquisitor of the faith. The superior of the priests of Aix, finding his own exorcisms of no avail, applied to the inquisitor Michaelis, by whose direction the two patients, Magdalen de la Palude, and Louise Capeau, were carried to the Sainte Baume. The demons now became more tractable, and the exorciser learnt that Magdalen was possessed by Belzebub, and her companion by a less potent imp, named Verrine, who confessed that they had taken possession of the sufferers by order of Louis Gaufridi, who was the prince and commander of all the magicians in Spain, France, England, and other countries, as far as Turkey, and who had Lucifer for his demon. This Gaufridi was a native of the mountains of Provence, born at Beauvezer lés Colmaret; he was now a priest at Marseilles, enjoying, it would appear, no very good reputation, especially on account of his intrigues with women, and he seems to have been an object of jealousy and ill-feeling among his fellow-clergy.

Sister Magdalen was induced to confess that when she was very young, Louis Gaufridi was a frequent visitor at her father's house in the country, and that one day when they were in the fields, he lured her away to a cavern at no great distance from her home. When they entered the cavern, she saw a great number of people, at which she was amazed, but her companion encouraged her and said, "These are our friends, you must be marked like them." The poor girl was in such astonishment that she made no resistance, but submitted to be marked and abused, and then she returned home, telling nobody, not even her father or mother, what had occurred. After this she was frequently carried to the meeting of the witches, of whom she was made princess, as Gaufridi was their prince. Although she still remained in her father's house, her intercourse with Gaufridi continued, until she suddenly took a fancy to enter the convent of the nuns of St. Ursula. When she consulted Gaufridi on this step, he earnestly dissuaded her from it, urged her to marry, and promised to find her a rich and handsome husband; but when he saw that she was fixed in her determination, he became angry, and threatened that, if she became a nun, his punishment should be not only upon her, but upon all the sisterhood, and the consequence was the visitation under which they were now suffering. Such was the statement made by Magdalen de la Palude to the inquisitor of the Sainte Baume.

The two nuns arrived at the Sainte Baume on the 27th of November, 1610, and the prior Michaelis seems to have taken a pleasure in exercising the office of exorcist, for he continued his examinations almost daily till the month of April follow-lowing. On their first arrival at the convent of the holy cave, the demons were extremely violent, and, irritated by the prior's exorcisms, they threw their victims into violent contortions, raised them up in the church, (the place of exorcising,) and attempted to carry them out by an opening over the choir, but they were prevented. In the course of a day or two the exorcisms began to produce their effect, and on the 7th of December, Verrine, who was the weaker demon and had possession of sister Louise, was compelled to talk. He said that Louise was possessed by three devils, himself and two others, named Gresil and Sonneillon. Next day Verrine gave a long account of the beauty, merits, and glory of the Virgin Mary. Meanwhile Belzebub, who possessed sister Magdalen, was enraged at the informations given by his fellow-demon, and during his discourse on the merits of the Virgin Mary, he began to bellow like a mad bull, turning his victim's head and eyes in dreadful contortions, and taking off one of her shoes, threw it at Verrine and struck sister Louise on the head. On the 9th of December, the demon Verrine accused sister Magdalen of being a witch, and exhorted her to repentance, but he said that sister Louise was innocent. Belzebub was again turbulent, and threatened Verrine with punishment, but the latter treated his menaces with contempt; he said he owed obedience to Belzebub when they were in hell together, but that under circumstances like the present he was his equal. On the 10th, Verrine entered into details relating to the punishments of the other world, and Belzebub was less unruly, though he tossed his victim, sister Magdalen, from one side of the church to the other, saying that was the way they tossed about the souls of sinners in the regions below. During all these strange proceedings, the church was crowded with pilgrims, who went away "much edified."

It was decided on the 12th of December that in future, while one priest exorcised and questioned the demons, another should commit their answers to writing. These depositions were collected and printed seriously by the exorciser Sebastian Michaelis, whose book made a great sensation, and went through several editions. It forms a sort of compendium of transcendental divinity; for the exorciser directed his examinations to the express object of obtaining "authentic" information on different points respecting which doubts might exist in the minds of christians. Among other things the demons told them that Antichrist was born; and when questioned as to the condition of Solomon and Nebuchadnezzar, whether Henri IV. (then lately dead) was saved, and on other similar matters, they gave replies which were highly satisfactory to all zealous Catholics. On one occasion Belzebub spoke with great bitterness against the art of printing, cursing the inventors of it, those who exercised it, and the doctors who gave their approbation to the books! These exorcisms, as I have stated above, were continued till the month of April, 1611; the demons appear to have suffered severely under the compulsion by which such confessions were extorted, and from time to time they became rebellious, and howled and shouted, invoking other demons to their assistance!

The priests who conducted this affair seem almost to have lost sight of Louis Gaufridi, in their anxiety to collect these important evidences of the true faith. It was not till towards the close of winter that the reputed wizard was again thought of. A warrant was then obtained against him, and he was taken into custody and confined in the prison of the conciergerie at Marseilles. On the 5th of March he was for the first time confronted with sister Magdalen, but without producing the result anticipated by his persecutors. Little information is given as to the subsequent proceedings against him, but he appears to have been treated with great severity, and to have persevered in asserting his innocence. Sister Magdalen, or rather the demon within her, gave information of certain marks on his body which had been placed there by the evil one, and on search they were found exactly as described. It is not to be wondered at, if, after the intercourse which had existed between them, sister Magdalen were able to give such information. Still Gaufridi continued unshaken, and he made no confession, until at length, on Easter Eve, the 26th of March, 1611, a full avowal of his guilt was drawn from him, we are not told through what means, by two capuchins of the convent of Aix, to which place he had been transferred for his trial. At the beginning of April, another witness, the demoiselle Victoire de Courbier, came forward to depose that she had been bewitched by the renegade priest, who had obtained her love by his charms, and he made no objection to their adding this new incident to his confession.

Gaufridi acknowledged the truth of all that had been said by sister Magdalen or by her demon. He said that an uncle, who had died many years ago, had left him his books, and that one day, about five or six years before his arrest on this accusation, he was looking them over, when he found amongst them a volume of magic, in which were some writings in French verse, accompanied with strange characters. His curiosity was excited, and he began to read it, when to his great astonishment and consternation, the demon appeared in a human form, and said to him, " What do you desire of me, for it is you who have called me?" Gaufridi was young, and easily tempted, and when he had recovered from his surprise, and was re-assured by the manner and conversation of his visitor, he replied to his offer, " If you have power to give me what I desire, I ask for two things; first, that I shall prevail with all the women I like; secondly, that I shall be esteemed and honoured above all the priests of this country, and enjoy the respect of men of wealth and honour." We may see perhaps through these wishes the reason why Gaufridi was persecuted by the rest of the clergy. The demon promised to grant him his desires, on condition that he would give up to him entirely his " body, soul, and works;" to which Gaufridi agreed, excepting only from the latter the administration of the holy sacrament, to which he was bound by his vocation as a priest of the church.

From this time Louis Gaufridi felt an extreme pleasure in reading the magical book, and it always had the effect of bringing the demon to attend upon him. At the end of two or three days the agreement was arranged and completed, and, it having been fairly written on parchment, the priest signed it with his blood. The tempter then told him that, whenever he breathed on maid or woman, provided his breath reached their nostrils, they would immediately become desperately in love with him. He soon made a trial of the demon's gift, and used it so copiously, that he became in a short time a general object of attraction to the women of the district. He said that he often amused himself with exciting their passions, when he had no intention of requiting them, and he declared that he had already made more than a thousand victims.

At length he took an extraordinary fancy to the young Magdalen de la Palude; but he found her difficult of approach on account of the watchfulness of her mother, and he only overcame the difficulty by breathing on the mother before he seduced the daughter. He thus gained his purpose, took the girl to the cave in the manner she had already described, and became so much attached to her that he often repeated his charm on her to make her more devoted in her love. Three days after their first visit to the cave, he gave her a familiar named Esmodes. Finding her now perfectly devoted to his will, he determined to marry her to Belzebub, the prince of the demons, and she readily agreed to his proposal. He immediately called the demon prince, who appeared in the form of a handsome gentleman; and she then renounced her baptism and christianity, signed the agreement with her blood, and received the demon's mark. When the book of magic and the various agreements, which Gaufridi said he had preserved, were sought for, they were not forthcoming; but he got over this difficulty by stating that he had burnt the one, when under fear of arrest, and that the evil one had carried away the others. He declared further, that he had had intercourse with sister Magdalen since she was at the Sainte Baume; that he had often been at Sabbaths at the Baume de Rolland, the Baume de Loubieres, and other places in the mountains about, and that two or three times he had wished that these meetings should be held at the Sainte Baume. Once the devil had sent him to fetch sister Magdalen thence, and he declared that he had dragged her from one place to another through all the woods around.

The priest gave an account of the Sabbaths, at which he was a regular attendant. When he was ready to go—it was usually at night—he either went to the open window of his chamber, or left the chamber, locking the door, and proceeded into the open air. There Lucifer made his appearance, and took him in an instant to their place of meeting, where the orgies of the witches and sorcerers lasted usually from three to four hours. Gaufridi divided the victims of the evil one into three classes,—the *masqués*, (perhaps the novices,) the sorcerers, and the magicians. On arriving at the meeting, they all worshipped the demon, according to their several ranks, the *masqués* falling flat on their faces, the sorcerers kneeling with their heads and bodies humbly bowed down, and the magicians, who stood highest in importance, only kneeling. After this, they all went through the formality of denying God and the saints. Then they had a diabolical service in burlesque of that of the church, at which the evil one served as priest in a violet chasuble; the elevation of the demon hoste was announced by a wooden bell, and the sacrament itself was made of unleaven bread. The scenes which followed resembled those of other witch-meetings. Gaufridi acknowledged that he took Magdalen thither, and that he made her swallow magical "characters," that were to increase her love to him; yet he proved unfaithful to her at these Sabbaths with a multitude of persons, and among the rest, with "a princess of Friesland." The unhappy sorcerer confessed, among other things, that his demon was his constant companion, though generally invisible to all but himself, and that he only left him when he entered the church of the Capuchins to perform his religious duties, and then he waited for him outside the church-door.

Gaufridi was tried before the court of parliament of Provence, at Aix. His confession, the declarations of the demons, the marks on his body, and other circumstances, left him no hope of mercy; judgment was given against him on the last day of April, and the same day it was put in execution. He was burnt alive.

All trùe Catholics had derived so much edification from the declarations of the demons of Aix, that cases of possession became more frequent, especially among the nuns. Among the more remarkable cases, we may merely cite those of the nuns of Louviers, in 1643, and of the nuns of Aussonne, in

1662. I will, however, content myself with one more narrative of this class, which is perhaps the most extraordinary of them all. We are left to guess at the reasons for the persecution of Louis Gaufridi, but our next chapter will detail a history of which the motives were more apparent.

CHAPTER XXII.

THE URSULINES OF LOUDUN.

Soon after the period of the persecution of Louis Gaufridi, there was in the town of Loudun in the ancient province of Anjou a priest named Urbain Grandier, a canon of the church there, and a man who was as remarkable for his learning and talent as for his handsome person and courtly manners. He was born towards the end of the sixteenth century at Bouvere near Sablé, at which latter place his father Pierre Grandier exercised the profession of a notary, and his uncle, Claude Grandier, was, like himself, a priest. Urbain Grandier had studied in the college of the Jesuits at Bordeaux, had distinguished himself so much by his attainments and by his eloquence that he became very popular at Loudun, where he obtained two benefices, as a preacher. This excited the jealousy and hatred of his brother clergy, whom his proud and resentful spirit hindered him from conciliating. He seems to have given them some hold upon him by certain irregularities in his life, especially by his familiarities with the other sex, which were a matter of scandal in the town. Loudun, moreover, contained a large population of Protestants, and Urbain Grandier perhaps had a leaning towards them.

Between the year 1620 and 1629, Urbain Grandier had had several serious quarrels and some lawsuits with the clergy of Loudun. A priest named Mounier had published libels upon him, and Urbain prosecuted and obtained a judgment against him, and exacted the full penalty with unfeeling rigour. He had gained an action against another priest named Mignon, a canon of the church of St. Croix, in a matter relating to a house which the latter claimed, and he had made Mignon his personal enemy by the offensive manner in which he exulted in his defeat. By such proceedings as these, and by his real or reputed amours, he had gained many enemies. In 1629, he was accused before the court of the bishop of Poitiers of scandalous intrigues, and even of having secretly introduced women into his church for improper purposes, and he was condemned by the official to be ejected from all his benefices. But some irregularity having been discovered in the proceedings, Urbain appealed, and obtained a decree of parliament, referring the case to the presidial of Poitiers, and he was acquitted of the charges brought against him, which his accusers were compelled to retract. This judgment was delivered on the 25th of May, 1631. It increased the exasperation of his enemies to such a degree, that the archbishop of Bordeaux, as Urbain's friend, advised him to quit Loudun, and establish himself in some other place out of the way of his persecutors. But the angry priest was too proud and resentful to listen to counsel like this.

In the year 1626, a small convent of Ursuline nuns had been established at Loudun, and being very poor, they rented a private house, and were allowed to support themselves by taking as boarders a few young ladies whom they educated. Their first confessor or "director of conscience," was a priest named Mussaut, who died soon after the acquittal of Urbain Grandier by the presidial of Poitiers. Urbain, rather imprudently, became a candidate for Mussaut's place, but was rejected, it was afterwards said, on account of his scandalous character. The office of director of conscience to the Ursulines was given to his old enemy Mignon. This affair seems to have caused a revival of animosities which might otherwise have sunk into oblivion.

Meanwhile the young scholars of the convent appear to have felt dull in the company of their teachers, and they determined to amuse themselves with frightening them. For this purpose they left their beds by night, made dreadful noises about the house, and took advantage of secret passages and peculiarities they had discovered in the building to play a variety of pranks, which they laid to the charge of the ghost of the late spiritual director, father Mussaut. The nuns communicated their terrors to Mussaut's successor, who soon suspected the intrigue; he saw to what advantage it might be turned, and obtained the confidence of the girls who were carrying it on. He not only encouraged them to proceed, but he soon brought the nuns themselves to join in his plans.

Mignon now proceeded more systematically in instructing his patients in the parts they were to act, and taught them to counterfeit all the strange postures and contortions of one supposed to be possessed. He gained the nuns to his purposes, not only by holding out to them the hope of enriching and glorifying their order, but by telling them that they would be the means of confounding and perhaps converting the numerous heretics in and about the town of Loudun, and he assured them that Urbain Grandier was himself a secret heretic. As far as we can judge, the motive which had most weight with the nuns was the prospect of enriching themselves by this "pious fraud," and the superior of the convent entered warmly into the design. Having prepared everything for his purpose, Mignon sent for a bigoted priest of the neighbourhood of Loudun, named Pierre Barré, a man who had assumed the character of a saint, to support which he performed a variety of extravagancies. With the assistance of this man, who was rejoiced at the opportunity of exhibiting the effects of his own holiness, Mignon began by exorcising the superior and two of her nuns, and they carried on their proceedings in great secret for two or three days They then entered into communication with another priest, who bore a very indifferent character, and made him their messenger to two magistrates, whom they invited to witness the exorcising of two nuns of the convent of the Ursulines possessed, as they said, by evil spirits. The first exhibition before the magistrates took place on the 11th of October, 1632. Before the proceedings began, Mignon informed the magistrates, that the nuns had been troubled for some time with a visitation of spectral appearances, which had ended in some of them being possessed with demons. He said that the superior of the nuns was possessed by the grand demon Astaroth, and that one of the nuns was in the possession of another devil whose name was Sabulon; and, although the nuns themselves, as he assured the magistrates, were totally ignorant of the learned languages, the demons knew all languages, and preferred making use of those which were no longer spoken. They were then ushered into a chamber where the superior lay in bed, and Mignon and his fellow exorcist began their operations. When the patient first saw the priests and their companions, she appeared to be seized with dreadful spasms and screamed fearfully; but under the hands of the exorcists she became calmer, and Mignon proceeded to interrogate her spirit in Latin. To his first question, "*Propter quam causam ingressus es in corpus hujus virginis?*" (for what cause did you enter the body of this virgin?) Astaroth answered with the utmost docility, "*Causa animositatis,*" (from animosity.) "*Per quod pactum?*" (by what pact?) said Mignon. "*Per flores,*" (by flowers,) replied the demon. "*Quales?*" (what flowers?) asked the priest. "*Rosas,*" was the reply. "*Quis misit?*" (who sent them?) "*Urbanus.*" "*Dic cognomen,*" (tell us his surname.) To this demand the demon replied with the utmost readiness,

"Grandier." Determined to possess all the particulars, the exorcist continued, "*Dic qualitatem,*" (tell us his profession.) "*Sacerdos,*" (a priest,) said the spirit. "*Cujus ecclesiæ?*" (of what church?) "*Sancti Petri,*" (of St. Peter's.) Then said the priest, "*Quæ persona attulit flores?*" (what person brought the flowers?) to which the instant reply was, "*diabolica,*" (a demon.)

With this, the fit ended, and of course the examination could be carried on no longer. Mignon took the magistrates aside, and discoursed with them on the extraordinary scene they had witnessed, pointing out to them its resemblance to the affair of Louis Gaufridi which had occurred twenty years before. The Romish clergy in general seemed inclined to believe implicitly in the possession, and the capuchins showed a particular animosity against Grandier. The laity were astonished at these extraordinary revelations, and it is not to be wondered at if a great portion of them were led by the priests, and thus easily prejudiced against the accused. The calling in of the magistrates had given the affair more importance; the two first invited had probably been selected as those most likely to be imposed upon by priestcraft. They were admitted to another experiment next day, (the 12th of October,) and after the demon who possessed the superior of the convent had been duly exorcised, he repeated the charges against Grandier, adding that he was not only a priest, but *magus* (a magician). On this occasion the guilty roses were asked for, and a bunch of those flowers were produced and burnt before the company, but to the disappointment of them all, they did not, as was expected, emit a noxious odour under the action of the fire. The principal civil officers of the municipality now interfered, and on the 13th of October the bailli of the town, with the lieutenant civil, the lieutenant criminal, the procureur du roi, the lieutenant à la prévôté, and other officers, went together to the convent of the Ursulines. It would appear that some of these municipal officers were Protestants, and the bailli, especially, was known as a man of good sense and justice. When they arrived at the house occupied by the nuns, they were shown into a waiting-room, where they were left a considerable time, until Mignon condescended to make his appearance, and inform them that the demon that morning had refused to answer except in private, that the examination had been a very extraordinary one, and that he would give them a report of it in writing.

Urbain Grandier professed to despise the intrigues of his enemies, but he could not help feeling alarmed at the formidable league which had been raised against him. He determined first to apply for protection to the spiritual power, and he hurried to lay his complaint before the bishop of Poitiers. This prelate, however, as we have seen before, was not friendly to Grandier, who could not obtain a personal audience, but was referred back to the civil authorities for redress. On his return to Loudun, Grandier went to the civil court, and presented a formal charge of conspiracy against the priest Mignon; and on the 28th of October, the bailli issued a public order of the court against the calumnies of the priests. Mignon protested earnestly against this proceeding, and the whole town became violently agitated by the dispute between the priests and the civil authorities. The bailli followed up his decree by taking a decided part against the nuns, and he gave Grandier warning of every new step which they took. The priests, however, now set the civil power at defiance, and, preparing to act under the authority of the bishop of Poitiers, they continued their exorcisms of the nuns, and, having collected together a number of the least reputable medical practitioners of the place, men they knew were willing from credulity or knavery to be their tools, they obtained their signature to a statement of the truth of the possession. Upon this the bailli publicly inhibited the priests from exorcising or further proceeding in this case, but they again refused to acknowledge his jurisdiction.

They accordingly went on exorcising more openly and boldly than ever. Another nun was now found to be possessed, and her demon confessed that he was Asmodeus, and that he had five companions in the possession of this single victim. He also declared that Urbain Grandier was the magician who had sent them. This occurred on the 24th of November; on the 25th, the civil officers, who were present, insisted on trying the pretended powers of the demons to speak all languages, and the bailli asked the patient what was the Hebrew word signifying water. She held down her head and muttered something, which one of the witnesses who stood very near her declared was a mere refusal in

French to answer. But one of the priests, who was suggesting to her, insisted that she said *zaquaq*, which he declared meant in Hebrew *aquam effudi!* On a previous occasion they had risked an exposure by making the demon speak bad Latin.* They now, therefore, began to be more cautious, and carried on their examination of the demons in a more secret manner. At the same time they tried to gain the bailli over, but in vain. The confessions of the demons still turned mainly upon the delinquences of Grandier, but they began also to talk against the huguenots, provoked no doubt by the incredulity of the civil magistrates. As the latter had exposed some of their tricks, and had given them considerable embarrassment, the nuns were now made to say in their fits that they would no longer give any answers in the presence of the bailli or other municipal officers.

The priests now made their appeal to the bishop of Poitiers, who at last openly espoused their cause, and on the 28th of November he appointed two commissioners, the deans of the canons of Champigni and of the canons of Thouars, to examine into this strange affair. With their countenance and assistance the exorcisms commenced anew, and when, on the 1st of December, the bailli went to the convent, and insisted upon being admitted to the examination and upon being permitted to put questions to the nuns when exorcised, he was refused by Barré, who now acted as chief exorcist.

* In allusion to their bad Latin, and to the classes in the schools, a wit of the day said, "*Que les diables de Loudun n'avoient étudié que jusqu'en troisième.*"

The bailli then formally forbade him to put any questions to the pretended demons tending to defame individuals; but Barré merely replied that it was his intention to use his own discretion in this respect. The priests had now everything at their own will, and they were sanguine of success, when their plot was deranged by the unexpected announcement that the archbishop of Bordeaux was on his way to Loudun. On several occasions the priests had declared, to explain some temporary intermission of the fits, that they had succeeded in driving away the demons, but that they had subsequently been sent back by the magician. When news came of the approach of the archbishop, they disappeared entirely, and the nuns became quiet and tranquil. Some prudent directions given by the archbishop seem to have put a stop to further proceedings, and even Mignon and Barré let the matter drop, so that little more was heard of it.

The Ursulines were now the sufferers. They fell into general discredit; people took away their daughters,* and they fell into distress. They laid the blame of their sufferings on their director, Mignon, who had led them into the expectation of deriving great profit from their imposture.

Before the embers of this flame were quite extinct, an unexpected circumstance rekindled them. Among the pamphlets which had appeared against

* Tallemant des Réaux, who has preserved so many anecdotes of this period, tells us that Le Couldray Montpensier, who had two daughters boarding with these nuns, immediately took them away, and had them well whipped, which he found an efficacious method of driving out the demons.

cardinal Richelieu, who then ruled the destinies of France, was a very bitter satire, entitled, in allusion to some low intrigue of the cardinals connected with this town, *La Cordonnière de Loudun*. M. de Laubardemont, a creature of the cardinal, who at this time held the office of master of the requests, was sent to Loudun, in 1633, to direct the demolition of the castle of that place. Mignon and his fellow-plotters immediately obtained an introduction to this minister, and they not only recounted to him the affair of the nuns, in a manner very disadvantageous to Urbain Grandier and his friends, but they persuaded him that Urbain was the author of the satire just mentioned. Laubardemont returned to Paris, and communicated what he had heard to the cardinal, who seldom spared the authors of personal attacks on himself when they were in his power, and who is said to have been urged on to sacrifice the curé of Loudun by his confidential adviser, the celebrated père Joseph. The result was, that Laubardemont returned to Loudun, commissioned by the king to inquire into the possession of the nuns, and into the charges against Grandier. He arrived at Loudun with this commission on the 6th of December, 1633.

The case now assumed a much more serious countenance. The demons returned to the sisters with redoubled fury, and with an increase of numbers, and nearly all the nuns were attacked by them. Mignon and his fellow-priest had already got up an exhibition of exorcism for Laubardemont before that functionary's departure for Paris, and he brought back with him a writ for the apprehension of Grandier, in which were blazoned forth all the crimes which had ever been imputed, rightly or wrongly, to that individual. Upon this he was thrown into prison, and his house searched for magical books, which were not found. Two only proofs against him, considered of any importance, were discovered among his papers, some French verses, which are characterised in the *procès verbal* as being *sales et impudiques*—a somewhat strange accusation in that licentious age, but they perhaps served to corroborate the suspicion that Grandier was the author of the libel on the cardinal—and a book which he had written, but never published, against the celibacy of the clergy. At the beginning of the year a series of examinations were taken, and being committed to writing and duly attested, Laubardemont carried them to Paris to lay them before the minister. He then received a new commission from the king to act as supreme judge of this cause, independent of all other jurisdiction whatever; and he returned to Loudun with this extensive power on the 9th of April, 1634.

Laubardemont began by selecting as judges a certain number of persons from the local magistracy who were most likely to be devoted to his will, and such physicians and others were chosen to assist in the examinations as were known to bear enmity to the accused. The numerous victims of the pretended possession were now distributed into two bands, for the convenience of the exorcists. On the 23rd of April the superior of the nuns declared that the demons who possessed her had entered her in the forms of a cat, a dog, a stag, and a goat. On the 24th, she declared the Grandier had the demon's marks on his body. On the authority of this statement, next day a surgeon, selected as being the bitterest of his enemies, was sent to Grandier in his prison to search for his marks, and the miserable victim was stripped and treated with extreme inhumanity. He ended by discovering, as he pretended, five marks, or insensible spots. The demons were not always very accurate in the information they gave to the exorcists. When questioned as to Grandier's books of magic, they indicated a certain *demoiselle* to whom he had entrusted them before his arrest, and in whose house they said that the books would be found. Laubardemont and others went immediately to the house indicated, which they examined from top to bottom, but they found no books of the description of those of which they were in search. They returned, and scolded the demons for their false information. The latter pretended that a niece of the *demoiselle* had carried them away after the information had been given. They then went to the niece, but they found that she was at church, and that she had been so occupied all day that it was impossible she could have acted as the demons stated. But the exorcists were not discouraged by a few slips like these, and they were especially active in their examinations at the beginning of the month of May. Some new demons then appeared on the scene, under the names of Eazas, Cerberus, Beherit, &c. Other statements of the demons were found to be false, and the conspirators had much difficulty in concealing some of the tricks they employed. But all these difficulties were passed over as matters of little moment.

The examinations were now exhibited publicly in the church, and a crowd of people, both Catholics and Huguenots, were always present. The matter had already created so much sensation throughout France, that many people of quality came from Paris and other parts, so that all the hostelries in the town were filled with visitors. Among the rest was Quillet, the court poet, who fell into temporary disgrace by his imprudence on this occasion. At one of the exhibitions, Satan, speaking from the mouth of one of the sisters, threatened that he would toss up to the ceiling of the church any one who should dare to deny the possession of the nuns. Quillet took him on his word, and was not tossed to the ceiling, but he provoked so much the anger of Laubardemont, that he is said to have found it advisable to make a journey to Rome. On another occasion the devil boasted that he would take the protestant minister of Loudun in his pulpit and carry him up to the top of the church steeple, but he did not put his threat in execution. This same protestant minister was present at one of the examinations, when the priests, who were administering the consecrated host, told him contemptuously, to show their superiority over the Huguenots, that he dared not put his fingers into the mouths of the nuns as they did. He is said to have replied, that "he had no familiarity with the devil, and would not presume to play with him." The priests made the nuns utter a great mass of nonsense, and much that was profane and indecent. They caused them to say many things irreverent even to those who conducted the prosecution, which was considered as proving how little they were influenced by them. One day the devil, by the mouth of one of the sisters, closed the examination by declaring, "*M. de Laubardemont est cocu.*" In the evening, as usual, Laubardemont took the written report, wrote under these words as a matter of course, "*Ce que j'atteste être vrai,*" and signed it with his name. When the depositions were sent to Paris, this circumstance was the source of no little amusement at court.

As the trial went on, doubts and ridicule began to be thrown upon it, which alarmed the commissioners, and it was resolved to hasten the proceedings. Every precaution was taken to secure the condemnation of Grandier. His brother, an advocate of parliament, was accused of sorcery and placed under arrest, that he might not be capable of appealing. Every circumstance that told in favour of the accused was carefully suppressed, while whatever could be turned against him was magnified into undue importance. Those who expressed any doubts were threatened with prosecution; and the bishop of Poitiers now came forward again, and not only gave the prosecution the full advantage of his ecclesiastical authority, but he caused placards to be exhibited about the town forbidding any one to speak disrespectfully of the nuns. This at once shut the mouths of all Grandier's friends.

His enemies had, however, another embarrassing circumstance to contend with. Some of the actors appear to have become ashamed of their parts, and to have been surprised with scruples of conscience. At the beginning of July, sister Clara declared before the multitude assembled in the church, that all her confessions for some months past had been mere falsehood and imposture, which had heen put into her mouth by Mignon and the priests, and she rushed from the church and endeavoured to make her escape; but she was seized and brought back. This, however, did not hinder another nun, sister Agnes, from following her example, and she made a similar declaration. The commissioner immediately adopted measures for hindering the recurrence of such accidents, and the priests declared that it was only one of the demon's vagaries, and that the unruly patients were at that moment under his influence. They carried their measures of intimidation so far, that they accused not only a sister of Grandier, but the wife of the bailli of Loudun, of being witches, intending thus at one blow to strike fear into his friends and relations. And they declared openly that the attempt to throw discredit on the proceedings was a mere trick of the Huguenots, who were afraid that the miracles performed by the priests on this occasion would throw discredit upon them.

Thus, overruling every form of law and justice, did the curé's enemies hurry on to their object. As soon as it was known that the all-powerful cardinal was resolved on the destruction of the victim, few were bold enough to stand up in his defence. On the 18th of August, 1634, the judges assembled in the convent of the Carmelites, and on the faith of evidence testified by Astaroth, the chief of the devils, and a host of other demons,* they pronounced judgment on Urbain Grandier, convicted of magic and sorcery, to the effect that he should perform penance before the public, and that then he should be conducted to the stake, and burnt alive along with his magical covenants and characters, (these were probably invented,) and with his manuscript treatise on the celibacy of the clergy. The sentence was put in execution the same day.

Thus perished another victim of superstition adopted as the instrument of personal revenge. The process of the curé of Loudun made an extraordinary noise, the bigotted priests holding it up as a miraculous proof of the truth and efficacy of the Romish faith, while the Protestants decried it as loudly as an infamous inposture. Even in England it excited considerable interest. It gave rise to many publications in France, where also the evidence was analysed and it weakness exposed, and the whole affair soon fell into discredit. Some years afterwards, the materials of this tragic story were collected together and arranged in a small volume printed at Amsterdam, in 1693, under the title of the *Histoire des Diables de Loudun*.

* The original depositions, with the autograph signatures of the demons (!), are still preserved among the manuscripts in the national library in Paris. The signatures are strange scrawls, evidently written by trembling hands guided by others.

CHAPTER XXIII.

THE LANCASHIRE WITCHES.

There was something extraordinary in the sudden prevalence of sorcery during the years 1610, 1611, and 1612, through most of the countries of western Europe. It was in the last of these years that occurred one of the most romantic, if not one of the most remarkable, cases of witchcraft in England.

One of the wildest districts in Lancashire, even at the present day, is that known as the forest of Pendle, on the borders of Yorkshire. Above it rises the dark and lofty mountain known as Pendle hill, from the declivity of which the forest extended over a descent of about five miles to a barren and dreary tract called the water of Pendle. The view from the summit of the hill was grand and extensive, and near at hand beneath lay the splendid remains of the abbey of Whalley. The tract included under the name of the forest was barren and desolate, thinly inhabited, and its population very rude and uncultivated. On a brow of the descent from Pendle hill, at a considerable distance from any other habitation, stood a solitary and deserted building, of some antiquity, no doubt in ruins, known popularly as the Malkin tower. It was inhabited at the time of which we are speaking by an old woman, whose real name was Elizabeth Southernes, but who was better known in the neighbourhood by that of old Demdike. She was at this time about eighty years of age, and exhibited all the characteteristics of a confirmed witch in their most exaggerated forms. She had a son named Christopher, and a daughter named Elizabeth, who married a labourer of the Pendle district, named John Device. The Devices had three children, James, Alizon, and Jennet, the latter being, in 1612, nine years of age. It is one of the doctrines of sorcery, that the descendants of a witch follow, from a sort of inevitable necessity, the same profession, and all the members of this family then living, through the three generations, bore the same evil reputation.

They were not, however, alone in their dealings with the evil one, for the district of Pendle was at this time little better famed in the north of England than the territory of Labourd in France. There was another family which held a high rank among the witches of Pendle, the principal member of which was Anne Whittle, who went by the popular name of old Chattox, and was of the same age as old Demdike; she had an only daughter named Anne, who was married to Thomas Redferne. Old Demdike was the senior or queen of the witches of Pendle and the neighbourhood, but she had a jealous rival in old Chattox, and the animosity created by their rivalry was shared by their families.

Mother Demdike, however, had long reigned supreme in her quarters, the terror of her neighbours. According to her own confession, she had been a witch fifty years, (the printed book says twenty, but there are other circumstances mentioned which show this was a misprint.) Her own account of herself, when brought to trial was, that at the period just mentioned, she was one day "coming homeward from begging, when there met her near unto a stone-pit in Goldshaw, in the said forest of Pendle, a spirit or devil, in the shape of a boy, the one half of his coat black, and the other brown, who bade her stay, saying to her, that if she would give him her soul, she should have anything that she would request. Whereupon she demanded his name, and the spirit answered his name was Tibb. And so in hope of such gain as was promised by the said devil or Tibb, she was contented to give her soul to the said spirit. And for the space of five or six years next after, the said spirit or devil appeared at sundry times unto her about daylight-gate, [twilight,] always bidding her stay, and asking her what she would have or do. To whom she replied, nay, nothing; for she said she wanted nothing yet. And so about the end of the said six years, upon a sabbath day, in the morning, this examinate, having a little child upon her knee, and she being in a slumber, the said spirit appeared unto her in the likeness of a brown dog, forcing himself to her knee, to get blood under her left arm ; and she being without any apparel saving her smock, the said devil did get blood under her left arm And she awaking, said, 'Jesus, save my child!' but had no power, nor could not say, Jesus save herself! whereupon the brown dog vanished out of her sight; after which she was almost stark mad for the space of eight weeks."

The child here spoken of must have been Elizabeth Device, one of the heroines of the present history, who in due time was betrayed by the evil ne, and made a witch by her mother. It was the old woman, also, who inducted her grand-children, or was the means of introducing them, to the same evil and dangerous calling. James Device, the eldest of these, said in his confession, "that upon Sheare Thursday was two years (Easter-eve, 1610,) his grandmother, Elisabeth Southernes, alias Demdike, did bid him, this examinate, go to the church to receive the communion, (the next day after being Good Friday,) and then not eat the bread the minister gave him, but to bring it and deliver it to such a thing as should meet him in his way homeward. Notwithstanding her persuasion, this examinate did eat the bread, and so in his coming homeward some forty roodes off the said church, there met him a thing in a shape of a hare, who spoke unto this examinate, and asked him whether he had brought the bread that his grandmother had bidden him, or no. Whereupon this examinate answered, he had not; and thereupon the said thing threatened to pull this examinate in pieces; and so this examinate thereupon marked himself to God, and so the said thing vanished out of this examinate's sight. And within some four days after that, there appeared in this examinate's sight, hard by the new church in Pendle, a thing like unto a brown dog, who asked this examinate to give him his soul, and he should be revenged of any whom he would; whereunto the examinate answered, that his soul was not his to give, but was his Saviour Jesus Christ's; but as much as was in him this examinate to give he was contented he should have it. And within two or three days after, this examinate went to the Carre Hall, and upon some speeches betwixt mistress Towneley and this examinate, she charging this examinate and his said mother to have stolen some turves of her, bad him pack the doores; and withall as he went forth of the door, the said mistress Towneley gave him a knock between the shoulders. And about a day or two after that, there appeared unto this examinate in his way a thing like unto a black dog, who put this examinate in mind of the said mistress Towneley's falling out with him, and bad him make a picture of clay like unto the said mistress Towneley; and he dried it the same night by the fire, and within a day after, he, this examinate, began to crumble the said picture, every day some, for the space of a week; and within two days after all was crumbled away, the said mistress Towneley died. And he further saith, that in Lent last one John Duckworth of the Launde promised this examinate an old shirt; and within a fortnight after, this examinate went to the said Duckworth's house, and demanded the said old shirt; but the said Duckworth denied him thereof. And going out of the said house, the said spirit Dandy appeared unto this examinate, and said, 'Thou didst touch the said Duckworth.' Whereunto this examinate answered, he did not touch him. 'Yes,' said the spirit again, 'thou didst touch him, and therefore I have power of him.' Whereupon this examinate agreed with the said spirit, and then wished the said spirit to kill the said Duckworth: and within one week, then next after, Duckworth died."

His sister Alizon's account of her conversion to witchcraft was as follows. She said, "that about two years agon, her grandmother (called Elisabeth Southernes, alias old Demdike) did sundry times in going or walking together as they went begging, persuade and advise this examinate to let a devil or familiar appear unto her; and that she, this examinate, would let him suck at some part of her, and she might have and do what she would. And she further saith, that one John Nutter, of the Bulhole in Pendle aforesaid, had a cow which was sick, and requested this examinate's grandmother to amend the said cow; and her said grandmother said she would, and so her said grandmother about ten of the clocke in the night, desired this examinate to lead her forth, which this examinate did, she being then blind; and her grandmother did remain about half an hour forth; and this examinate's sister did fetch her in again; but what she did when she was so forth, this examinate cannot tell. But the next morning this examinate heard that the said cow was dead. And this examinate verily thinketh that her said grandmother did bewitch the said cow to death. And further, this examinate saith, that about two years agon, this examinate having gotten a piggin full of blue milk by begging, brought it into the house of her grandmother, where (this examinate going forth presently, and staying about half an hour) there was butter to the quantity of a quartern of a pound in the said milk, and the quantity of the said milk still remaining; and her grandmother had no butter in the house when this examinate went forth, during which time this examinate's grandmother still lay in her bed. And further, this examinate saith, that Richard Baldwin of Weethead, within the forest of Pendle, about two years ago, fell out with this examinate's grandmother, and so would not let her come upon his land: and about four or five days then next after, her said grandmother did request this examinate to lead her forth about ten of the clocke in the night, which this examinate accordingly did, and she stayed forth then about an houre, and this examinate's sister fetched her in again. And this examinate heard the next morning that a woman child of the said Richard Baldwin was fallen sick; and as this examinate did then hear, the said child did languish afterwards by the space of a year, or thereabouts, and died. And this examinate verily thinketh that her said grandmother did bewitch the said child to death."

The youngest of the Devices, Jennet, a child of nine years, was as yet too young to be a witch herself, but she had been a careful watcher of the doings of her relatives, and appears to have been usually admitted to their secret meetings.

Old Demdike must certainly have obtained the special favour of the evil one, if it was to be gained by the number of her converts, for she was not only the perverter of those of her own party, but of those of the rival faction also ; for old Chattox, her equal in age and decrepitude, if not in power, confessed that it was mother Demdike who first seduced her to listen to the tempter. The records of the court testify that " the said Anne Whittle, alias Chattox, said, that about fourteen years past she entered, through the wicked persuasions and counsel of Elizabeth Southernes, alias Demdike, and was seduced to condescend and agree to become subject unto that devilish abominable profession of witchcraft. Soon after which, the devil appeared unto her in the likeness of a man, about midnight, at the house of the said Demdike ; and thereupon the said Demdike and she went forth of the said house unto him ; whereupon the said wicked spirit moved this examinate that she would become his subject and give her soul unto him. The which at first she refused to assent unto ; but after, by the great persuasions made by the said Demdike, she yielded to be at his commandment and appointment. Whereupon the said wicked spirit then said unto her, that he must have one part of her body for him to suck upon ; the which she denied then to grant unto him ; and withall asked him, what part of her body he would have for that use ; who said, he would have a place of her right side, near to her ribs, for him to suck upon ; whereunto she assented. And she further said, that at the same time there was a thing in the likeness of a spotted bitch, that came with the said spirit unto the said Demdike, which then did speak unto her in this examinate's hearing, and said, that she should have gold, silver, and worldly wealth, at her will; and at the same time she saith there was victuals, viz. flesh, butter, cheese, bread, and drink, and bid them eat enough. And after their eating, the devil called Fancy, and the other spirit calling himself Tibb, carried the remnant away. And she saith, that although they did eat, they were never the fuller nor better for the same; and that at their said banquet the said spirits gave them light to see what they did, although they neither had fire nor candle-light; and that they were both she spirits and devils."

Anne Redferne, mother Chattox's daughter, held a special rank among these miserable people, for she was the most skilful of them all in making those terrible instruments of evil, the images of clay. Old Demdike, in her confession, declared, "that about half a year before Robert Nutter died, as this examinate thinketh, this examinate went to the house of Thomas Redferne, which was about midsummer, as this examinate remembereth it. And there, within three yards of the east end of the said house, she saw the said Anne Whittle, alias Chattox, and Anne Redferne, wife of the said Thomas Redferne, and daughter of the said Anne Whittle, alias Chattox, the one of the one side of the ditch, and the other on the other, and two pictures of clay or marle lying by them; and the third picture the said Anne Whittle, alias Chattox, was making; and the said Anne Redferne, her said daughter, wrought her clay or marle to make the third picture withall. And this examinate passing by them, the said spirit, called Tibb, in the shape of a black cat, appeared unto her this examinate, and said, 'Turn back again, and do as they do. To whom this examinate said, 'What are they doing?' Whereunto the said spirit said, 'They are making three pictures.' Whereupon she asked whose pictures they were. Whereunto the said spirit said, 'They are the pictures of Christopher Nutter, Robert Nutter, and Mary, wife of the said Robert Nutter.' But this examinate denying to go back to help them to make the pictures aforesaid, the said spirit, seeming to be angry therefore, shove or pushed this examinate into the ditch, and so shed the milk which this examinate had in a can or kit, and so thereupon the spirit at that time vanished out of this examinate's sight. But presently after that, the said spirit appeared to this examinate again in the shape of a hare, and so went with her about a quarter of a mile, but said nothing to this examinate, nor she to it."

The two factions under these two rivals in mischief—the Erictho and Canidia, as they have been aptly termed, of the forest of Pendle—were the terror of the neighbourhood. Those who were not witches themselves, were glad to buy on any terms the favour of mother Demdike and her familiar Tibb, or that of mother Chattox and her imp Fancy; and those who offended the two powerful sorceresses or their friends, or who failed to propitiate them, were sure to meet with some kind of severe punishment Several of their deeds are recounted in the examinations taken down at the trials. Their vengeance was often the result of very trifling provocations, and they at times exerted their blighting influence without any provocation at all. In her second examination, Alizon Device, after telling the manner of her seduction by her grandmother, says that not long after, "being walking, towards the Rough-Lee, in a close of one John Robinson's, there appeared unto her a thing like unto a black dog, speaking unto her, and desiring her to give him her soul, and he would give her power to do anything she would: whereupon this examinate being therewithall inticed, and setting her down, the said black dog did with his mouth (as this examinate then thought) suck at her breast, a little below her paps, which place did remain blue half a yeare next after; which said black dog did not appear to this examinate, until the eighteenth day of March last; at which time this examinate met with a pedlar on the highway called Colne-field, near unto Colne; and this examinate demanded of the said pedlar to buy some pins of him; but the said pedlar sturdily answered that he would not loose his pack; and so this examinate parting with him, presently there appeareth to this examinate the black dog which appeared unto her as before; which black dog spake unto her in English, saying, 'What wouldst thou have me to do with yonder man?' To whom this examinate said, 'What canst thou do at him?' And the dog answered again, 'I can lame him.' Whereupon this examinate answered, and said to the said black dog, 'Lame him;' and before the pedlar was gone forty rods further, he fell down lame; and this examinate then went after the said pedlar; and in a house about the distance aforesaid, he was lying lame."

We have seen that Alizon Device accused her grandmother Demdike of causing the death of a daughter of Richard Baldwin, the millar, about two years before the time of her arrest. The feud between them seems to have been lasting, for the old woman confessed that, a little before the Christmas of 1611 her daughter Elizabeth Device had been employed "in helping the folks at the mill," and asked her to call upon Richard Baldwin to demand some remuneration for her work. Probably Elizabeth Device had given some cause of anger to the millar, for, as old Demdike, led by her granddaughter Alizon, (for she was herself blind,) approached his house, he met them, and applying certain opprobrious epithets to both, threatened he would burn the one and hang the other unless they went their ways. As they were passing the next hedge, the old witch's familiar Tibb made his appearance, and obtained a commission to take vengeance "of the millar or his." What that vengeance was, we are not informed.

As far as we can discover from the facts deposed at the trial, the hostility between mother Demdike and mother Chattox arose from the depredations of the latter or of her family, which happened about the close of the reign of queen Elizabeth. Elizabeth Device was robbed, and some of the articles stolen were found immediately afterwards on the person of Anne, the daughter of Chattox, (she was not at this time married to Redferne,) and reclaimed. The anger of mother Chattox was now great against the

Devices, and, she being apparently powerless against old Demdike and her blood, her son-in-law John Device, the husband of Elizabeth, became so alarmed for his own safety, that he covenanted with Chattox to pay her yearly a measure of meal on condition that she should not hurt him or his goods by her charms. "This," said Alizon, "was yearly paid, until the year which her father died in, which was about eleven years since; her father, upon his then death-bead, taking it that the said Anne Whittle, *alias* Chattox, did bewitch him to death, because the said meal was not paid the last year!"

Many other persons seem to have been gradually drawn into this feud, among whom were some branches of the Nutters, a family rather extensively spread among the lesser gentry and yeomanry of this district. The Redfernes were tenants of the Nutters of Pendle in the time of old Robert Nutter, whose wife, Elizabeth Nutter, had employed mother Chattox to effect the destruction of her own grandson, known as "young Robert Nutter," in order that her husband's lands might go to some member of the same family who stood higher in her favour. This circumstance we learn from the confession of mother Chattox herself, who tells us that "Elizabeth Nutter, wife to old Robert Nutter, did request this examinate, and Loomeshaw's wife of Burley, and one Jane Boothman of the same, who are now both dead, to get young Robert Nutter his death, if they could, all being together then at that time, to that end, that if Robert were dead, then the women their cousins might have the land; by whose persuasion they all consented unto it. After which time, this examinate's son-in-law Thomas Redferne did persuade this examinate not to kill or hurt the said Robert Nutter; for which persuasion the said Loomeshaw's wife had like to have killed the said Redferne, but that one Mr. Baldwyn (the late schoolmaster at Coln) did by his learning stay the said Loomeshaw's wife, and therefor had a capon from Redferne."

Baldwyn the schoolmaster, was probably a "white wizard."

Robert Nutter was thus saved from death, but his fate was only deferred, for not long after, as mother Chattox further informs us, Robert Nutter who was probably ignorant of the plot from which he had already escaped, "did desire her daughter, Redferne's wife, to have his will of her, being then in Redferne's house; but the said Redferne's wife denied the said Robert. Whereupon the said Robert seeming to be greatly displeased therewith, in a great anger took his horse and went away, saying in a great rage, that if ever the ground came to him she should never dwell upon his land." Anne Redferne told her mother of the threat and the circumstance which had given rise to it, and the latter immediately consulted her familiar Fancy, "who came to her in the likeness of a man, in a parcel of ground called the Launde, asking this examinate what she would have him to do; and this examinate bade him go and revenge her of the said Robert Nutter." The result was the death not only of Robert Nutter, but of his father, Christopher Nutter, the particulars of which were told at the trial by young Robert's brother John and his sister Margaret.

Elizabeth Nutter had now fully obtained her desire, and the Redfernes were allowed to remain in their house. Some years after, however, we still find hostility existing between the Redfernes and the Nutters of Pendle. Anthony Nutter had now, perhaps, inherited Elizabeth Nutter's property, and lived in the house at Pendle with his daughter Anne. One day they offended mother Chattox, when she came to their house, and next day Anne Nutter fell sick, and, after languishing three weeks, died. James Device, on his examination at the trial, told a strange story connected with this event. He said, "that twelve years ago, Anne Chattox, at a burial at the new church in Pendle, did take three scalps of people which had been buried and then cast out of a grave, as she the said Chattox told this examinate; and took eight teeth out of the said scalps, whereof she kept four to herself, and gave other four to the said Demdike, this examinate's grandmother; which four teeth now shown to this examinate are the four teeth that the said Chattox gave to his said grandmother as aforesaid; which said teeth have ever since been kept, until now found by Henry Hargreaves and this examinate, at the west-end of this examinate's grandmother's house, and there buried in the earth, and a picture of clay there likewise found by them about half a yard over in the earth where the said teeth lay, which said picture so found was almost withered away, and was the picture of Anne, Anthony Nutter's daughter."

We have no account of the circumstances which, after these witches had so long enjoyed impunity, led at last to their seizure. Perhaps the enmity of the Nutters had something to do with it; but Thomas Potts, who collected and printed the records of a trial in which he seems to have taken a very particular interest,* ascribes their discovery and arrest to the zealous endeavours of that "very religious honest gentleman," Roger Nowell, esq., "one of his majesty's justices in these parts," the representative of the old family of the Nowells of Read in the Pendle district. Four of the most notorious of these witches, Demdike and Chattox, with Alizon Device and Anne Redferne, were captured by Nowell's orders, and, having each made a "full" confession, probably in the hope of saving their lives, he committed them as prisoners to Lancaster castle on the second of April, 1612, to take their trials at the next assizes.

Their chief place of resort, Malkin tower, remained as yet unvisited and untouched. It was a place looked upon with awe by the peasantry, and

* Potts was the author of "The Wonderful Discoverie of Witches in the Countie of Lancaster," (4to. Lond. 1613,) a book of some rarity, of which a reprint, with a considerable mass of valuable information, was edited, in 1845, for the Chetham Society, by James Crossley, esq. of Manchester. The present account of the Lancashire witches is compiled entirely from the materials preserved by Potts, which are the authentic copies of the confessions of the offenders and the depositions of witnesses. The common chap-book tract, entitled "The Lancashire Witches," which has been inserted by Mr. Halliwell in his "Palatine Anthology," was a mere catch-penny invention.

The reader will remember the admirably conceived character of master Thomas Potts, in Ainsworth's romance.

few but old Demdike and her confederates cared to approach it. Strange noises were heard about it, and it was haunted by beings still more strange. James Device, in his examination before justice Nowell, deposed that, "about a month ago, as this examinate was coming towards his mother's house, and at day-gate [twilight] of the same night, he met a brown dog coming from his grandmother's house, about ten roods distant from the same house; and about two or three nights after, he heard a voice of a great number of children shrieking and crying pitifully, about daylight-gate, and likewise about ten roods distant of this examinate's said grandmother's house. And about five nights then next following, within twenty roods of the said Elizabeth Southerne's house, he heard a foul yelling like unto a great number of cats; but what they were, this examinate cannot tell."

It was here that, during mother Demdike's life, the witches of these parts held their grand and solemn meetings, which took place annually on Good Friday. The day of assembly was just at hand when Demdike was arrested, but many of the witches who had escaped met as usual, in spite of her absence. In fact, the meeting at the Malkin tower, on the Good Friday of 1612, seems to have been better attended than usual. There was, we are told, "great cheer, merry company, and much conference." The objects of this conference were of some importance. It was Elizabeth Device who presided, and of course now the object of most interest to her was the delivery of her mother. It was, we are told, proposed to kill the jailer of Lancaster castle, set all the prisoners at liberty, and blow up the castle itself, by a few old women assembled in an old ruinous tower. But what might not old women do, when they had Satan to assist them? The matters which were intended to be originally debated or performed at this meeting were the christening of a familiar for Alizon Device, and the bewitching of certain individuals who had recently given them offence.

But while thus consulting, the witches were not aware that a young traitor was sitting amongst them. This was Jennet Device, the youngest of the granddaughters of old Device and the child of the very woman who was presiding over the meeting in her absence. This ill-conditioned child, a girl of nine years old, gave information to the zealous justice Nowell of the meeting at the Malkin tower, and told him who were present. Within a few days the number of persons implicated in this affair, imprisoned in Lancaster castle, was increased to twelve, among whom were Elizabeth Device, her son James, and Alice Nutter of Rough Lee, a lady of fortune.

From the informer Jennet Device, the worthy justice extracted a more particular account of the feast at the Malkin tower. She said there were about twenty persons present, of whom three only were men, and that the hour of meeting was twelve o'clock of the day. They had to their dinner, beef, bacon, and roasted mutton; "which mutton, as this examinate's brother said, was of a wether of Christopher Swyer's of Barley; which wether was brought in the night before into this examinate's mother's house by the said James Device, and in this examinate's sight was killed and eaten as aforesaid." John Balcock, one of the men present at this meeting, turned the spit. A woman named Preston, of Craven in Yorkshire, was brought by her familiar, who had taken the form of a white foal for that purpose. James Device, who confessed that he had been present at the meeting in Malkin tower, added, "that all the witches went out of the said house in their own shapes and likenesses. And they all, by that they were forth of the doors, got on horseback like unto foals, some of one colour, some of another; and Preston's wife was the last: and when she got on horseback, they all presently vanished out of this examinate's sight. And before their said parting away, they all appointed to meet at the said Preston's wife's house that day twelvemonths; at which time the said Preston's wife promised to make them a great feast. And if they had occasion to meet in the mean time, there should warning be given, that they all should meet upon Romleyes Moor."

Several of the persons at this meeting were related in some way or other to the Devices or to their rivals, and they appear to have been generally of a very equivocal character in other respects. One person now implicated in this affair, Alice Nutter of Rough Lee, alone excites much sympathy. She was a woman of considerable property, and held a respectable position among the better families in the county. Rough Lee, her residence, is still standing, and is a good specimen of the gentleman's house of that period. Jennet Device, the little girl, was evidently suborned to swear away the lives of her relatives, and there appeared good reason for believing that she introduced Alice Nutter into the plot at the desire of some of that lady's relatives, who were eager to obtain her property, which would come to them by heritage on her death. It has been further handed down by tradition that justice Nowell owed the lady a grudge on account of a long-disputed question of a boundary between their lands, and that he at least gave encouragement to this conspiracy against her.

The charges brought against Alice Nutter on the trial were chiefly remarkable for their weakness. Jennet Device and her brother James declared that she was at the meeting at the Malkin tower on Good Friday, and Elizabeth Device said she joined with her and old Demdike in bewitching a man named Mitton to death, merely because the said Mitton had refused to give Demdike a penny.

Old Demdike escaped the cruelty of the law by dying in prison a few days after she had been committed. Thus mother Chattox became the chief of the witches who were brought into court for trial on the 19th of August. She is described as "a very old, withered, spent, and decrepid creature, her sight almost gone." Mother Chattox was quite blind; her lips were "ever chattering and talking, but no man knew what;" and she was "always more ready to do mischief to men's goods than themselves;" in this respect the contrary of Demdike, who took delight in killing and tormenting the persons of her enemies. She was, nevertheless, notorious as "a dangerous witch," and was "always opposite to old Demdike, for whom the one favoured, the other hated deadly." Between them no doubt the forest of Pendle must have been an agreeable neighbourhood. Yet mother Chattox had some feelings of affection, for when judgment was pronounced upon her, she cried out in a distracted manner that God would be merciful to her, and falling on her knees, supplicated the judge that he would "be merciful unto Anne Redferne, her daughter." Demdike's daughter, Elizabeth Device, was next brought to the bar. "This odious witch was branded with a preposterous mark in nature, even from her birth, which was her left eye standing lower than the other; the one looking down, the other looking up, so strangely deformed that the best that were present in that honourable assembly and great audience did affirm they had not often seen the like." When this woman saw her own child stand up in evidence against her, she burst into a violent passion, "according to her accustomed manner, outrageously cursing, cried out against the child in such a fearful manner, as all the court did not a little wonder at her, and so amazed the child, as with weeping tears she cried out to my lord the judge, and told him she was not able to speak in the presence of her mother." In the end they were obliged to take Elizabeth Device away, and then the daughter gave her evidence unconcerned. The other prisoners were then brought to their trial in succession. Four, Chattox, Elizabeth Device, and the two children of the latter, (James and Alizon,) had made confessions, and therefore they had little to hope. With them were convicted Anne Redferne, Alice Nutter, Katharine Hewit, John Bulcock and his wife Jane, all of Pendle, and Isabel Roby of Windle, in the parish of Prescot, who maintained their innocence to the last. They were all burnt the day after their trial, "at the common place of execution near to Lancaster." One Margaret Pearson of Padiham, though convicted of being a witch, was dealt more leniently with, being only condemned to exposure on the pillory. Two others were acquitted.

Young Jennet Device, who for her age appears to have possessed at least as evil disposition as any of them, was spared as the principal evidence against the accused. Her declaration proved that she was not unacquainted with the practices of her parents, and she confessed, "that her mother had taught her two prayers, the one to cure the bewitched, and the other to get drink." *

* The prayer, or rather charm, to cure those bewitched, which Jennet Device had learnt from her mother, was as follows, and from its phraseology was evidently then of considerable antiquity.

Upon Good Friday, I will fast while I may
Untill I heare them knell
Our Lord's owne bell.
Lord in his messe
With his twelve apostles good,
What hath he in his hand?
Ligh in leath wand.
What hath he in his other hand?
Heaven's doore key.
Open, open, heaven doore keyes.
Steck, steck, hell doore.
Let crizum child
Goe to its mother mild.

One other of the witches who met at the fatal assembly in Malkin tower was brought to the scaffold at the same time. This was Jennet Preston, of Gisborne in Craven, who was tried at York for bewitching some members of the family of Lister in Craven, and for other similar offences; but the principal evidence against her was derived from the confessions of Elizabeth, James, and Jennet Device. It was she who rode to the Malkin tower on a white foal. She died without confession.

Jennet Device only escaped the scaffold on this occasion, as it has been supposed, to undergo somewhat later the same dreadful punishment that she had brought on so many of her relatives. Twenty years after the events detailed above, the witches still continued to hold their meetings in the forest of Pendle,

What is yonder that casts a light so farrandly?
Mine owne deare sonne that's naild to the tree.
He is naild sore by the heart and hand,
And holy harne panne.
Well is that man,
That Fryday spell can,
His child to learne;
A cross of blew, and another of red,
As good Lord was to the roode.
Gabriel laid him downe to sleepe
Upon the ground of holy weepe;
Good Lord came walking by,
Sleepst thou, wakst thou, Gabriel?
No, Lord, I am sted with sticke and stake,
That I can neither sleepe nor wake.
Rise up, Gabriel, and goe with me,
The stick nor the stake shall never deere thee.
Sweet Jesus, our Lord, amen.

It is a mere farrago of popish religious verses.

in greater numbers than ever, but for some reason or other the old rendezvous at Malkin tower seems to have been deserted, and they now assembled at a place at some distance from it named the Hoar-stones, a house which is said to be still standing. On the 10th of February, 1633, a lad named Edmund Robinson, the son of a poor mason in Pendle forest, made the following strange declaration before two justices of the peace. He said that on All Saints' day, in the preceding year, he was gathering bullies or wild plums in Wheatley-lane, when he saw two greyhounds, one black and the other brown, running over the next field towards him. They came to him familiarly, and then he perceived they had each a collar, which "did shine like gold," and to which a string was attached. Seeing that nobody followed the greyhounds, he imagined they belonged to some of the neighbours and had broke loose, and, as at that moment a hare started up at a short distance from him, he thought he would set them to hunt it, and pointing at it, he cried, "Loo, loo!" but to no purpose, for the dogs would not run. "Whereupon, being very angry, he took them, and with the strings that were at their collars, tied either of them to a little bush at the next hedge, and with a rod that he had in his hand he beat them; and instead of the black greyhound one Dickinson's wife stood up, a neighbour whom this informer knoweth, and instead of the brown greyhound a little boy whom this informer knoweth not." Young Robinson proceeded to state that, in his terror, he attempted to run away, but was arrested by the woman, who "put her hand into her pocket, and pulled out a piece of silver much like unto a fair shilling, and offered to give him to hold his tongue, and not to tell, which he refused, saying, 'Nay, thou art a witch!' Whereupon she put her hand into her pocket again, and pulled out a string like unto a bridle that jingled, which she put upon the little boy's head that stood up in the brown greyhound's stead, whereupon the said boy stood up a white horse." The woman now seized upon Edmund Robinson, placed him on the horse before her, and rode with him to Hoar-stones, where "there were divers persons about the door, and he saw divers others coming riding upon horses of several colours towards the house, which tied their horses to a hedge near to the said house; and which persons went into the said house, to the number of threescore or thereabouts, as this informer thinketh, where they had a fire and meat roasting, and some other meat stirring in the house, whereof a young woman, whom he this informer knoweth not, gave him flesh and bread upon a trencher, and drink in a glass, which after the first taste he refused, and would have no more, and said it was naught. And presently after, seeing divers of the company going to a barn near adjoining, he followed after, and there he saw six of them kneeling and pulling at six several ropes which were fastened or tied to the top of the house, at or with which pulling came then in this informer's sight flesh smoking, butter in lumps, and milk, as it were, syleing (*straining*) from the said ropes, all which fell into basins which were placed under the said ropes. And after that these six had done, there came other six which did likewise, and during all the time of their so pulling, they made such foul faces that feared this informer, so as he was glad to steal out and run home." He further stated that the women in the barn had there "pictures" or images, which they were pricking with thorns.

No sooner was young Robinson's flight discovered, than a party of the witches, of whom the foremost were Dickinson's wife just mentioned, the wife of a man named Loynd or Loyne, and Jennet Device,* joined in the pursuit, and they had nearly overtaken him at a spot which bore the somewhat ominous name of Boggard-hole, when the appearance of two horsemen caused them to desist. His troubles, however, were not thus ended, for on his return home in the evening, "his father bade him go fetch home two kyne to seale (*tie up in their stalls*), and in the way, in a field called the Ollers, he chanced to hap upon a boy who began to quarrel with him, and they fought so together till this informer had his ears made very bloody by fighting, and looking down he saw the boy had a cloven foot, at which sight he was afraid, and ran away from him to seek the kyne. And in the way he saw a light like a lantern, towards which he made haste, supposing it to be carried by some of Mr. Robinson's people [one of their more wealthy neighbours]; but when he came to the place, he only

* There is some room, after all, for doubt if this Jennet Device be the same who figured in the trials in 1612. In the copy of the deposition in lord Londesborough's manuscript she is described as "Jennet Device uxor Willielmi Device."

found a woman standing on a bridge, whom, when he saw her, he knew to be Loynds' wife, and knowing her, he turned back again, and immediately he met with the aforesaid boy, from whom he offered to run, which boy gave him a blow on the back which caused him to cry." The boy's father, in confirmation of this story, acknowledged sending him for the two kyne, and added that, thinking he stayed longer than he should have done, "he went to seek him, and in seeking him heard him cry very pitifully, and found him so afraid and distracted, that he neither knew his father, nor did know where he was, and so continued very near a quarter of an hour before he came to himself," when he told his father the same story which he now repeated before the magistrates.

The boy Robinson, in his deposition, mentioned the names of such of the persons present at the meeting at Hoar-stones as he knew, who were immediately seized and committed to Lancaster castle. As he said that he should recognize the others if he saw them, he was carried about by his father and others to the churches of the neighbouring parishes to examine the congregations, and in this way he gained a considerable sum of money. John Webster, whose "Displaying of Witchcraft" is one of the best books on the subject published during the seventeenth century, has given us a curious account of these proceedings. "It came to pass," he says, "that this said boy was brought into the church of Kildwick, a large parish church where I (being then curate there) was preaching in the afternoon, and was set upon a stall (he being but about ten or eleven years old) to look about him, which moved some little disturbance in the congregation for a while. And after prayers I inquiring what the matter was, the people told me that it was the boy that discovered witches, upon which I went to the house where he was to stay all night, where I found him and two very unlikely (*ill-looking*) persons that did conduct him and manage his business. I desired to have some discourse with the boy in private, but that they utterly refused. Then, in the presence of a great many people, I took the boy near me, and said, 'Good boy, tell me truly, and in earnest, did thou see and hear such strange things of the meeting of witches as is reported by many that thou dost relate, or did not some person teach thee to say such things of thyself?' But the two men not giving the boy leave to answer, did pluck him from me, and said he had been examined by two able justices of the peace, and they did never ask him such a question; to whom I replied, the persons accused therefore had the more wrong."

By means like these, a number of wretched persons were thrown into prison, to the amount of nearly thirty. They were no sooner arrested, than people were found to accuse them of a variety of crimes, chiefly that of killing or seriously injuring people by witchcraft. It is rather a singular coincidence of names, that Jennet Device was charged with killing Isabelle the wife of William Nutter. The crime of another, Mary Spencer, was "causeing a pale or cellocke to come to her full of water fourteen yards up a hill from a well." Another, named Margaret Johnson, was accused of killing Henry Heape, and of wasting and impairing the body of Jennet Shackleton. As the evidence appears to have been otherwise rather deficient, all these persons were searched for marks, which were found in great abundance, and it is stated, at the end of the list, that against one person put on her trial, there was "no evidence found, only in search a mark found on her body." * At the ensuing assizes at Lancaster the prisoners were all put upon their trial, and no less than seventeen were on such evidence found guilty. One of them at least, Margaret Johnson, had made a confession, which, as containing apparently an abstract of the full character of a witch according to the belief of Lancashire at this period, deserves to be printed. It is here given, verbatim, from lord Londesborough's manuscript. Margaret Johnson, on the 9th of March, 1633, before the same justices who had taken the deposition of the boy Robinson, said, "that betweene seven or eight yeares since, shee beeing in her house at Marsden in greate passion and anger, and discontented, and withall oppressed with some want, there appeared unto her a spirit or devill in the similitude and proportion of a man,

* A very curious volume of manuscripts relating to magic and sorcery, recently published by lord Londesborough, contains early copies of the depositions of Edmund Robinson and his father, of the confession of Margaret Johnson, which is given farther on, and of the list of persons brought to trial, with the description of their marks, and an enumeration of the crimes with which they were charged. The marks are described too minutely to allow of this curious paper being printed in a work like the present.

apparrelled in a suite of blacke, tied about with silke pointes, whoe offered her, yf shee would give him her soule, hee would supply all her wantes, and bring to her whatsoever shee wanted or needed, and at her appointment would helpe her to kill and revenge her either of men or beaste, or what she desired; and after a sollicitacion or two, shee contracted and condicioned with the said devill or spiritt for her soule. And the said devill bad her call him by the name of Memillion, and when shee called hee would bee ready to doe her will. And shee saith that in all her talke and conference shee called the said Mamillion her gou ... And shee furthersaith that shee was not at the greate meetinge of the witches at Harestones in the forrest of Pendle on All Saintes day last past, but saith that shee was at a second meetinge the Sunday after All Saintes day at the place aforesaid, where there was at that time betweene thirty and forty witches, which did all ride to the said meetinge. And thend of the said meetinge was to consult for the killing and hurting of man and beastes; and that there was one devill or spiritt that was more greate and grand devill then the rest, and yf anie witch desired to have such an one, they might have such an one to kill or hurt anie body. And shee further saith, that such witches as have sharpe boanes are generally for the devill to prick them with which have no papps nor duggs, but raiseth blood from the place pricked with the boane, which witches are more greate and grand witches then they which have papps or dugs. And shee beeing further asked what persons were at their last meetinge, she named one Carpnall and his wife, Rason and his wife, Pickhamer and his wife, Duffy and his wife, and one Jane Carbonell, whereof Pickhamer's wife is the most greate, grand, and auncyent witch; and that one witch alone can kill a beast, and yf they bidd their spirit or devill to goe and pricke or hurt anie man in anie particuler place, hee presently will doe it. And that their spiritts have usually knowledge of their bodies. And shee further saith the men witches have woemen spiritts, and woemen witches have men spiritts; and that Good Friday is one of their constant daies of their generall meetinge, and that on Good Friday last they had a meetinge neere Pendle water side; and saith that their spirit doeth tell them where their meetinge must bee, and in what place; and saith that if a witch desire to bee in anie place upon a suddaine, that on a dogg or a rod or a catt their spiritt will presently convey them thither, or into any roome in any man's house. But shee saith it is not the substance of their bodies that doeth goe into anie such roomes, but their spiritts that assume such shape and forme. And shee further saith that the devill, after hee begins to sucke, will make a papp or a dug in a short time, and the matter hee sucketh is blood. And further saith that the devill can raise foule wether and stormes, and soe hee did at their meetinges. And she further saith that when the devill came to suck her pappe, he came to her in the lickness of a catt, sometimes of one collour and sometimes of another. And since this trouble befell her, her spiritt hath left her, and shee never sawe him since."

Although the jury were satisfied with the evidence in this case, such was not the case with the judge, who respited the prisoners, and the affair was reported to the king in council. Charles I. had not the same weak prejudices in these matters as his father, and by his orders, an inquiry was instituted at Chester, under the direction of the bishop, the result of which was that four of the convicted witches, Margaret Johnson, (whose confession has just been given,) Frances Dickenson, Mary Spencer, and the wife of one of the Hargreaves, were sent to London, and there examined, first by the king's physicians, and then by the king in person. Strong suspicions having arisen, the boy was separated from his father, (they had both been brought to London,) and then he confessed that the whole was an imposture, and that he had been taught to say what he had said by his father and some other persons who had conspired to get up this story as a profitable speculation. He declared that on the day when he said he was carried to the meeting at Hoar-stones, he was a mile off gathering plums in another man's orchard. Fortunately none of the pretended witches had been executed.

Such was the end of the second great case of witchcraft in Lancashire, which became from many circumstances, but especially by the king's interference and the transferring of the case to London, one of the most celebrated in England. The Lancashire witches have gained a new celebrity at the present day by furnishing the plot of one of the best romances of one of the most popular and admired of our writers, Harrison Ainsworth. The term itself had become so famous that it has long been in that county transferred to a class of witches of the same sex, but of a very different character, and no festival there is now considered perfect until the toast of "the Lancashire Witches" of the present day has been drunk.

CHAPTER XXIV.

WITCHCRAFT IN ENGLAND DURING THE EARLIER PART OF THE SEVENTEENTH CENTURY.

The case of the Lancashire witches, in 1612, seems to have been the first grand exemplification of king James's witchcraft doctrines in England. Yet though the published cases of witchcraft during that monarch's reign are not very numerous, there can be no doubt that the superstition itself was widely prevalent throughout the country, and that it gave rise to innumerable instances of persecution. In the same year, 1612, five witches were executed at Northampton, of whom one only, a man, made a confession. He said that he had three spirits, whom he called Grissill, Ball, and Jack. In 1615, there was a rather remarkable case of witchcraft at Lynn, in Norfolk. Relations of both these cases were printed, and dispersed abroad. In 1618, an event of this kind occurred on the borders of the counties of Leicester and Lincoln, which was still more remarkable as having occurred in one of the noblest families in the land.

Sir Francis Manners succeeded his brother Roger in the earldom of Rutland in 1612, and soon distinguished himself by the magnificent hospitality which he exercised at his castle of Belvoir. He had two sons, Henry and Francis, and a daughter Katherine; the first of these died about the year 1614, and he was followed to the grave by his younger brother within two years. The only remaining child, who afterwards married the duke of Buckingham, was also taken with a severe illness, from which she was hardly expected to recover. In the hamlet adjoining to the castle there lived an old woman named Joan Flower, with two daughters, whose poverty excited the compassion of the earl and his lady, and the mother was employed in the castle as a chairwoman, while her eldest daughter Margaret was received into the household as a servant. It was soon found. however, that mother Flowers was undeserving of the kindness thus shown to her; she gave offence by her evil manners, and by the disorders of her house, where people of no good reputation came to visit her younger daughter Philip, and at last Margaret Flower was discharged from her place for purloining the provisions of the castle to furnish the visitors at her mother's house. All this had occurred before the death of the earl's children, and, as the countess had acted generously towards the daughter when she was discharged, they were never suspected of malice.

However, reports of a sinister character touching the proceedings of the family of Joan Flower soon spread abroad. They had gained the reputation of being witches, and it began to be whispered about that the earl's children had perished by their agency. Witches appear to have been rather numerous in this vicinity, and as the reports became more rife, a number of arrests, including the three Flowers and other persons, were made just before the Christmas of 1617, and the prisoners were lodged in Lincoln jail. The mother, Joan Flowers, when she was committed to prison, is said to have asked for bread and butter, which she wished impiously might be her death if she were guilty of the crime of which she was accused; but she no sooner attempted to swallow it, than she was choked and instantly expired. The earl of Rutland was at the time in London; when, however, he heard of the imprisonment of the witches, and the crimes that were imputed to them, he hastened with his brother, sir George Manners, to Lincoln, and assisted at their examination. They all confessed, were, as might be expected, duly convicted, and were executed early in the March of the year 1618.*

Among the witnesses on this occasion was a woman—apparently an old one—named Joan Willimott, of Goodby in Leicestershire, who confessed "that she hath a spirit which she calleth Pretty, which was given unto her by William Berry of Langholme in Rutlandshire, whom she served three years; and that her master, when he gave it unto her, willed her to open her mouth, and he would

* The earl and the countess were so far satisfied that their children died by witchcraft, that it was stated in the inscription on their monument in Bottesford church.

blow into her a fairy which should do her good; and that she opened her mouth, and he did blow into her mouth; and that presently after his blowing there came out of her mouth a spirit, which stood upon the ground, in the shape and form of a woman, which spirit asked of her her soul, which she then promised unto it, being willed thereunto by her master. She further confessed, that she never hurt anybody, but did help divers that sent for her, which were stricken or forespoken; and that her spirit came weekly to her, and would tell her of divers persons that were stricken and forespoken. And she saith, that the use which she had of the spirit, was to know how those did which she had undertaken to amend; and that she did help them by certain prayers which she used, and not by her own spirit; neither did she employ her spirit in anything, but only to bring word how those did which she had undertaken to cure."

Another witness, named Ellen Green, of Stathorne in the same county, said, "that one Joan Willimott of Goodby came about six years since to her in the Wolds, and persuaded this examinate to forsake God, and betake her to the devil, and she would give her two spirits, to which she gave her consent, and thereupon the said Joan Willimott called two spirits, one in the likeness of a kitten, and the other of a moldiwarp (*a mole*); the first, the said Willimott called Pusse, the other Hiffe-hiffe, and they presently came to her; and she departing left them with the examinate, and they leaped on her shoulder; and the kitten sucked under her right ear or her neck, and the moldiwarp on the left side in the like place. After they had sucked her, she sent the kitten to a baker of that town, whose name she remembers not, who had called her witch and struck her; and bade her said spirit go and bewitch him to death. The moldiwarp she then bade go to Anne Dawse of the same town and bewitch her to death, because she had called this examinate witch and jade; and within one fortnight they both died. And further, this examinate saith, that she sent both her spirits to Stonesby, to one Willison, a husbandman, and Robert Williman, a husbandman's son, and bade the kitten go to Willison and bewitch him to death, and the moldiwarp to the other and bewitch him to death, which they did, and within ten days they died. These four were bewitched while this examinate dwelt at Waltham aforesaid. About three years since, this examinate removed thence to Stathorne, where she now dwelt; upon a difference between the said Willimott and the wife of John Patchet of the said Stathorne, yeoman, she, the said Willimott, called her, this examinate, to go and touch the said John Patchet's wife and her child, which she did, touching the said John Patchet's wife in her bed, and the child in the grace-wife's arms, and then sent her said spirits to bewitch them to death, which they did, and so the woman lay languishing by the space of a month and more, for then she died: the child died the next day after she touched it. And she further saith, that the said Joan Willimott had a spirit sucking on her under the left flank in the likeness of a little white dog, which this examinate saith that she saw the same sucking in barley-harvest last, being then at the house of the said Joan Willimott."

Both the daughters of mother Flowers confessed, and Margaret gave the following account of the proceedings relating to the earl of Rutland's family. "She saith and confesseth, that about four or five years since her mother sent her for the right-hand glove of Henry lord Rosse, afterward that her mother bade her go again into the castle of Belvoir, and bring down the glove or some other thing of Henry lord Rosse; whereupon she brought down a glove, and delivered the same to her mother, who stroked Rutterkin, her cat, with it; after it was dipped in hot water, and so pricked it often, after which Henry lord Rosse fell sick within a week, and was much tormented with the same. She further saith, that finding a glove about two or three years since of Francis lord Rosse on a dung-hill, she delivered it to her mother, who put it into hot water; and after took it out and rubbed it on Rutterkin the cat, and bade him go upwards; and after her mother buried it in the yard, and said a mischief light on him, but he will not mend again. She further said, that her mother and she, and her sister, agreed together to bewitch the earl and his lady, that they might have no more children; and being demanded the cause of this their malice and ill-will, she saith, that about four years since the countess (growing into some mislike with her) gave her forty shillings, a bolster, and a mattress, and bade her bide at home and come no more to dwell at the castle; which she not only took in ill part, but grudged at it exceedingly, swearing in her heart to be revenged;

after this her mother complained to the earl against one Peake, who had offered her some wrong, wherein she conceived that the earl took not her part, as she expected, which dislike with the rest exasperated her displeasure against him, and so she watched the opportunity to be revenged: whereupon she took wool out of the said mattress, and a pair of gloves, which were given her by Mr. Vavasor, and put them into warm water, mingling them with some blood, and stirring it together; then she took the wool and gloves out of the water, and rubbed them on the body of Rutterkin her cat, saying the lord and the lady should have more children, but it should be long first. She further confessed, that by her mother's commandment, she brought to her a piece of a handkerchief of the lady Katherine, the earl's daughter; and her mother put it into hot water, and then taking it out rubbed it on Rutterkin, bidding him fly and go, whereupon Rutterkin whined and cried 'Mew;' whereupon she said, that Rutterkin had no power over the lady Katherine to hurt her." Her sister, Philip Flowers, declared, "that about the 30th of January last past, being Saturday, four devils appeared unto her in Lincoln jail, at eleven or twelve o'clock at midnight; the one stood at her bed's foot, with a black head like an ape, and spake unto her, but what she cannot well remember, at which she was very angry, because he would speak no plainer, or let her understand his meaning: the other three were Rutterkin, little Robin, and Spirit, but she never mistrusted them, nor suspected herself till then."

The Roman Catholics in England were very active

during the reign of James I., and they attempted to take advantage of the popular credulity in getting up cases of possession in imitation of their brethren on the continent; one of the most remarkable cases of this kind occurred in Lancaster in 1612, and led to a trial on the same day with that of the witches of Pendle.

The village of Samlesbury is at some distance from the Pendle district, nearer to Preston, but it was probably the reports of the deeds of mothers Demdike and Chattox that suggested the plot now to be related. The principal family in this township were the Southworths, who had their head seat at Samlesbury park, and who seem to have been much divided among themselves—a division which was increased by religious differences, for some of them were Protestants and others Catholics. Lancashire was at this time remarkable for the number of papists which it harboured—it was the grand asylum of the English seminary priests, and there are documents which show that Samlesbury-park was a well-known resort of the partizans of Rome. One of these priests was Christopher Southworth, who for concealment had assumed the name of Thompson, and who appears to have been nearly related to sir John Southworth, the occupier of the park, who was then recently dead. Between sir John and one of his female relations, Jane Southworth, there was a bitter feud, for what reason is not stated; a servant of sir John's, named John Singleton, deposed, that "he had often heard his old master say, that the said Jane Southworth was, as he thought, an evil woman and a witch;" and he added, "that the said sir John Southworth, in his coming or going between his own house at Samlesbury and the town of Preston, did for the most part forbear to pass by the house where the said wife dwelt, though it was his nearest and best way, and rode another way, only for fear of the said wife, as this examinate verily thinketh." This statement was confirmed by another witness, a yeoman of Samlesbury, named William Alker, who deposed, "that he had seen the said sir John Southworth shun the said wife when he came near where she was, and hath heard the said sir John say that he liked her not, and that he doubted she would bewitch him." As far as we can gather, it appears further, that Jane Southworth was a recent convert from Romanism to the Church of England.

There was in the same village a family of the name of Bierley. Jennet Bierley was an aged woman, who appears to have lived with a daughter-in-law, Ellen Bierley; her own daughter had married Thomas Sowerbuts of Samlesbury, a husbandman, and by her he had a daughter, Grace Sowerbuts, who was at this time about fourteen years of age. Jennet and Ellen Bierley were Protestants, while Thomas Sowerbuts was a Catholic, and there was probably a quarrel between them on account of the religion of the child, which Thomas Sowerbut resolved should be that of Rome, and for that purpose he sent her for religious instruction to the priest Thompson (*alias* Southworth).

Soon after or about the time of the seizure of the witches of Pendle, Grace Sowerbuts pretended to be seized with strange fits, and she was found in a sort of trance among the hay and straw in a barn, whence she was taken to her father's house, and there told a story which led to the arrest of Jane Southworth, and Jennet and Ellen Bierley, and they were committed to Lancaster jail. They were brought to trial on the 19th of August, 1612, and then Grace Sowerbut made a statement in court, to the effect that, after having been "haunted and vexed" for some years by the prisoners and another confederate, named old Doewife, these four women had lately drawn her by the hair of the head to the top of a hay-mow, where they left her. Not long after this, Jennet Bierley met her near her home, appearing to her first in human likeness, "and after that in the likeness of a black dog," and attempted to terrify her. The girl told her father what had happened, and how she had often been "haunted" in this manner; and being asked by the court why she never told anybody before, she said, "She could not speak thereof, though she desired so to do." Soon after this, on the fourth of April, "going towards Samlesbury back to meet her mother, coming from Preston, she saw the said Jennet Bierley, who met this examinate at a place called the Two Brigs, first in her own shape, and afterwards in the likeness of a black dog with two legs, which dog went close by the left side of this examinate till they came to a pit of water, and then the said dog spake, and persuaded this examinate to drown herself therein, saying it was a fair and an easy death; whereupon this examinate thought there came one to her in a white sheet, and carried her away from the said pit, upon the coming whereof the said black dog departed away." The dog subsequently returned, and carried her to a neighbour's barn, where it left her in a trance on the floor. She went on to describe other instances of persecution by the witches, and declared that on one occasion her grandmother and aunt had taken her by night to the house of a man named Thomas Walshman, which they entered "she knew not how," and Jennet Bierley caused the death of an infant child; and the night after the burial of the child, "the said Jennet Bierley, and Ellen Bierley, taking this examinate with them, went to Samlesbury church, and there did take up the said child, and the said Jennet did carry it out of the churchyard in her arms, and then did put it in her lap and carried it home to her own house, and having it there, did boil some thereof in a pot, and some did broil on the coals, of both which the said Jennet and Ellen did eat, and would have had this examinate, and one Grace Brierley, daughter of the said Ellen, to have eaten with them, but they refused so to do. And afterward the said Jennet and Ellen did seethe (*boil*) the bones of the said child in a pot, and with the fat that came out of the said bones they said they would anoint themselves, that thereby they might sometimes change themselves into other shapes. And after all this being done, they said they would lay the bones again in the grave the next night following, but whether they did so or not this examinate knoweth not; neither doth she know how they got it out of the grave at the first taking of it up." She next stated, that "about half a year ago, the said Jennet

Bierley, Ellen Bierley, Jane Southworth, and this examinate, (who went by the appointment of the said Jennet, her grandmother,) did meet at a place called Redbank, upon the north side of the water of Ribble, every Thursday and Sunday at night, by the space of a fortnight, and at the water-side there came unto them, as they went thither, four black things, going upright, and yet not like men in the face, which four did carry the said three women and this examinate over the water; and when they came to the said Redbank, they found something there which they did eat. . . . . And after they had eaten, the said three women and this examinate danced, every one of them with one of the black things aforesaid." . . . . She proceeded to describe further acts, familiar to those who enter into the minutiæ of sorcery, and which seem to have been taken from the foreign books on the subject, and then described other persecutions to which she had been subjected, until the time of the arrest of the prisoners.

It was not the fashion at this time to submit witnesses in such cases to a strict cross-examination, nor did any one think of opening the grave of the child to ascertain in what condition the body might then be; but Thomas Walshman deposed that his child died about the time stated, though he said that it had been sick for some time. Witnesses were also examined as to Grace Sowerbuts' fits, and the father and one or two other witnesses gave their evidence in corroboration of her statements. The evidence was thus in due order taken, and the jury was no doubt ready to give a verdict against the prisoners, when the judge, sir Edward Bromley, demanded of the latter what they had to say for themselves. The sequel may be told best in the rather dramatic language of the report of the trial. The three prisoners, instead of being abashed as persons under such circumstances usually were, "humbly upon their knees, with weeping tears, desired him for God's cause to examine Grace Sowerbuts, who set her on, or by whose means this accusation came against them. Immediately the countenance of this Grace Sowerbuts changed; the witnesses, being behind, began to quarrel and accuse one another. In the end his lordship examined the girl, who could not for her life make any direct answer, but strangely amazed, told him she was put to a master to learn, but he told her nothing of this. But here, as his lordship's care and pains were great to discover the practices of these odious witches of the forest of Pendle and other places now upon their trial before him, so was he desirous to discover this damnable practice to accuse these poor women and bring their lives in danger, and thereby to deliver the innocent. And as he openly delivered it upon the bench, in the hearing of this great audience, that if a priest or Jesuit had a hand in one end of it, there would appear to be knavery and practice in the other end of it, and that it might the better appear to the whole world, examined Thomas Sowerbuts what master taught his daughter; in general terms he denied all. The wench had nothing to say, but her master told her nothing of that. In the end, some that were present told his lordship the truth, and the prisoners informed him how she went to learn with one Thompson, a seminary priest, who had instructed and taught her this accusation against them, because they were once obstinate papists, and now came to church. Here is the discovery of this priest, and of his whole practice. Still this fire increased more and more, and, one witness accusing another, all things were laid open at large. In the end, his lordship took away the girl from her father, and committed her to Mr. Leigh, a very religious preacher, and Mr. Chisnal, two justices of the peace, to be carefully examined."

Grace Sowerbuts now made a full confession; she declared that all she said before had been taught her by the priest; that it was a mere invention; that her fits were counterfeit; and that she had, by her own will, gone into the barn and other places where she was found.

Eight years after this trial, in 1620, occurred a somewhat similar case, which made a great sensation at the time. There was at Bilston, in Staffordshire, a poor boy of twelve years old, named William Percy, the son of a husbandman of that place. One day as he was coming home from school, he met an old woman whom he had never seen before, but who, as it was afterwards pretended, was a poor woman of the neighbourhood, named Joan Cock; she taxed him that he did not wish her good day, and told him that he was a foul thing, and that it had been better for him if he had saluted her. This was the account which the lad gave, and he had no sooner reached home than he was seized with dreadful fits. It appears that there were many Roman Catholics residing in the neighbourhood of Bilston, and to some of these the boy's parents applied for advice and assistance. As soon as the boy was exorcised according to the forms directed by the Romish church, he became calm, and in reply to questions put to him, he declared that he was bewitched, and that he was possessed by three devils. Besides the exorcisms, the priests were very liberal with holy water and with holy oil, by the plentiful application of which, "with extreme fits and hearings, he brought up pins, wool, knotted thread, thrums, rosemary, walnut leaves, feathers, &c." This we learn from the priest, who drew up the account of the "miracle," which was afterwards printed, and who informs us, among other things, that "on Thursday, being Corpus Christi day, I came again, and found the child in great extremities In this time he had brought up eleven pins, and a knitting needle folded up in divers folds, &c. He said the spirit bad him not to hearken to me in any case; that the witch said she should make an end of him, &c. I wished him to pray for the witch, which he did; then the child did declare that now he was perfectly himself, and desired that his books, pens, ink, cloaths, might be blessed, wishing his parents, sisters, and brothers, to bless themselves, and become Catholics; out of which faith, by God's grace, he said, he would never live or die. On Sunday I exorcised him, and learned of him, that while puritans were in place, he saw the devil assault him in form of a blackbird."

The boy's fits and trances continued, sometimes

apparently yielding to the exorcisms of the priests, and then again returning as violent as ever. Meanwhile the woman accused of the witchcraft by the possessing devils, was arrested and carried before the chancellor of the bishop of Litchfield, by whose directions William Perry was brought to confront her, when he immediately fell into his usual fits, declaring that she was his tormenter. On this evidence she was committed to Stafford jail, and brought to trial on the tenth of August, but the jury, not satisfied with the evidence, acquitted her.

The judges, who seem to have suspected the truth, committed the boy to the care of the bishop of Coventry and Litchfield, who happened to be present, and he carried him home with him to Eccleshall castle. There his fits and convulsions were repeated, and the bishop for some time could make nothing of him. At length he bethought himself of an experiment which would at least satisfy himself. It appears that the trial verse used by the priests was the first verse of the first chapter of the gospel of St. John, the words of which were no sooner commenced than the boy was seized with the most violent symptoms. The bishop took a Greek Testament in his hand, and said to the patient, "Boy, it is either thou or the devil that abhorrest those words of the Gospel, and if it be the devil, he (being so ancient a scholar as of almost six thousand years' standing) knows and understands all languages, so that he cannot but know when I recite the same sentence out of the Greek text; but if it be thyself, then art thou an execrable wretch, who plays the devil's part, wherefore look to thyself, for now thou art to be put to trial, and mark diligently whether it be that same scripture which shall be read." Then the bishop read the twelfth verse of the chapter, and the boy supposing it was the first, fell into his usual convulsions: but, after the fit was passed over, and the bishop read the first verse, the boy thinking it was some other passage, was not affected at all.

The bishop was thus convinced of the imposture, but there were still some extraordinary features about the case which required explanation, and he let it go on, that it might be in the end more fully exposed. At length a hole was made through the partition of the room in which the boy slept, and the bishop placed one of his servants secretly to watch. A discovery was thus made which left no further doubt on the matter, and when the boy found himself detected, he changed countenance and confessed. The story he told was, that an old man called Thomas, with gray hair and "a cradle of glasse," met him not far from his father's house, and, entering into conversation with him, suggested this imposture as a means of staying from school. He then taught him to roll about, groan, cast up his eyes, &c., and told him to accuse somebody who was reputed a witch. Some papists, he said, recommended him to seek help of the Catholic priests. When the bishop asked him if he did not design to yield to their exorcisms, he replied that he did, but that he had continued the imposture so long, because much people resorted to him, and brought him good things, and because he was not willing to go to school again. It is not impossible that the story of the old man had been suggested by the priests themselves, in order to conceal their own complicity in case of a discovery of the fraud.

The dangerous doctrine, which had long before been acted upon in the case of the witches of Warboys, was now widely promulgated, that the declaration of the person bewitched, while in the fits caused by witchcraft, was sufficient evidence against the supposed offender. This was opening a door for the indulgence of personal enmity which could not fail to be often taken advantage of, and such cases appear to have been of very frequent occurrence. In lord Londesborough's volume of manuscripts already alluded to, there are the notes of two very curious affairs of this kind. The first of these cases occurred in and near London in the year 1622. The lady Jennings, living at Thistleworth, had a daughter named Elizabeth, of the age of thirteen years. One day she was "frighted with the sight of an old woman who suddainly appeared to her att the dore and demaunded a pin of her,"—this seems to have been the usual article which the witches asked of those they were going to torment—and from that time the child suffered from convulsive fits of the most painful description. A variety of remedies were tried in vain, and in the course of this treatment a woman named Margaret Russell, who went by the name of Countess, frequently attended—she appears to have been well known at the house, and to have interfered with the medical arrangements. On the 25th of April, at the end of one of her fits, Elizabeth Jennings uttered the names of this woman and three others, and then went on talking incoherently, "These have bewitched all my mother's children — east, west, north, and south, all these lie—all these are witches. Set up a great sprig of rosemary in the middle of the house—I have sent this child to speak to show all these witches. Put Countess in prison this child will be well.—If she had been long ago, all together had been alive [it appears some other children of the lady Jennings had died]. —Them she bewitched with a cat-stick —Till then I shall lie in great pain.—Till then by fits I shall be in great extremity.—They died in great misery." These and some other speeches are duly attested by nine persons, among whom was the medical attendant.

The same day Countess was arrested and carried before sir William Slingsby, a justice of the peace, and her account of herself is a curious picture of the time. She said, "that yesterday she went to Mrs. Dromondbye in Blacke-and-White-court in the Old Baylye, and told her that the lady Jennings had a daughter strangely sicke, whereuppon the said Dromondbye wished her to goe to inquire att Clerkenwell for a minister's wiffe that cold helpe people that were sicke, but she must not aske for a witch or a cunning woman, but for one that is a phisition woman, and there this examinate found her and a woman sitting with her, and told her in what case the child was, and she said shee wold come this day, but shee ought her noe service, and said she had bin there before and lefte receiptes there, but the child did not take them. And she said further, that there was two children that the lady Jennins had by this husband that were bewitched and dead, for there was controversie betweene two howses, and that as long as they dwelt there they cold not prosper, and that there shold be noe blessing in that house by this man. And being demaunded what she meant by the difference betwixt two howses, she answered it was betwixt the house of God and the house of the world; but being urged to expresse it better, she said wee knewe it well enough, it was the difference betwixt Higgins the apothecarie, the next neighbour, and the lady Jennins. And shee further confesseth that above a moneth agoe she went to Mrs. Saxey, in Gunpouder-alley, who was forespoken herselfe, and that had a booke that cold helpe all those that were fore-spoken, and that shee wold come and shewe her the booke and helpe her under God. And further said to this examinate, that none but a seminary preist cold cure her." We have here another instance how busy the seminary priests, or Jesuits, were in obtruding themselves in such cases.

Countess was now committed to Newgate, and next day new revelations were obtained from the bewitched child confirmatory of the former accusation. But meanwhile the minister's wife, (Mrs. Goodcole,) with her husband and some friends, went to the Old Bailey, and being confronted with the prisoner, the latter denied the most important part of what she had said. In fact, the accusation seems to have arisen out of a private quarrel, and on application to an experienced physician, Dr Napier, the lady Jennings was set at ease as to the ailment of her daughter—so we learn from a note at the end of the paper.

The other case recorded in lord Londesborough's manuscript occurred in 1626, and is still more remarkable. On the 13th of August in that year, a man named Edward Bull and a woman named Joan Greedie were indicted at Taunton assizes for bewitching one Edward Dinham. This man, when in his fits, had two voices besides his own, "whereof one is a very pleasant voice and shrill, the other deadly and hollow;" the third was his own voice. When the two first (who were good and evil spirits that possessed him) spoke, there was no motion of his lips or tongue, which however moved as was usual with a man talking when his own voice was heard. No doubt he was a ventriloquist. The dialogue, as taken down in the paper before me, bears a close resemblance to the conversations of the possessed nuns in France—it is too gross an imposture to deceive any one for a moment. (I use *good* and *bad*, for the two spiritual voices, and *man* for the natural voice, as more simple than the mode of expressing than in the manuscript.) The conversation began as follows:—

" *Good.* Howe comes this man to bee thus tormented?

" *Bad.* He is bewitched.

" *Good.* Who hath done it?

" *Bad.* That I may not tell.

" *Good.* Aske him agayne.

" *Man.* Come, come, prithee tell me who hath bewitched me.

" *Bad.* A woman in greene cloathes and a blacke

hatt, with a longe poll; and a man in gray srite with blewe stockinges.

"*Good.* But where are they?

"*Bad.* Shee is at her house; and hee is at a taverne in Yeohull in Ireland.

"*Good.* But what are theire names?

"*Bad.* Nay, that I will not tell.

"*Good.* Aske him againe.

"*Man.* Come, come, prithee tell me what are their names.

"*Bad.* I am bound not to tell.

"*Good.* Then tell half of their names.

"*Bad.* The one is Johane, and the other Edward.

"*Good.* Nowe tell me the other half.

"*Bad.* That I may not.

"*Good.* Aske him agayne.

"*Man.* Come, come, prithee tell me the other half.

"*Bad.* The one is Greedie, and the other Bull."

Having obtained this information, a messenger was sent to a house "suspected," and finding a woman dressed according to the description, he caused her to be arrested and committed to safe custody. The conversation then went on as follows.

"*Good.* But are these witches?

"*Bad.* Yes, that they are.

"*Good.* Howe came they to bee soe?

"*Bad.* By discent.

"*Good.* But howe by discent?

"*Bad.* From the grandmother to the mother, and from the mother to the children.

"*Good.* But howe were they soe?

"*Bad.* They were bound to us, and wee to them.

"*Good.* Lett me see the bond.

"*Bad.* Thou shalt not.

"*Good.* Let me see it, and if I like I will seale alsoe.

"*Bad.* Thou shalt if thou wilt not reveale the contentes thereof.

"*Good.* I will not."

The bond is now supposed to be shown, on which the good spirit exclaims,—

"*Good.* Alas! oh pittifull, pittifull, pittifull! what? eight seales, bloody seales, four dead, and four alive? ah, miserable!

"*Man.* Come, come, prithee tell me, why did they bewitche me?

"*Bad.* "Because thou didst call Johane Greedie witche.

"*Man.* Why, is shee not a witche?

"*Bad.* Yes, but thou shouldest not have said soe.

"*Good.* But why did Bull bewitche him?

"*Bad.* Because Greedie was not stronge enough."

Inquiry is again made after Bull, and on following the direction given by the spirit, the messenger finds the spot from which he had just escaped, and meets with people who had seen him running away. A conversation follows on the mischiefs which the witches had perpetrated before they attacked this man, and we learn that they had bewitched a person to death. The conversation is resumed in another fit six days after, and another attempt to catch Bull failed. The bad spirit now declares his intention to have Dinham's soul, but the good spirit opposes him, and a violent struggle arises, and the evil one has the advantage. The conversation between them is then resumed :—

"*Bad.* I will have him, or else I will torment him eight tymes more.

"*Good.* Thou shalt not have thy will in all thinges, thou shalt torment him but four tymes more.

"*Bad.* I will have thy soule.

"*Good.* If thou wilt answere me three questions, I will seale and goe with thee.

"*Bad.* I will.

"*Good.* Who made the world?

"*Bad.* God.

"*Good.* Who created mankynde?

"*Bad.* God.

"*Good.* Wherefore was Christ Jesus his precious blood shed?

"*Bad.* I'le no more of that."

Upon this, the patient was seized with terrible convulsions. A few days afterwards, in another fit, the struggle to obtain possession of the soul is renewed.

"*Bad.* If thou wilt give me thy soule, I will give thee gold enough.

"*Good.* Thy gold will scald my fingers.

"*Bad.* If thou wilt give me thy soule, I will give the dice, and thou shalt winne infinite somes of treasure by play.

"*Good.* If thou canst make every letter in this booke [*the man had a prayer-book in his hand*] a die, I will.

"*Bad.* That I cannott.

"*Good.* Laudes, laudes, laudes!

"*Bad.* Ladies, ladies, ladies, thou shalt have ladies enough, and if thou wilt they shall come to bedd to thee." [The bad spirit evidently did not understand Latin!]

"*Good.* If thou canst make every letter in this book a ladie, I will."

The bad spirit now attempted to cast the book away, but after a violent struggle he was overcome, and then the good spirit made "the sweetest musicke that ever was heard." After another attempt to trace and catch Bull, by the spirit's directions, he was at last captured in his bed. Now that the prisoners were secured, Dinham was delivered from his persecutor, and was no more tormented. The witches were indicted for similar offences, but we are not told what was their fate, or whether any "seminary priests" were here concerned.

The influence of the doctrine and example of king James might now be considered as passed, and the witchcraft agitation would perhaps have gradually subsided, had not a new influence arisen to revive the flame. Among the writers on the subject of witchcraft during James's reign, one took it up in a more rational view than was usual among his contemporaries. This was John Cotta, an eminent physician of Northampton, the author of a work entitled "The Trial of Witchcraft." Cotta did not dispute the existence of the witches, but he objected to the evidence which was received against them; and the arguments which he used to support his opinions would, if followed out, have led him much further than he would venture then to go. Cotta requires that the evidence against persons accused of witchcraft should be of a direct and practical description. He recommended that in all cases of supposed witchcraft or possession, skilful physicians should be employed to ascertain if the patient might not be suffering from a natural malady, and he pointed out the fallacy which attended the doctrine of witches' marks. He showed how little faith could generally be placed in the confessions of the witches, both from the manner in which they were obtained, and the characters of the individuals who made them. He exposed in the same rational manner the uncertainty of such objectionable modes of trying witches, as swimming them in the waters, scratching, beating, pinching, or drawing blood from them. He objected also to taking the supernatural revelations in those who were bewitched as evidence against those who were accused of bewitching them. It will be seen that all the evidence at that time considered conclusive would thus have been rendered of no account. But Cotta was in advance of his age; he published his book in 1616, when king James's doctrines prevailed in full force, and it attracted little attention; a new and much enlarged edition, published in 1624, does not appear to have been much better received—at least it had no effect in checking the persecution to which so many unfortunate creatures were exposed.

CHAPTER XXV.

WITCHCRAFT UNDER THE COMMONWEALTH: MATTHEW HOPKINS, THE WITCH-FINDER.

THE great witch persecution in England arose under the commonwealth. The ardent religious feelings of the puritans led them to believe not only that they were themselves supported by divine inspiration and favoured with special revelations, but that Satan was as actively at work against them, and that, as with the heroes of the Homeric age, the warfare in which they were thrown engaged the spiritual no less than the carnal world. It was natural, therefore, that they should look with especial horror and hostility on that union of Satan and mankind which was embodied in the witch or sorcerer. They were the more apparent manifestations of the devil's own interference in the attempt to bring back the double tyranny of kingship and popery. It is impossible now to say how far the prosecutions of witches at this period belonged to the personal animosities of religious and political party, but there can be little doubt that some at least of those who suffered were martyrs to their loyalty. The first name which ushers in the melancholy list during this period is that of Dr. Lamb, who had been the favourite Buckingham's domestic magician, and who was torn to pieces by the London mob in 1640.

The great outbreak of fanaticism and superstition which followed began in the county of Essex. In the spring of 1645, several witches were seized at Manningtree, and were subsequently condemned and hanged One of these was an old woman named Elizabeth Clarke, and the most important witness against her was "Matthew Hopkins of Manningtree, gent." It appears that this Hopkins had watched with her several nights in a room in the house of a Mr. Edwards, in which she was confined, to keep her from sleeping until she made a confession, and to see if she were visited by her familiars. He declared, among other things, that on the night of the 24th of March, which appears to have been the third night of watching, after he had refused to let her call one of her imps or familiars, she confessed that about six or seven years before she had surrendered herself to the devil, who came to her in the form of "a proper gentleman, with a laced band." Soon after this a little dog appeared, fat and short in the legs, in colour white with sandy spots, which, when he hindered it from approaching her, vanished from his sight. She confessed that it was one of her imps, named Jarmara. Immediately after this had disappeared, another came in the form of a greyhound, which she called Vinegar

Tom; and it was followed by another in the shape of a polecat. "And this informant [Hopkins] further saith, that going from the house of the said Mr. Edwards to his own house about nine or ten of the clock that night, with his greyhound with him, he saw the greyhound suddenly give a jump, and ran as she had been in a full course after a hare; and that when the informant made haste to see what his greyhound so eagerly pursued, he espied a white thing about the bigness of a kitlin, (*kitten*,) and the greyhound standing aloof from it; and that by and by the said white imp or kitten danced about the said greyhound, and by all likelihood bit a piece of the flesh of the shoulder of the greyhound, for the greyhound came shrieking and crying to this informant with a piece of flesh torn from her shoulder. And this informant further saith, that coming into his own yard that night, he espied a black thing, proportioned like a cat, only it was thrice as big, sitting on a strawberry-bed, and fixing its eyes on this informant; and when he went towards it, it leaped over the pale towards this informant, as he thought, but ran quite through the yard, with his greyhound after it to a great gate, which was underset with a pair of tumbrill-strings, and did throw the said gate wide open, and then vanished; and the said greyhound returned again to this informant, shaking and trembling exceedingly."

Hopkins had not ventured to remain with the witch alone in his watchings, for he had with him one John Sterne, of Manningtree, who also added "gentleman" to his name, and who confirmed everything that Hopkins had said, deposing to the coming of the imps, and adding that the third imp was called Sack-and-sugar. They watched at night with another woman, named Rebecca West, and saw her imps in the same manner. She confessed, and stated that the first time she saw Satan, he came to her at night, told her he must be her husband, and married her. The severe treatment to which the persons accused were exposed soon forced confessions from them all, and they avowed themselves guilty of mischiefs of every description, from the taking away of human life to the spoiling of milk. Some of their imps had caused storms at sea, and thus the ships of people against whom they were provoked were cast away. The names and forms of their imps were equally fantastic. Rebecca Jones, a witch brought from St. Osythe's, said that she had met a man in a ragged suit, with great eyes that terrified her exceedingly, and that he gave her three things like moles, but without tails, which she fed with milk. Another had an imp in the form of a white dog, which she called Elimanzer, and which she fed with milk-pottage. One had three imps, which she called Prick-ear, Jack, and Frog; another had four, named James, Prick-ear, Robin, and Sparrow. Several witnesses—poor and ignorant people—were brought to testify to the mischief which had been done by these means; and some declared that they had seen their imps. A countryman gravely related how, passing at day-break by the house of one of the women accused, named Anne West, he was surprised to find her door open at that early hour, and looking in, he saw three or four things like black rabbits, one of which ran after him. He seized upon it and tried to kill it, but it seemed in his hands like a piece of wool, and stretched out in length as he pulled it without any apparent injury. Then recollecting that there was a spring near at hand, he hurried thither and attempted to drown it, but it vanished from his sight as soon as he put it in the water. He then returned towards the house, and seeing Anne West standing outside the door in her smock, he asked her why she sent her imps to torment him.

This seems to have been the first appearance of Matthew Hopkins in the character of a witch-finder, for which he became afterwards so notorious, and which he now assumed as a legal profession. He proceeded in a regular circuit through Suffolk, Norfolk, Cambridgeshire, and Huntingdon, accompanied with John Sterne and a woman whose business it was to examine the bodies of the females in search of their marks. In August of 1645, we find them at Bury, in Suffolk, where, on the 27th of that month, no less than eighteen witches were executed at once, and a hundred and twenty more were to have been tried, but a sudden movement of the king's troops in that direction obliged the judges to adjourn the session. Some of the imps here appeared in the shapes of snakes, wasps, and hornets, and even of snails. They were mostly employed in petty offences; one man and his wife were guilty only of having bewitched the beer in a brewhouse and making it stink. Others, however, confessed that they had raised tempests and storms, and caused mischief of a much more serious character. One woman declared that she had conceived two children by the devil, "but as soon as she was delivered of them they ran away in most horrid long ugly shapes." Anne Leach, of Mistley, Essex, who was tried here, said that the imps "did mischief wherever they went, and that when this examinant did not send and employ them abroad to do mischief, she had not her health, but when they were employed she was healthful and well."

The most remarkable victim of this inquisition at Bury was an aged clergyman named Lowes, who had been vicar of Brandeston near Framlingham in that county, fifty years, a well-known opponent of the new church government. This man, we are told by Sterne, one of the inquisitors, "had been indicted for a common imbarrator, and for witchcraft, above thirty years before, and the grand jury (as I have heard) found the bill for a common imbarrator, who now, after he was found with the marks, in his confession he confessed that in pride of heart to be equal, or rather above God, the devil took advantage of him, and he covenanted with the devil, and sealed it with his blood, and had those familiars or spirits, which sucked on the marks found on his body, and did much harm both by sea and land, especially by sea, for he confessed, that he being at Lungarfort [Landguard-fort] in Suffolk, where he preached, as he walked upon the wall or works there, he saw a great sail of ships pass by, and that, as they were sailing by, one of his three imps, namely, his yellow one, forthwith appeared to him and asked him what he should do, and he bad it go and sink such a ship, and showed his imp a new ship amongst the middle of the rest, (as I remember,) one that belonged to Ipswich, so he confessed the imp went forthwith away, and he stood still and viewed the ships on the sea as they were a sailing, and perceived that ship immediately to be in more trouble and danger than the rest; for he said the water was more boisterous near that than the rest, tumbling up and down with waves, as if water had been boiled in a pot, and soon after (he said) in a short time it sunk directly down into the sea as he stood and viewed it, when all the rest sailed down in safety; then he confessed he made fourteen widows in one quarter of an hour. Then Mr. Hopkins, as he told me, (for he took his confession,) asked him, if it did not grieve him to see so many men cast away in a short time, and that he should be the cause of so many poor widows on a sudden; but he swore by his Maker, no, he was joyful to see what power his imps had: and so likewise confessed many other mischiefs, and had a charm to keep him out of the jail and hanging, as he paraphrased it himself, but therein the devil deceived him; for he was hanged that Michaelmas time, 1645, at Bury St. Edmunds; but he made a very far larger confession, which I have heard hath been printed; but if it were so, it was neither of Mr. Hopkins' doing nor mine own, for we never printed anything until now."

Perhaps Hopkins, when scared by the royal troops, returned homeward from Bury to Ipswich, where a poor woman named Lakelaw was burnt on the ninth of September. She confessed that she had been a witch nearly twenty years, and that she had bewitched to death her own husband and a person who had refused to give her a needle, besides destroying several ships, yet she had always appeared to be a very religious woman, and was a constant attendant at church. She had three imps in the shapes of two little dogs and a mole.

At Yarmouth, Hopkins sacrificed sixteen persons, all of whom made confessions. One woman had been in the habit of doing work for one of the aldermen, who was a stocking merchant. One day, when he was absent from home, she went to his house to ask for work, and was turned away contemptuously by his man. She then applied to the maid-servant for some knitting, but was received no more favourably. She went home in great distress and anger, and in the middle of the night, hearing a knock at the door, she rose from her bed to look out at the window, and there saw a tall black man. He told her he knew of the ill-treatment she had received, and that he was come to give her the means of revenge; and, after having made her write her name in a book he drew from his pocket, he gave her some money, and went away. Next night he appeared again, and told her he had not the power to injure the man because he went regularly to hear pious ministers and said his prayers night and morning; and it was then agreed that he should punish the maid. The night following he returned with the same story as regarded the maid, but he said there was a child in the family that might be injured. The woman having consented, he came next night with an image of wax intended to represent the child, and they went together to the churchyard and buried it. The child was immediately taken ill, and it had languished in this condition eighteen months, when the witch was seized and brought to the witch-finder's "justice." She was taken to the room where the child lay, and she had no sooner repeated her confession there, than it began to recover. They took the woman next morning to the churchyard, where she pointed to the exact spot where the waxen image was buried, but when they dug they found nothing. The devil, it seems, had carried it away. This woman's familiar came to her in the shape of a blackbird.

The infection thus set a going by Hopkins in one part of the kingdom, soon spread itself to others, and the whole island seemed on a sudden to be filled with malignant witches. In this same month of September, 1645, three witches were executed at Faversham in Kent. They had signed covenants to the evil one with their blood. One of them said, that about three-quarters of a year before, when she first became a witch, "as she was in the bed about twelve or one of the clock in the night, there lay a ragged soft thing upon her bosom, which was very soft, and she thrust it off with her hand; and she saith that when she had thrust it away, she thought God forsook her, for she could never pray so well since as she could before; and further saith, that she verily thinks it was alive." Another, who had been twenty years acquainted with a demon which first appeared to her in the shape of a hedgehog, but as soft as a cat, "at her first coming into the jail spake very much to the others that were apprehended before her to confess if they were guilty; and stood to it very perversely that she was clear of any such thing, and that if they put her into the water to try her, she should certainly sink. But when she was put into the water, and it was apparent that she did float upon the water, being taken forth, a gentleman to whom before she had so confidently spoken, and with whom she offered to lay twenty shillings to one that she could not swim, asked her how it was possible that she could be so impudent as not to confess herself, when she had so much persuaded the others to confess; to whom she answered, that the devil went with her all the way, and told her that she should sink, but, when she was in the water, he sat upon a cross-beam and laughed at her." The third of the Faversham witches, whose term of twenty years for which she had sold herself to Satan was nearly expired, and whose familiar was a little dog named Bun, deposed "that the devil promised her that she should not lack, and that she had money sometimes brought her she knew not whence, sometimes one shilling, sometimes sixpence, never more at once." The incapacity of the tempter to give more than a small sum of money at a time to any of his victims was a peculiar article in the English popular creed. "In 1645," says Baxter, "in Dorsetshire, I lodged at a village on a hill, called (I think) Evershot, in the house of the minister, a grave man, who had with him, a son, also a learned minister, that had been chaplain to sir Thomas Adams in London. They both told me, that they had a neighbour that had long lain bed-rid, that told all the occasion; that for a long time, being a poor labouring man, every morning when he went out of his door, he found a shilling under his door, of which he told no man, so that in a long time, he buying some sheep or swine, and seeming rich, his neighbours marvelled how he came by it. At last he told them, and was suddenly struck lame and bed-rid. They would have me speak with the man; but the snow covering the ground, and I being ill, and the witnesses fully credible, I forbore."

Hopkins and his colleagues were encouraged in their new profession by the tacit recognition of parliament, who sent a commission of puritanical ministers to assist the judges in the assizes. We can trace his course imperfectly by the pamphlets of the time, which give reports of at least some of the different trials in which he figured as grand accuser, but some of these are now exceedingly rare, and many no doubt are lost. He was perhaps at Cambridge towards the end of the year 1645, as a witch was hanged there who had an imp in the form of a frog. Towards spring the witch-finder-general reached Huntingdon, where a rich harvest awaited him.

The imps of the witches of Huntingdon often assumed the form of mice, and they were transferable from one person to another. They had different powers, some being able to kill men, others only cattle and animals, while the power of others extended only to inanimate things. This was the reason why one witch had often several familiars. John Winnick, a husbandman, said that having lost his purse with seven shillings in it, at which he was much grieved, he was one day at noon in the barn, making hay-bottles for horses, "swearing, cursing, and raging," and wishing he might have help to restore his loss, when the evil one appeared to him in the form of a black shaggy beast, with paws like a bear, but not quite so large as a coney or rabbit, and tempted him by a promise of restitution. One of the Huntingdon witches, Joan Wallis, said that she one day met a man in black clothes, who said his name was Blackman, and asked her if she was poor. She "saw he had ugly feet," and was afraid. He told her that he would send her two familiars named Grissell and Greedigut, and "within three or four days Grissell and Greedigut came to her, in the shapes of dogs with great bristles of hog's hair upon their backs, and said to her they were come from Blackman to do what she would command them, and did ask her if she did want anything, and they would fetch her anything; and she said she lacked nothing. Then they prayed her to give them some victuals, and she said she was poor and had none to give them, and so they departed." Yet she confessed that Blackman, Grissell, and Greedigut, divers times came to her afterwards, and brought her two or three shillings at a time. Elizabeth Chandler was accused of having two imps named Belzebub and Trullibub; but she denied it, and stated that she called a certain log of wood Belzebub, and a stick near it Trullibub. Another woman was constrained to confess that she sent her familiar, named Pretty, to kill a man's capons. The man being brought forward as a witness, deposed, "that she coming to bake a loaf at his house about three or four years since, being denied, his capons did fall a fluttering, and would never eat after. And also saith, that about the same time, she having a hog in his yard, some of his servants set a dog on the same; for which she said she would be revenged, and the next day one of his hogs died."

It was apparently just before his visit to Huntingdon to undertake these examinations, which took place during the months of March and April of the year 1646, that Hopkins went to Kimbolton. The reports of his sanguinary proceedings had spread consternation far and wide, and it was only here and there that any one durst raise a voice against him. One of these courageous individuals was John Gaule, the minister of Great Staughton, near Kimbolton in Huntingdonshire, who took up the cudgels against Hopkins, and provoked his wrath to such a degree, that he wrote the following insolent letter to one of the chief persons in his parish. "My service to your worship presented, I have this day received a letter to come to a town called Great Staughton, to search for evil-disposed persons called witches, (though I hear your minister is far against us through ignorance,) I intend to come (God willing) the sooner to hear his singular judgment in the behalf of such parties. I have known a minister in Suffolk preach as much against the discovery in a pulpit, and forced to recant it (by the committee) in the same place. I much marvel such evil members should have any, much more any of the clergy who should daily preach terror to convince such offenders, stand up to take their parts against such as are complainants for the king and sufferers themselves with their families and estates. I intend to give your town a visit suddenly. I am to come to Kimbolton this week, and it shall be ten to one but I will come to your town first; but I would certainly know afore whether your town affords many sticklers for such cattle, or willing to give and afford us good welcome and entertainment, as other where I have been, else I shall waive your shire, (not as yet beginning in any part of it myself,) and betake me to such places where I do and may persist without controll, but with thanks and recompence. So I humbly take my leave, and rest your servant to be commanded. Matthew Hopkins."

So far was John Gaule from being terrified by this threatening epistle, that he immediately made it the text of a treatise against the witch-finder and his followers, which he published the same year under the title of "Select Cases of Conscience touching Witches and Witchcraft." Gaule was not in advance of his age in point of intelligence, though his better and more generous feelings revolted at the wholesale cruelties which had been provokėd by Hopkins and his accomplices. He fully believed in the existence of the witches, and in the evils which they perpetrated, but he wished, like Cotta, that the evidence should be more cautiously sifted and discriminated. In his enumeration of the objectionable methods of trying witches, he lets us into a secret of Hopkins's practices, which show us at once the horrible character of the persecution that was carried on under the direction of the witch-finder general. "To all these signs," says Gaule, "I cannot but add one at large, which

I have lately learnt, partly from some communications I had with one of the witch-finders, (as they call them,) partly from the confessions (which I heard) of a suspected and committed witch, so handled as she said, and partly as the country people talk of it. Having taken the suspected witch, she is placed in the middle of a room, upon a stool or table, cross-legged, or in some other uneasy posture, to which, if she submits not, she is then bound with cords; there is she watched and kept without meat or sleep for the space of four-and-twenty hours (for they say within that time they shall see her imp come and suck). A little hole is likewise made in the door for the imp to come in at; and lest they should come in some less discernible shape, they that watch are taught to be ever and anon sweeping the room, and if they see any spiders or flies, to kill them, and if they cannot kill them, then they may be sure they are her imps."

The provision of making a hole in the door shows no very intelligent appreciation of the nature of spirits, but it agrees tolerably well with the confessions of several of Hopkins' victims. Elizabeth Clarke, at Manningtree, is said to have confessed that when the devil visited her at night, she was obliged to rise and let him in when he knocked at the door. One witch kept her imp a year and a half with oatmeal, and then lost it. Another *killed* her imp; and another had imps which sucked one another.

The horror at first excited by the atrocities committed under the regime of the witch-finder-general soon gave place to a widely-extended feeling of indignation. A lady who lived near Hoxne in Suffolk, told Dr. Hutchinson (the author of the Essay on Witchcraft) that when the witch-finders came into that neighbourhood, they took a poor woman, and by keeping her fasting and without sleep, induced her to confess that she had an imp named Nan. "This good gentlewoman told me that her husband (a very learned ingenious gentleman) having indignation at the thing, he and she went to the house, and put the people out of doors, and gave the poor woman some meat, and let her go to bed; and when she had slept and come to herself she knew not what she had confessed, and had nothing she called Nan but a pullet, that she sometimes called by that name." Tortures like these, and even worse, were exercised on parson Lowes of Brandeston, to force a confession from him. Dr. Hutchinson learnt "from them that watched with him, that they kept him awake several nights together, and run him backwards and forwards about the room, until he was out of breath; then they rested him a little, and then ran him again; and thus they did for several days and nights together, till he was weary of his life, and was scarce sensible of what he said or did. They swam him at Framlingham, but that was no true rule to try him by; for they put in honest people at the same time, and they swam as well as he."

To escape the odium which pursued him through the counties in which he had made himself so conspicuous, Hopkins appears to have now removed the scene of his labours into other parts of the kingdom. We find him not long after this at Worcester. On the fourth of March, probably of the year 1647, four witches were condemned in that city, and Matthew Hopkins was one of the principal witnesses. After the same process of watching her, he extracted from one of them a confession that Satan had appeared to her as a handsome young man, that he said he came to marry her, and that he accordingly took her as his wife. Another said that she only enjoyed her health while her imp was employed in doing mischief. These were imitations of the confessions made in Essex and Suffolk. The witches at Worcester said they tormented and killed people by making figures of wax, and sticking pins and needles into them. On their trial, one of them denied their confession, and said that when they confessed they were not in their senses.

On his return to his native county, Hopkins was assailed on every side by the outcries of his enemies, and he was alarmed at the indignation which his cruelties had excited. The extraordinary scale on which he had carried on his prosecutions, gave rise to a popular report that he was not himself unacquainted with Satan, from whom it was pretended by some that he had obtained the list of his subjects. Complaints had been publicly made against him, and his method of proceeding was laid aside as too rigorous and tyrannical. In fact, a great reaction had followed him in his course, and the witch-finder was now in disgrace. Hopkins felt this, and winced under the popular attacks. It appears that he was of a weak constitution, and vexation and regret hastened the hereditary consumption to which he was a prey. He returned to Manningtree in 1647, printed a pamphlet in his own defence,* and then died. This we learn from his coadjutor Sterne, who assures us that he had "no trouble of conscience for what he had done, as was falsely reported of him." A report was afterwards circulated, apparently without any foundation in truth, although adopted by Butler, that in the midst of the popular indignation against the witch-finder, some gentlemen had seized on him and put him to the trial of swimming, on which, as he happened to swim, he was adjudged to be himself a wizard.† Upon the death of Hopkins, the popular

* "The Discovery of Witches, in answer to several queries lately delivered to the judge of assize for the county of Norfolk; and was published by Matthew Hopkins, witch-finder, for the benefit of the whole kingdom. Printed for R. Royston, at the Angel, in Iron Lane. 1647." This is a very rare tract, and the only copy I know of was in the possession of sir Walter Scott, from whose "Letters on Demonology and Witchcraft" I take the title.

† The lines of Hudibras have been often quoted—

Hath not this present parliament
A lieger to the devil sent,
Fully empower'd to set about
Finding revolted witches out?
And has he not within a year
Hang'd threescore of them in one shire?
Some only for not being drown'd,
And some for sitting above ground
Whole days and nights upon their breeches,
And feeling pain, were hang'd for witches.
And some for putting knavish tricks
Upon green geese or Turkey chicks;

odium seems to have fallen on his colleague Sterne, who had taken up his residence at Lawshall, near Bury St. Edmunds. In 1648, provoked by the reflections that had been cast on himself and his colleague Hopkins, he published a defence of their conduct, under the title of "A Confirmation and Discovery of Witchcraft," in which he boasts that he had been part an agent in convicting about two hundred witches in Essex, Suffolk, Northamptonshire, Huntingdonshire, Bedfordshire, Norfolk, Cambridgeshire, and the Isle of Ely. He assures us "that in many places I never received penny as yet, nor any am like, notwithstanding I have hands for satisfaction, except I should sue; but many rather fall upon me for what hath been received, but I hope such suits will be disannulled, and that where I have been out of moneys for towns in charges and otherwise, such course will be taken that I may be satisfied and paid with reason." * Hopkins himself, in defending himself against the charge of interestedness, tells us that his regular charge was twenty shillings for each town, including the expenses of living, and journeying thither and back. In his book, he confesses that

Or pigs that suddenly deceased
Of griefs unnatural, as he guess'd,
Who proved himself at length a witch,
And made a rod for his own breech.

HUDIBRAS, Part ii. Canto 3.

* A copy of this excessively rare book is in the rich library of works on demonology of Mr. James Crossley of Manchester. I only know it through the extracts given in that gentleman's recent edition of Potts' Discovery of Witches.

besides the other practices of stripping the victims naked, and thrusting pins into various parts of their body, in search of marks, and swimming them, he had practised the new torture of keeping them awake, and forcing them to walk, which was an invention of his own; but he acknowledges that he had been so far obliged to yield to public opinion in the latter part of his course, as to lay aside this his own favourite remedy.

The violent persecution excited by Hopkins had now subsided, and it was followed by a calm, during which we hear but little of accusations of witchcraft. The independents, who had gained the ascendancy, seem to have discouraged prosecutions of this kind. Yet, in 1649, soon after the execution of the king, we perceive an inclination to revive the prosecutions against witches. In the May of that year, the city of Worcester was again the scene of a tragedy of this kind. A boy, at Droitwich, whose mother, a poor woman, had a cow that had strayed, was sent in search of it. As he came near a brake, he thought he saw the bullrushes move in one place, and, imagining the cow might be grazing amongst them, he approached the spot; but he had no sooner come near, than an old woman suddenly jumped up and cried "boh!" The lad was seized with sudden terror, became speechless, and hurried home in a state of distraction. He remained in the house till the evening. and then he was seized with a sudden fit, ran out, and directed his steps towards the house of sir Richard Barret, where, as was usual in the olden time, a number of poor people were collected at the door feeding upon the charity of the family. Among these the lad discovered the old woman of the brake, who it appears was a vagrant from Lancashire, sitting down and supping upon a mass of hot pottage, and he ran furiously at her, thew her pottage in her face, and struck her. The people who stood round interfered, and, when the state of the case was known, the old woman was taken and committed to the prison, which was there called the "Chequer." About the middle of the night, the boy's mother heard a noise above her, and hurried up to the garret where the boy slept, where she found him out of bed, with the leg of a stool in his hand, striking furiously at the window. He then put on his clothes, ran down into the street, and went direct to the prison. It appears that in the meantime the jailor, who compassionated the sufferings of the boy, had threatened his prisoner that she should have nothing to eat until she had said the Lord's prayer and a blessing on her victim, which with some difficulty she was prevailed upon to do. The consequence of this was, that when the boy arrived at the prison, he had recovered his speech, and was enabled to ask the jailor why he had allowed his prisoner to go at large. The jailor insisted that she was safe under lock and key. "Nay," replied the boy, "I have just seen her myself," and he proceeded to tell him how the old woman had come in at his window while he was in bed, and how he had jumped up and struck her two blows with a stool-leg as she was making her exit, which must have left their marks on her body. A woman was sent to examine the prisoner's person, and to her great astonishment she found distinct marks of blows, just as the boy had described them. These circumstances were deposed to at the assizes at Worcester by the boy, his mother, the jailor, and the woman who searched, and the witch of course stood duly convicted. About the same time a man at Tewkesbury had a sow with a numerous litter of pigs, and was surprised at the short allowance of milk she gave to them. Suspecting there might be something wrong, he watched at night, and saw a black thing like a polecat come and suck the old sow greedily. He immediately struck at the depredator with a fork he held in his hand, and stuck the prongs into its thigh; but it made its escape through the door, and he lost sight of it. He followed, however, in the direction which he supposed it had taken, and meeting with a man he knew, asked him if he had not seen such an animal as he described. The man declared he had seen nothing but a "wench," who passed him apparently in great haste. This wench was taken and examined, and the wounds caused by the prongs of the fork were found on her thigh. She was taken to Gloucester, and at the next assizes tried and convicted. In the month of July following, a man and woman were executed at St. Albans; the man confessed he had been a witch sixty years, and that he had generally exercised his profession as a white or beneficent witch. He was probably one of those miserable impostors who gained their living by conjuring to cure diseases, and help people to what was lost or stolen. His accomplice was a kinswoman, who lived with him, and had a familiar in the shape of a cat. She acknowledged that this familiar had promised to bring her anything she wanted, *except money.* They said there were plenty of other witches about the neighbourhood, and accused several persons by name.

This year, however, witnessed a much more remarkable affair than any of these, and one which made a considerable sensation. It has gained in modern times an additional importance from the circumstance that our great historical novelist, sir Walter Scott, has made it the foundation of one of his romances. I shall give it nearly in the words of the report written at or near the time.

After Charles's death, the royal property was confiscated to the state, and commissioners were appointed by parliament to survey and sell the crown lands. Among the royal estates was the manor of Woodstock, of which the parliamentary commissioners were sent to take possession in the month of October, 1649. The more fanatical part of the opponents of royalty had always taught that, through witches and otherwise, the devil was actively engaged in the service of their opponents, battling against them; and they now found him resolved upon more open hostilities than ever. On the 3rd of October the commissioners, with their servants, went to the manor-hall, and took up their lodgings in the king's own rooms, the bed-chamber and withdrawing-room: the former they used as their kitchen, the council-hall was their brewhouse, the chamber of presence served as their place of sitting to dispatch business, and the dining-room was used as a wood-house, where they laid the wood of "that ancient standard in the high park, known of all by the name of the king's oak, which (that nothing might remain that had the name of king affixed to it) they digged up by the roots." On the 14th and 15th they had little disturbance; but on the 16th there came, as they thought, something into the bed-chamber, where two of the commissioners and their servant lay, in the shape of a dog, which going under their bed, did, as it were, gnaw their bed-cords; but on the morrow finding them whole, and a quarter of beef which lay on the ground untouched, they "began to entertain other thoughts." October 17th.—Something, to their thinking, removed all the wood of the king's oak out of the dining-room to the presence-chamber, and hurled the chairs and stools up and down that room; from whence it came into the two chambers where the two commissioners and their servants lay, and hoisted up their bed feet so much higher than their heads, that they thought they should have been turned over and over, and then let them fall down with such force, that their bodies rebounded from the bed a good distance; and then shook the bedsteads so violently, that they declared their bodies were sore with it. On the 18th something came into the chamber and walked up and down, and fetching the warming-pan out of the withdrawing-room, made so much noise that they thought fire-bells could not have made more. Next day trenchers were thrown up and down the dining-room, and at those who slept there; one of them being wakened, put forth his head to see what was the matter, and had trenchers thrown at him. On the 20th, the curtains of the bed in the withdrawing-room were drawn to and fro; the bedstead was much shaken, and eight great pewter dishes and three dozen of trenchers thrown about the bedchamber again. This night they also thought a whole armful of the wood of the king's oak was thrown down in their chamber, but of that in the morning they found nothing had been moved. On the 21st, the keeper of their ordinary and his bitch lay in one of the rooms with them, and on that night they were not disturbed at all. But on the 22nd, though the bitch slept there again, to which circumstance they had ascribed their former night's rest, both they and it were in "a pitiful taking," the latter "opening but once, and then with a whining fearful yelp." October 23.—They had all their clothes plucked off them in the withdrawing-room, and the bricks fell out of the chimney into the room. On the 24th they thought in the dining-room that all the wood of the king's oak had been brought thither, and thrown down close by their bed-side, which being heard by those of the withdrawing-room, "one of them rose to see what was done, fearing indeed his fellow-commissioners had been killed, but found no such matter. Whereupon returning to his bed again, he found two or three dozen of trenchers thrown into it, and handsomely covered with the bed-clothes."

The commissioners persisted in retaining possession, and were subjected to new persecutions. On the 25th of October the curtains of the bed in the withdrawing-room were drawn to and fro, and the bedstead shaken, as before; and in the bed-chamber, glass flew about so thick (and yet not one of the chamber-windows broken,) that they thought it had rained money; whereupon they lighted candles, but "to their grief they found nothing but glass." On the 29th something going to the window opened and shut it, them going into the bed-chamber, it threw great stones for half an hour's time, some whereof fell on the high-bed, others on the truckle-bed, to the number in all of above fourscore. This night there was also a very great noise, as if forty pieces of ordnance had been shot off together. It astonished all the neighbourhood, and it was thought it must have been heard a great way off. During these noises, which were heard in both rooms together, the commissioners and their servants were struck with so great horror, that they cried out one to another for help; whereupon one of them recovering himself out of a "strange agony" he had been in, snatched a sword, and had like to have killed one of his brethren coming out of his bed in his shirt, whom he took for the spirit that did the mischief. However, at length they got all together, yet the noise continued so great and terrible, and shook the walls so much, that they thought the whole manor would have fallen on their heads. At the departure of the supernatural disturber of their repose, "it took all the glass of the windows away with it." On the first of November, something, as the commissioners thought, walked up and down the withdrawing-room, and then made a noise in the dining-room. The stones which were left before, and laid up in the withdrawing-room, were all fetcht away this night, and a great deal of glass (not like the former) thrown about again.

On the second of November, there came something into the withdrawing-room, treading, as they conceived, much like a bear, which began by walking about for a quarter of an hour, and then at length it made a noise about the table and threw the warming-pan so violently that it was quite spoiled. It threw also a glass and great stones at the commissioners again, and the bones of horses; and all so violently, that the bedstead and the walls were bruised by them. That night they planted candles all about the rooms, and made fires up to the "rantle-trees" of the chimney, but all were put out, nobody knew how, the fire and burnt wood being thrown up and down the room; the curtains were torn with the rods from their beds, and the bed-posts pulled away, that the tester fell down upon them, and the feet of the bedstead were cloven into two The servants in the truckle-bed, who lay all the time sweating for fear, were treated even worse, for there came upon them first a little which made them begin to stir, but before they could get out, it was followed by a whole tubful, as it were, of stinking ditch water, so green, that it made their shirts and sheets of that colour too. The same night the windows were all broke by throwing of stones, and there was most terrible noises in three several places together near them. Nay, the very rabbit-stealers who were abroad that night were so affrighted with the dismal thundering, that for haste they left their ferrets in the holes behind them, beyond Rosamond's well. Notwithstanding all this, one of them had the boldness to ask, in the name of God, what it was, what it would have, and what they had done that they should be so disturbed after this manner. To which no answer was given, but the noise ceased for a while. At length it came again, and, as all of them said, brought seven devils worse than itself. Whereupon one of them lighted a candle again, and set it between the two chambers in the doorway, on which another fixing his eyes saw the similitude of a hoof, striking the candle and candlestick into the middle of the bedchamber, and afterwards making three scrapes on the snuff to put it out. Upon this, the same person was so bold as to draw his sword, but he had scarce got it out, but there was another invisible hand had hold of it too, and tugged with him for it; and prevailing, struck him so violently, that he was stunned with the blow. Then began violent noises again, insomuch that they, calling to one another, got together, and went into the presence chamber, where they said prayers, and sang psalms; notwithstanding all which, the thundering noises still continued in other rooms. After this, on the 3rd of November, they removed their lodging over the gate; and next day, being Sunday, went to Ewelm, "where, how they escaped the authors of the relation knew not, but returning on Monday, the devil (for that was the name they gave their nightly guest) left them not unvisited, nor on the Tuesday following, which was the last day they stayed." The courage even of the devout commissioners of the parliament was not proof against a persecution like this, and the manor of Woodstock was relieved from their presence. It is said that one of the old retainers of the house, years afterwards, confessed that he had entered the service of the commissioners, in order by playing these tricks upon them, which he was enabled to do by his intimate acquaintance with the secret passages of the lodge, to rescue it from their grasp.

Hopkins and Sterne were not without their imitators in other parts of the country. About the end of the year of which we have just been speaking, the magistrates of Newcastle-upon-Tyne were alarmed at the reports of witches in that town, and they sent into Scotland for a practiser in the art of discovering them. They agreed to pay his travelling expenses, and give him twenty shillings for every witch who should be convicted—an excellent method of increasing their number. No sooner was the Scotchman arrived in Newcastle, than the bellman was sent round the town to invite all persons to bring their complaints against women suspected, and about thirty were brought to the town hall, and subjected, in the sight of all the people collected there, to his examination. We are told that his practise was to lay the body of the person suspected naked to the waist, and then run a pin into her thigh, after which he suddenly let her coats fall, and asked her if she had nothing of his in her body which did not bleed; the woman was hindered from replying by shame and fear, and he immediately took out the pin and set her aside as a convicted witch. By this atrocious process, he ascertained that twenty-seven persons were practisers of sorcery, and at the ensuing assizes fourteen women and a man were found guilty and executed. The names of the sufferers are recorded in the register of the parish of St. Andrew's.

Just at the time when the commonwealth was merging into the protectorate, in the years 1652 and 1653, we find cases of witchcraft becoming suddenly more numerous, or, which is perhaps nearer the truth, there were for some cause or other more printed reports of them. In the former year a witch was hanged at Worcester. On the 11th of April, 1652, one Joan Peterson, known as the witch of Wapping, was hanged at Tyburn. She lived in Spruce Island, near Shadwell, and was said to have done on the whole more good than harm, for she practised chiefly as a white witch. Strange things, however, were told of her. A man deposed that he was sitting with her in her house and saw her familiar, in the shape of a black dog, come in and suck her. And two women said that, as they were watching with a child of one of their neighbours that was strangely distempered, "about midnight they espied (to their thinking) a great black cat come to the cradle's side and stopt the cradling, whereupon one of the women took up the fire-fork to strike at it, and it immediately vanished. About an hour after the cat came again to the cradle side; whereupon the other woman kicked at it, but it presently vanished, and that leg that she kicked with began to swell and be very sore, whereupon they were both afraid, and calling upon the master of the house, took their leave. As they were going to their own homes, they met a baker, who was likewise a neighbour's servant, who told them that he saw a great black cat that had so frightened him that his hair stood an end; whereupon the women told him what they had seen, who said he thought in his conscience that Peterson had bewitched the aforesaid child, for, (quoth the baker,) I met the witch a little before going down the island." The baker gave his testimony in court, and when asked by the judge the very pertinent question, "whether he had not at other times as well as that been afraid of a cat, he answered, no, and that he never saw such a cat before, and hoped in God he should never see the like again."

On the 30th of July, 1652, no less than six witches were condemned at Maidstone in Kent. In addition to the usual circumstances in such cases, they confessed that the devil had given them a piece of flesh, "which whensoever they should touch they should thereby effect their desires; that this flesh lay hid amongst grass, in a certain place which she named, where upon search it was found accordingly." The flesh was brought into court as an evidence against them, and the author of the printed report informs us that it "was of a sinewy substance, and scorched, and was seen and felt by this observator, and reserved for public view at the sign of the Swan in Maidstone." Other witches were brought to trial, and some found guilty, but four only were hanged. "Some there were that wished rather they might be burnt to ashes; alledging, that it was a received opinion amongst many that the body of a witch being burnt, her blood is prevented thereby from becoming hereditary to her progeny in the same evil, while by hanging it is not; but whether this opinion be erroneous or not, I," says the narrator, "am not to dispute."

The following year (1653) witnessed the execution at Salisbury of a woman who had been in her younger days the servant of the famous Dr. Lamb. Her name was Anne Bodenham, and she appears to have been initiated into Lamb's practices, and to have settled at Salisbury in the character of a wise woman. She helped people to recover things stolen, cured diseases, and seems to have carried on the practice of poisoning. Many of those charged with the crime of witchcraft appear to have been secret professors of the art of poisoning. The depositions against Anne Bodenham were of a remarkable character. It appears that a little girl had been bewitched, and the wise woman Bodenham was accused of being in some way or other concerned in it. A servant girl was sent to consult her, and she deposed that Anne Bodenham, having taken her into a room in her house, made a circle on the floor and carefully swept the space within it. She then looked in a glass, and in a book, uttering certain mysterious words, and placed an earthen pan full of coals in the middle of the circle. Five spirits then appeared in the shape of ragged boys, and at the same time there arose a high wind which shook the house. She gave the spirits crumbs of bread, which they picked from the floor and ate, and then, after they had all leaped over the pan of coals, they danced with the witch and the maid servant. The latter had witnessed this scene more than once, and on one occasion she was carried to a meadow at Wilton to gather vervain and dill. She declared that she had seen Anne Bodenham transform herself into a great black cat.

The improvement in intelligence and liberality under the protectorate is shown by the publication of two treatises, which contained the boldest protests against the iniquity of the witch persecution that had appeared since the days of Reginald Scott. The trials at Maidstone in 1653 had so much shocked the good sense of some of the gentlemen of Kent, that it produced from one of them, sir Robert Filmor, a tract entitled, " An Advertisement to the Jury-men of England, touching Witches," in which he pointed out the ridiculous absurdity of the proofs by which this class of offenders were usually convicted. " The late execution of witches at the summer assizes in Kent," he says, " occasioned this brief exercitation, which addresses itself to such as have not deliberately thought upon the great difficulty in discovering what or who a witch is. To have nothing but the public faith of the present age, is none of the best evidence, unless the universality of elder times do concur with these doctrines, which ignorance in the times of darkness brought forth, and credulity in these days of light hath continued." Language like this must have sounded strange within six or seven years after the fury of persecution which had been excited by Matthew Hopkins ; yet in this spirit Filmor proceeds calmly to consider and refute each of the reasons on which the witch-finders depended, ending with the crowning proof supposed to be derived from the devil himself declaring against his victims, "which, how it can be well done, except the devil be bound over to give in evidence against the witch, cannot be understood."

This book, which marked the commencement of the protectorate, was published anonymously; but two years after, in 1655, a minister of the name of Thomas Ady put forth in the same, or even in a more enlightened, spirit, a book entitled, "A Candle in the Dark, or a treatise concerning the nature of witches and witchcraft; being advice to judges, sheriffs, justices of the peace, and grand jurymen, what to do before they pass sentence on such as are arraigned for their lives as witches." Ady has enlivened his book with a variety of anecdotes and scraps of information relating to the popular superstitions of the day, and in speaking of charms, which he regards as mere relics of popery, he gives the following as the most approved remedy against the bewitching of milk when it will not work properly in the churn. The maid, while churning, was to repeat the words,—

> Come, butter, come; come, butter, come;
> Peter stands at the gate,
> Waiting for a butter'd cake;
> Come, butter, come.

This, Ady says, was told by an old witch who declared that her grandmother had learnt it in the good days of queen Mary.

The reign of the protector Oliver was certainly not favourable to the persecution of witches. Yet two persons, a mother and daughter, were hanged at

Bury St. Edmunds about the year 1655, and in the November of 1657 a rather remarkable case occurred at Shepton Mallet in Somersetshire. A woman named Jane Brooks was accused of bewitching a boy named Jones, by giving him an apple, which he roasted and ate. He was immediately seized with strange fits, and while under their influence he cried out against Jane Brooks and her sister as the cause of his suffering. It was deposed at the trial that, one Sunday afternoon, in company with his father and a cousin named Gibson, he was suddenly visited with a fit, and he said that he saw Jane Brooks against the wall of the room, pointing to the spot where he pretended she stood. Gibson took up a knife and struck at the part of the wall to which the boy pointed, and the latter immediately exclaimed, "Oh, father! cousin Gibson hath cut Jane Brooks's hand, and it is bloody!" They immediately took a constable, and went with him to the woman's house, where they found her sitting on a stool, with her hands before her, one placed on the other. The constable inquired how she did, and she replied, not well. He then asked her why she sat in that position, with her hands before her, to which she replied that it was her wont to do so. When he asked further if nothing ailed her hand, she said, "No, it was well enough." Still not satisfied, he forced one hand from under the other, and found it bleeding just as the boy had described. On being asked how this happened, she said she had scratched her hand with a great pin.* This was sufficient matter for

* The following story is given in Dr. Hutchinson's Histo-

carrying the woman to prison. It was pretended that the boy was often lifted about in an extraordinary manner; and one woman declared that on the 25th of February, 1658, being seized with one of her fits while in her house, he went out of the house into the garden, and she followed him. There she saw him gradually lifted up into the air, and pass away over a wall, and she saw no more of him till he was found lying at the door of a house at some distance, when he declared that he had been carried there by Jane Brooks. She was tried at Chard assizes, on the 26th of March, 1658, and, as might be expected from such conclusive evidence, condemned.

About the period of the protector's death, a witch was hanged at Norwich, and several punished in the same way in Cornwall; and in 1659, two were hanged at Lancaster, who protested their in-

rical Essay on Witchcraft. "About the year 1645, there was at Chelmsford an afflicted person, that in her fits cried out against a woman, a neighbour, which Mr. Clark, the minister of the gospel there, could not believe to be guilty of such a crime. And it happened, while that woman milked her cow, the cow struck her with one horn upon the forehead, and fetched blood; and while she was thus bleeding, a spectre in her likeness appeared to the person afflicted, who, pointing at the spectre, one struck at the place, and the afflicted said, 'You have made her forehead bleed.' Hereupon some went to the woman, and found her forehead bloody, and acquainted Mr. Clark with it; who forthwith went to the woman, and asked how her forehead became bloody; and she answered, 'by a blow of the cow's horn;' whereby he was satisfied that it was a design of Satan to render an innocent person suspected."

nocence to the last. The approach of a great political change, and the animosities of party which attended it, always furnished the opportunity, even in humble life, of gratifying personal resentments; and we shall find immediately after the restoration that the cases of witchcraft were again numerous. At the beginning of the period of the interregnum, the devil was the enemy of the republicans,—at its close he was opposed to the royalists. On the 14th of May, 1660, four persons at Kidderminster, a widow, her two daughters, and a man, were charged with various acts of witchcraft, and carried to Worcester jail. The eldest daughter was accused of saying that, if they had not been taken, the king should never have come to England, "and, though he now doth come, yet he shall not live long, but shall die as ill a death as they; and that they would have made corn like pepper." These were the mere ravings of puritanical discontent, repetitions probably of sentiments they had heard among their neighbours. The relator continues, "Many great charges against them, and little proved, they were put to the ducking in the river: they would not sink, but swam aloft. The man had five teats, the women three, and the eldest daughter one. When they went to search the women, none were visible; one advised to lay them on their backs and keep open their mouths, and then they would appear; and so they presently appeared in sight."

CHAPTER XXVI.

WITCHCRAFT IN GERMANY, IN THE EARLIER PART OF THE SEVENTEENTH CENTURY.

In Germany, since the fifteenth century, sorcery had been undergoing much the same fate as in France and Spain. In the writers of the sixteenth century we trace a system of demonology differing only in some of its details from that of the other countries which we have reviewed, and in some respects perhaps more complete. It has more bold and striking points, a circumstance arising no doubt from the fact that here the ancient Teutonic mythology retained a stronger hold upon the popular mind. The sites of primitive worship are more distinctly marked; and such mountains as Blocksberg, Inselsberg, Weckingstein near Minden, Staffelstein near Bamberg, Kreidenberg near Würzburg, Bönnigsberg near Loccum, Fellerberg near Treves, Kandel in Brisgau, and Heuberg in the Schwarz forest, which occur as the scenes of the great sabbaths of the witches of this period, were no doubt sacred places of the early Germans.

The witchcraft trials in Germany during the sixteenth century were numerous and curious, and there as elsewhere we can trace their origin often in personal feuds, in political enmities, and more especially in religious differences.* It was, however, at the commencement of the seventeenth century, on the eve of those terrible religious wars which tore Germany to pieces, that the prosecutions against witchcraft took there their grand developement. They were most remarkable at the cities of Bamberg and Würzburg, and other places where the Roman Catholic religion was prevalent, and which were under the immediate influence of the Jesuits. Some of the earlier writers on sorcery had declared that the increasing number of witches in the sixteenth century was owing to the spread of protestantism, and the Jesuits now seized upon this doctrine as a means of influencing the minds of the vulgar against the heretics. It is probable, therefore, that of the multitudes of persons who perished at the stake in Germany during the first half of the seventeenth century for sorcery, the only crime of

* The best general treatise on witchcraft in the German language is, I believe, that by Dr. W. G. Soldan, " Geschichte der Hexenprocesse, aus den Quellen dargestellt." (Stuttgart, 1843.) The great collections of materials are Horst's Zauber-Bibliothek, and Hauber's Bibliotheca Magica. The present chapter is taken chiefly from Soldan's book, with which I was not acquainted when the earlier part of this book was written.

many was their attachment to the religion of Luther.

The period of the great persecutions of witches in Würzburg and Bamberg was one of great suffering, when the country had been reduced to poverty by a merciless war, and when the petty princes of the empire were not unwilling to seize upon any pretence to fill their coffers; and it has been remarked that in Bamberg, at least, the persons prosecuted were in general those, the confiscation of whose property was a matter of consideration. At Bamberg, as well as at Würzburg, the bishop was a sovereign prince in his dominions. There had long been a silent war in this place between catholicism and the reformation, for the latter had gained a footing in the preceding age from which its opponents had not yet been able to drive it. The prince-bishop John George II., who ruled Bamberg from 1622 to 1633, after several unsuccessful attempts to root out Lutheranism from his dominions, commenced his attacks upon it in 1625, under another name, and the rest of his reign was distinguished by a series of sanguinary witch-trials which disgrace the annals of that city. His grand agent in these proceedings was Frederic Forner, suffragan of Bamberg, a blind supporter of the Jesuits and a great enemy of heretics and sorcerers, against whom he published a treatise under the formidable title of *Panoplia armaturæ Dei*. We may form some notion of the proceedings of this worthy from the statement of the most authentic historians of this city that between 1625 and 1630, not less than nine hundred trials took place in the two courts of Bamberg and Zeil; and a pamphlet published at Bamberg by authority, in 1659, states the number of persons which bishop John George had caused to be burnt for sorcery to have been six hundred.

Among the persons thus sacrificed were the chancellor, his son doctor Horn, with his wife and two daughters, and many of the lords and councillers of the bishop's court, and these are stated to have confessed that above twelve hundred of them had confederated together, and that if their sorcery had not been brought to light, they would have brought it to pass within four years, that there would have been neither wine nor corn in the country, and that thereby man and beast would have perished with hunger, and men be driven to eat one another. There were even some catholic priests, we are told, among them, who had been led into practices too dreadful to be described, and they confessed, among other things, that they had baptized many children in the devil's name. It must be stated that these confessions were made under tortures of the most fearful kind, far more so than anything that was practised in France or other countries. Two of the city magistrates, (*bürgermeisters,*) besides other extraordinary things they had done, said that they had often raised such terrible storms, that houses were thrown down and trees torn up by the roots, and that it had been their intention to raise such a wind as should overthrow the great tower of Bamberg. The wives of one of the burgomasters and of the town butcher declared that it was their task to make the ointment for the sorcerers, from each of which they received two pennies a-week, and that this amounted in a year to six hundred *gülders* or florins. The burgomaster Neidecker acknowledged that he had assisted in poisoning the wells by sorcery, so that whoever drank of them would immediately be struck with pestilence, and that thus great multitudes had perished. The history of Germany shows how easy it was at this time to point out the ravages of war, pestilence, and famine. It was also acknowledged that no less than three thousand sorcerers and witches assembled at the dance on the Kreidenberg mountain near Würzburg, on the night of St. Walpurgis, and that each having given a *kreuzer* to the musician, he gained no less than forty *gülders*, and that at the same dance they drunk seven "fudder" of wine which they had stolen from the bishop of Würzburg's cellar. There were little girls of from seven to ten years of age among the witches, and seven-and-twenty of them were convicted and burnt. The numbers brought to trial in these terrible proceedings were so great, and they were treated with so little consideration, that it was usual not even to take the trouble of setting down their names, but they were cited as the accused No. 1, 2, 3, and so on. The Jesuits took their confessions in private, and they made up the lists of those who were understood to have been denounced by them.

Lutheranism had been gaining ground in Würzburg more even than in Bamberg, and when bishop Julius came to the see in 1575, the majority of the population was protestant. The energy with which he set about making converts alarmed many of those who had anything to lose in the world, and the number of "heretics" was thus soon diminished. Nevertheless, bishop Philip Adolph, who came to the see in 1623, found a sufficient number of Protestants to excite his alarm, and not daring, in the political position of Germany at that moment, to persecute them openly for their religion, he adopted the plan of his neighbour of Bamberg. A great confederacy of sorcerers was suddenly discovered, and during two or three years hundreds of people of all ages and conditions were hurried to the stake. A catalogue of nine-and-twenty *brände,* or burnings, during a very short period of time previous to the February of 1629, will give the best notion of the horrible character of these proceedings; it is printed from the original record in Hauber's *Bibliotheca Magica.*

"*In the first burning, four persons.*

The wife of Liebler.
Old Ancker's widow.
The wife of Gutbrodt.
The wife of Höcker.

In the second burning, four persons.

The old wife of Beutler.
Two strange women.
The old woman who kept the pot-house.

In the third burning, five persons.

Tungersleber, a minstrel.
The wife of Kuler.

The wife of Stier, a proctor.
The brushmaker's wife.
The goldsmith's wife.

In the fourth burning, five persons.

The wife of Siegmund the glazier, a burgomaster.
Brickmann's wife.
The midwife. N.B. She was the origin of all the mischief.
Old Rume's wife.
A strange man.

In the fifth burning, nine persons.

Lutz, an eminent shop-keeper.
Rutscher, a shop-keeper.
The housekeeper of the dean of the cathedral.
The old wife of the court rope-maker.
Jo. Stembach's housekeeper.
The wife of Baunach, a senator.
A woman named Znickel Babel.
An old woman.

In the sixth burning, six persons.

The steward of the senate, named Gering.
Old Mrs. Canzler.
The fat tailor's wife.
The woman cook of Mr. Mengerdorf.
A strange man.
A strange woman.

In the seventh burning, seven persons.

A strange girl of twelve years old.

A strange man.
A strange woman.*
A strange bailiff (*schultheiss*).
Three strange women.

In the eighth burning, seven persons.

Baunach, a senator, the fattest citizen in Würzburg.
The steward of the dean of the cathedral.
A strange man.
The knife-grinder.
The gauger's wife
Two strange women.

In the ninth burning, five persons.

Wunth, the wheelright.
A strange man.
Bentze's daughter.
Bentze's wife herself.
The wife of Eyering.

In the tenth burning, three persons.

Steinacher, a very rich man.
A strange woman.
A strange man.

In the eleventh burning, four persons.

Schwerdt, a vicar-choral in the cathedral.
Rensacker's housekeeper.

* It must be understood that *strange* means, not a citizen of Würzburg. Perhaps the numerous strange men and women were Protestant refugees from other parts.

The wife of Stiecher.
Silberhans, a minstrel.

In the twelfth burning, two persons.

Two strange women.

In the thirteenth burning, four persons.

The old smith of the court.
An old woman.
A little girl nine or ten years old.
A younger girl, her little sister.

In the fourteenth burning, two persons.

The mother of the two little girls before-mentioned.
Liebler's daughter, aged twenty-four years.

In the fifteenth burning, two persons.

A boy of twelve years of age, in the first school.
A butcher's wife.

In the sixteenth burning, six persons.

A noble page of Ratzenstein, was executed in the chancellor's yard at six o'clock in the morning, and left upon his bier all day, and then next day burnt with the following:—

A boy of ten years of age.

The two daughters of the steward of the senate, and his maid.

The fat rope-maker's wife.

In the seventeenth burning, four persons.

The inn-keeper of the Baumgarten.

A boy eleven years old.

The wife of the apothecary at the Hirsch (*the Stag*), and her daughter.

N.B. A woman who played the harp had hanged herself.

In the eighteenth burning, six persons.

Batsch, a tanner.

Two boys of twelve years old.

The daughter of Dr. Junge.

A girl of fifteen years of age.

A strange woman.

In the nineteenth burning, six persons.

A noble page of Rotenham was beheaded at six o'clock in the chancellor's yard, and burnt the following day.

The wife of the secretary Schellhar.

A woman.

A boy of ten years of age.

Another boy twelve years old.

Brugler's wife, a cymbal-player (*beckin*), was burnt alive.

In the twentieth burning, six persons

Göbel's child, the most beautiful girl in Würzburg.

A student on the fifth form, who knew many languages, and was an excellent musician *vocaliter et instrumentaliter*.

Two boys from the new minster, each twelve years old.

Stepper's little daughter.

The woman who kept the bridge-gate.

In the twenty-first burning, six persons.

The master of the Dietricher hospital, a very learned man.

Stoffel Holtzmann.

A boy fourteen years old.

The little son of senator Stolzenberger.

Two *alumni.*

In the twenty-second burning, six persons.

Stürman, a rich cooper.

A strange boy.

The grown-up daughter of senator Stolzenberger.

The wife of Stolzenberger herself.

The washerwoman in the new building.

A strange woman.

In the twenty-third burning, nine persons.

David Croten's boy, of nine years old, on the second form.

The two sons of the prince's cook, one of fourteen years, the other of ten years, from the first school.

Melchior Hammelmann, vicar at Hach.

Nicodemus Hirsch, a canon in the new minster.

Christopher Berger, vicar in the new minster.

An *alumnus.*

N.B. the bailiff in the Brennerbach court and an *alumnus* were burnt alive.

In the twenty-fourth burning, seven persons.

Two boys in the hospital.

A rich cooper.

Lorenz Stüber, vicar in the new minster.

Batz, vicar in the new minster.
Lorenz Roth, vicar in the new minster.
A woman named Rossleins Martin.

In the twenty-fifth burning, six persons.

Frederick Basser, vicar in the cathedral.
Stab, vicar at Hach.
Lambrecht, canon in the new minster.
The wife of Gallus Hansen.
A strange boy.
Schelmerei the huckstress.

In the twenty-sixth burning, seven persons.

David Hans, a canon in the new minster.
Weydenbusch, a senator.
The innkeeper's wife of the Baumgarten.
An old woman.
The little daughter of Valkenberger was privately executed and burnt on her bier.
The little son of the town council bailiff.
Herr Wagner, vicar in the cathedral, was burnt alive.

In the twenty-seventh burning, seven persons.

A butcher, named Kilian Hans.
The keeper of the bridge-gate.
A strange boy.
A strange woman.
The son of the female minstrel, vicar at Hach.
Michel Wagner, vicar at Hach.
Knor, vicar at Hach.

In the twenty-eighth burning, after Candlemas, 1629, *six persons.*

The wife of Knertz the butcher.

The infant daughter of Dr. Schütz.

A blind girl.

Schwartz, canon at Hach.

Ehling, a vicar.

Bernhard Mark, vicar in the cathedral, was burnt alive.

In the twenty-ninth burning, seven persons.

Viertel Beck.

The innkeeper at Klingen.

The bailiff of Mergelsheim.

The wife of Beck at the Ox-tower.

The fat noble lady (*edelfrau*).

N.B. A doctor of divinity at Hach and a canon were executed early at five o'clock in the morning, and burnt on their bier.

A gentleman of Adel, called Junker Fleischbaum."

We are assured at the end of this document that there were many other burnings besides those here enumerated. It appears that, except in particular cases, the judges showed so much mercy as to cause their victims to be put to death by beheading before they were burnt.

One of the victims on this occasion excited especial commiseration, because he was of high rank, a kinsman of the bishop himself, on whom he attended as a page of the court, and because he was young, handsome, and interesting. The youthful Ernst von Ehrenberg, we are told, was remarkable chiefly for the the attention he paid to his studies in the university of Würzburg, and for the progress which he made in them, until he was seduced by his aunt, a lady of rank in that city, who received him as a kinsman into her family. This lady, the Jesuits tell us, was an abandoned witch—perhaps she was a Protestant—and she soon taught her nephew to pursue evil courses, until from an undue familiarity with herself he proceeded to become a familiar of the devil. For a while he had sufficient dissimulation to conceal his wickedness, until the change became evident from his increasing neglect of his studies and his religious duties, and instead of being as before, remarkable for his attention to his books, he now spent his time at play and among the ladies. The Jesuit inquisitors were alarmed at his conduct, and undertook to discover the cause. They found, or pretended to find, by the confessions of some of the sorcerers brought to the stake, that, through the seductions of his aunt, he had sold himself to the devil, and that he had attended the sabbaths of the witches. The bishop determined to convert his kinsman, if possible, to a different life. On his profession of repentance and promise of amendment, he was delivered to the care of the Jesuits, that he might profit by their teaching, and they took him to their house, where they loaded him with holy amulets, agnus-Deis, relics, and holy water, and appointed one of their order to attend upon him both day and night, to protect him against the attempts of the fiend. The Jesuits, however, soon found, as they declared, that no distemper was so incurable as sorcery. Whenever he had the opportunity, he lay aside the holy articles with which he was encumbered at night, and then the devil came to him and carried him away to the witches' meetings, from whence he contrived to return before four o'clock in the morning, the hour when his spiritual instructors rose. Once or twice, however, perhaps rising earlier than usual, they found his bed empty, and they discovered from this and some other circumstances how he spent his nights. They now declared that all his promises of amendment were only intended to deceive, and that they entertained no further hopes of him. He was accordingly condemned to death, and the judgment was held over him *in terrorem* with the hope that he might still be induced to repent. The conclusion of his story is dramatically told by the Jesuit who has left us a relation of it. The Jesuits were to prepare him for death. Early on the morning of the day appointed for his execution,—it appears that he had not been made acquainted with his sentence,—they went to him and told him, in ambiguous language, that he was to prepare for a better life than that he had hitherto led, and then toek him into the castle. Here he recognized with an innocent joy the scenes of his childish gambols; "There," said he, "I played, there I drank, there I danced," and went on making remarks of this kind, until he was conducted into a room hung with black, where a scaffold was erected. Then he turned pale, and for a few minutes stood trembling and speechless; but when the executioners attempted to lay their hands upon him, he raised such a cry of distress that the judges themselves were moved by it, and they went to intercede with the bishop in his favour. The prince made a last attempt, and sent a messenger to offer him forgiveness if he would promise a thorough reformation. But the messenger returned with an answer that all was in vain, for the devil had so hardened the youth, that he boldly declared he would remain as he was, that he had no need of repentance or change, and that if he were not so already, he would wish to become so. Then the prince sternly signified his will that justice should take its course. They dragged the youth again into the dark chamber, supported on each side by a Jesuit, who urged him to repentance; but he persisted in saying that he needed no repentance, begged for his life, tried to wrest himself from the grasp of the officers, and gave no attention to the exhortations of the priests. At last the executioner seized a favourable moment, and in the midst of his struggles to escape struck the head from his body at a blow.

We will not multiply our list of executions of witches in Germany. The persecution raised by the Jesuits against the sorcerers seemed increasing rather than otherwise, when one of their order, a pious and learned man, named Frederick Spee, a native of Cologne, raised his voice against its cruelty, by publishing, in the year 1631, a treatise on the subject, under the title of *Cautio Criminalis*, in which he pointed out the necessity of taking with more caution the sort of evidence which it was usual to adduce against offenders of this class

It was, as its author states in the title, "a book very necessary at that time for the magistracy throughout Germany," (*liber ad magistratus Germaniæ hoc tempore necessarius,*) and it no doubt had a great influence in putting a stop to the wholesale prosecutions which had become so prevalent.

CHAPTER XXVII.

THE WITCHES OF SCOTLAND UNDER KING JAMES AFTER HIS ACCESSION TO THE ENGLISH THRONE.

In the earlier ages of society, the practice of medicine, which consisted in a curing of wounds, was usually entrusted to the women. It was their business to gather the best herbs, and to know their several virtues. The remedies were often very simple, and required no great knowledge to prepare and apply them, and the professed healers, who themselves believed in the efficacy of charms and "characters," and imagined that the properties of different herbs were given to them by the spirits who presided over woods and fields, found an advantage at the same time in clothing their remedies in adventitious mystery. To what an extent this was practised will be fully understood by any one who is conversant with the collections of medicinal receipts in mediæval manuscripts. After the Roman civilization had introduced itself among the various branches of the Teutonic race, and schools of medicine were established, a new race of practitioners sprang up, superior to the others by their learning and theoretic knowledge, but still judging it convenient to create a popular reverence for their art by clothing it in a similar garb of mystery. Thus medicine, in whatever circumstances it was found, was deeply intermixed with superstition.

In process of time these two classes of medical practitioners became more and more widely separated from each other, the scholastic physicians rising in professional character, while the others went on degenerating until they became literally "old women doctors." This vulgar medicinal knowledge became at last united with sorcery in the person of the witch, as it had formerly been united with the religious worship of the people in the functions of the priestess. The latter received her knowledge by the inspiration of the gods; the former derived her knowledge of the virtues of herbs by the gift of the fairies or of the devil. Many of them added to these a profession of a far more horrible character. They were acquainted with herbs of which the properties were noxious, as well as with those which were beneficial, and they acquired at times an extraordinary skill in concocting poisons of different degrees of force, and which acted in different manners. The witches were the great poisoners of the middle ages, and their practice was no doubt far more extensive than, even with what we have recently witnessed among our peasantry, we can easily imagine.

Nearly all the Scottish witches of the first half

of the seventeenth century were such vulgar practitioners in the healing art, and some of them at least were poisoners. Our materials are again furnished almost entirely by Robert Pitcairn, whose collection of early Scottish criminal trials is one of the most curious works of the kind that has ever been published.

The first instance of an offender of this class in the seventeenth century that occurs in these registers is that of James Reid of Musselburgh, who was brought to trial as a "common sorcerer, charmer, and abuser," on the 21st of July, 1602. James Reid professed to heal all kinds of diseases, "quhilk craft he lernit fra the devill, his maister, in Bynnie craigis and Corstorphin craigis, quhair he met with him and consultit with him to lerne the said craft; quha (i. e. James Reid) gaif him thrie pennies at ane tyme, and a peice creische (*grease*) out of his bag at ane uther tyme." The devil's terms, on this occasion, were not very exorbitant. This first interview took place some thirteen years before the time of his trial, and he had since that had frequent meetings with the evil one, who appeared sometimes in the form of a man, and sometimes in that of a horse. His grand specific in effecting his cures was water from a south-running stream. Among the crimes enumerated in his indictment were several "cures" performed, to use the words of the record, "in his devilish manner;" but the most serious charge against him was a conspiracy against the life of one David Libbertoun, a baker of Edinburgh. There was a feud between this man and the family of John Crystie, of Crystiesoun's mylne, or mill, arising perhaps from some dishonest transactions between them, for in former days the roguery of bakers and millers was proverbial. Crystie's daughter Jonet, and some other women of the family, applied to James Reid for revenge, and he held a consultation with the fiend for the purpose of bringing destruction on Libbertoun, his family, goods, and corn. James's instructor made him take a piece of raw flesh, on which he made nine nicks or notches, and "enchanted the same." The flesh was given to Jonet Crystie, one half to be laid under the door of Libbertoun's mill, and the other under the door of his stable; the object of the latter being to bewitch his horses and cattle. Satan also enchanted nine stones, which were to be thrown on David Libbertoun's lands, to destroy his corn. They next made a "picture" of wax, which the fiend also "enchanted;" and this the women roasted at a fire in Crystie's house, to effect the destruction of Libbertoun himself. The latter in due course died.

In England they were contented with the cheaper and easier process of hanging the witches, but in Scotland, as in Germany, the good old system of burning was still persevered in, although they now generally put the victims to death by strangling, or some other means, before they were committed to the flames. This act of mercy was probably occasioned by the horrible scenes that burning alive continually gave rise to. We learn from the minutes of the Scotch privy council, that, on the 1st of December, 1608, "the earl of Mar declared to the council that some women were taken in

Broughton (the suburb of Edinburgh) as witches, and, being put to an assize, and convicted, albeit they persevered constant in their denial to the end, yet they were burnt quick, after such a cruel manner, that some of them died in despair, renouncing and blaspheming; and others, half-burnt, broke out of the fire, and were cast quick in it again, till they were burnt to death."

James Reid was wirreit, or strangled, and then burnt.

We learn from these same registers, that a man named Patrick Lowrie, of Halie in Ayrshire, commonly known by the name of Pat the witch, suffered the same fate in the July of the year 1605. This man had been in confederacy with several women witches, and on the Whitsunday of 1604 they had held a meeting with the evil one on the Sandhills in Kyle, near the burgh of Irvine. On Hallow-Eve, the same year, they assembled again on Lowdon-hill, where a spirit, in the likeness of a woman, who called herself Helen M'Brune, appeared to them, and after a long consultation, gave Patrick a hair-belt, "in one of the ends of which belt appeared the similitude of four fingers and a thumb, not far different from the claws of the devil." They afterwards visited the neighbouring churches and churchyards, to dig up the dead from their graves, and dismember them, "for the practising of their witchcraft and sorcery." This man, like the former, injured some people, and performed cures for others; he was charged especially with curing a child of "ane strange *incureabill* disease."

The practices of Isobel Griersoune, the wife of a

labourer at Preston-pans named John Bull, were still more extraordinary. She was tried on the 10th of March, 1607, and it appeared that, having conceived a "cruel hatred and malice" against one Adam Clark, of the same place, she used during a year and a half "all devilish and ungodly means" to be avenged upon him. One night, in the November of 1606, between eleven o'clock and midnight, when the whole family, consisting of Adam, his wife, and a woman servant, were asleep in their beds, she entered their house in the likeness of her own cat, accompanied with a great number of other cats, and made such an uproar that the inmates went nearly mad. Then, to increase the tumult, the devil, in the shape of a black man, made his appearance, and, in a fearful manner, seizing the servant as she stood in the middle of the floor, tore her cap from her head and threw it in the fire, and dragged her up and down the house with so much violence that she was obliged to keep her bed for six weeks after. Such scenes as this seldom occur in the stories of English witchery. Previous to this occurrence, at the beginning of the year 1600, the same Isobel had taken offence against a man of the same town, named William Burnet. She threw a piece of raw "enchanted" flesh at his door, and he was immediately struck with a dreadful malady, and for the space of a year the demon haunted the house nightly, in the shape of a "naked infant bairn." In consequence of these and other similar persecutions, William Burnet languished three years and died. Another man refused to pay her the sum of nine shillings and fourpence, which he owed her, and he was seized with a grievous sickness, which never left him till the debt was discharged. An ale-house keeper affronted her, and all his ale became "thick likė gutter dirt," and smelt so bad that nobody would touch it. An innkeeper's wife gave her some cause of offence, and she went "under silence and cloud of night," and, entering the house "after a devilish and unknown way," dragged her by the hair out of bed from the side of her husband, and threw her on the floor, "whereby her spirit failed her," and she continued in a helpless state during five or six days. On this occasion, Isobel Griersoune was publicly accused of being the cause of the woman's sickness, and she therefore employed her neighbours to bring her and the innkeeper's wife to drink together, after which the latter recovered; but she again called her a witch, whereupon Isobel, who appears to have possessed anything but a gentle temper, flew into a rage, and said to her, "The faggot of hell light on thee, and hell's cauldron may thou seeth in!" Her weakness returned, and remained with her till the time of Isobel's trial. Isobel Griersoune was burnt on the Castle-hill at Edinburgh. In the December of the same year a man was burnt there for the same crime; he was accused of poisoning people, as well as curing. Other similar cases occur in the following years, and no doubt many might be instanced from other parts of Scotland.

On the 27th of May, 1608, a woman named Beigis Tod, of "Lang Nydrie," was tried for sorcery, and condemned to the stake. It was stated that in the August of 1594, she, with her sister and some others, met another party of witches at "Deane-fute of Lang Nydrie," where the devil appeared to them, and reproved Beigis Tod "very sharply" for her long tarrying. She said, "Sir, I could win na sooner." They all passed together to Beigis's house in Lang Nydrie, where, after they had drunk together "a certain space," they took a cat and drew it nine times through the "cruik," or iron on which the pot was hung over the fire; and then they went with all speed to Seatoun thorn, to the north of the gate. Thorns were always favourite meeting-places of witches and spirits. When they came to the thorn, the devil left them to fetch Cristiane Tod, a sister of Beigis, "and passed to Robert Smart's house, and brought her out; and as she was coming with him, she took a great fright, and said to the devil, 'Sir, what will you do with me?' who answered her, 'Tak na feir, for ye sall gang to your sister Beigis, and to the rest of hir cumpanie quha ar stayand upon your cuming at the thorn.'" Then they all went with Satan to the iron gate of Seatoun, where they again took a cat, and drew it nine times through the iron gate. Immediately afterwards they went to a barn, where they christened the cat, and called her Margaret. They then returned to Deane-fute, where they first met, and cast the cat to the evil one. We are not told the object of these strange proceedings.

The year 1613 was rendered remarkable in the annals of Scottish sorcery by two very extraordinary cases, one of which belonged to high life. John Erskine, laird of Dun in the county of Angus, and grandson of the celebrated John Erskine who held the office of superintendent of Angus and Mearnes, and distinguished himself by his exertions in support of the Reformation, had two sons, David, who inherited the lordship, and Robert, and three daughters, Helen, Isobel, and Anne. David Erskine, the elder brother, died young, leaving two boys, John and Alexander, the former of whom was acknowledged as the young laird. Robert Erskine and his three sisters seem to have been more attached to one another than to their late brother; the sisters especially seem to have been wicked women, and, now that only two children stood between him and the hereditary estates of the family, they urged their surviving brother to secure the lairdship and property by one of those bold bad actions which were so common in feudal times. It appears that a dispute had arisen relating to the wardship of the children, and that Robert Erskine was disappointed at not getting his nephews into his own ward. About the midsummer of 1610, a meeting between Robert and his three sisters took place in his mansion of Logy, and it was resolved that the children, of whom one seems to have been on a visit to Logy and the other was residing with his mother in Montrose, should be carried off by poison, which must be prepared and rendered effectual by witchcraft. Two of the sisters, who appear to have been the most active in this affair, proposed to one David Blewhouse that he should find a witch and see the work done without their direct interference, and in return for this service he was to receive five hundred marks of silver and a piece of land. An agreement to this effect was drawn up, but for some reason or other it was subsequently broken off, and the two sisters, Anne and Helen, determined to take the matter in hand themselves. They accordingly set off together, and went over the Cairnemouth towards "Mure-ailhouse," to a notorious witch named Janet Irwing, from whom they received a "great quantity" of herbs, with particular directions how to use them These they carried home to Logy, but Robert Erskine was not satisfied that they were sufficiently powerful for his purpose, and paid a visit in person to the witch, who took away all his scruples on this head. They now proceeded to make the poisonous drink, according to the witch's directions, and everything being ready, Robert Erskine rode over to Montrose, taking the boy who was with him home to his brother and mother. There the drink was secretly administered, and the victims were suddenly plunged into dreadful sufferings, and exhibited every symptoms of being poisoned, till they both died, "and sa was crewallie and tressonabillie murthoret," to use the expressive words of the record. The murderers did not long enjoy the result of their crime; how the discovery was made is not told, but it seems probable that David Blewhouse turned traitor. On the 30th of November, 1613, Robert Erskine was brought for examination before the Scottish privy council, and though he denied all knowledge of the murder at first, he ended by making a full confession. The course of justice was quick at this time, and he was beheaded on the 1st of December at the "Mercat" cross in Edinburgh. His sisters seem to have possessed stronger nerves, for in face of his confession, and the evidence of Blewhouse and other witnesses, they continued "obdurate in a constant denial." They were not brought to a trial till the 22nd of June, 1614, but the evidence against them was so conclusive, that they were at once found guilty, and two of them were like their brother beheaded at the Mercat-cross. The third obtained a respite from the king, who subsequently changed her punishment from death to perpetual banishment.

The other Scottish tragedy of the year 1613 was, in some respects, of a more romantic character, and we only know it from a copy of the record of the trial sent to sir Walter Scott. Two brothers, Archibald and John Dein, lived in the town of Irvine, of which they were burgesses; the first had married a woman named Janet Lyal, while the wife of Alexander was Margaret Barclay. It appears that there was a quarrel between the two families, and John Dein and his wife publicly accused Margaret Barclay of theft. Margaret Barclay raised an action of slander before the church court, which was discharged, and the opponents were directed to be reconciled. But Margaret did not possess a conciliating temper, and she declared that she only gave her hand in obedience to the kirk-session, but that her animosity against John Dein and his spouse was unabated. Soon after this occurrence, John Dein's ship prepared to sail for France, and he took with him the provost of the burgh of Irvine, Andrew Tran, who was one of the owners of the vessel. As they were starting, Margaret Barclay was heard to pray that sea nor salt water might never bear the ship, and that partans, or crabs, might eat the crew at the bottom of the sea. The first news of the ship which reached Irvine came by a wandering juggler named John Stewart, who called at the house of the provost, and dropped broad hints that he knew by some mysterious means that the vessel was lost, and that the provost himself had perished. After a short period of anxiety in the provost's family, all doubt was removed by the arrival of two of the crew, who stated that their ship had been wrecked on the coast of England near Padstow, and that they were the sole survivors of all who who were on board. People remembered Margaret Barclay's imprecations, and suspicions of sorcery were immediately excited against her and John Stewart, whose knowledge of the state of the ship seemed so extraordinary.

Margaret Barclay appears to have been no favourite in the town of Irvine, and proceedings were commenced in a way most likely to turn to her confusion. The wandering juggler was first arrested, and fear or torture wrung from him a confession, in which he cleared himself by seriously compromising the other person suspected. He said that Margaret Barclay, presuming perhaps on his character of a juggler, had applied to him to teach her some magic arts, "in order that she might get gear, kyes milk, love of man, her heart's desire on such persons as had done her wrong, and finally that she might obtain the fruit of sea and land." He replied that he neither possessed such arts, nor was able to communicate them to others, and thus the matter ended. But he said that subsequent to this, and shortly after the ship set sail, he came accidentally one night to Margaret's house, and there he found her with two other women making clay figures, one of which was made handsome and with fair hair, he supposed to represent provost Tran. They proceeded to make a figure of a ship in clay, and while they were thus occupied, the devil appeared in the shape of a handsome black lap-dog. When the ship was made, the whole party, Satan and all, left the house together, and went into an empty waste-house near the sea-port. They afterwards proceeded to the sea-side, and cast in the figures of clay representing the ship and the men, and immediately the sea raged, roared, and became red like the juice of madder in a dyer's cauldron. Márgaret Barclay's female acquaintances were next convened, and when John Steward was introduced to them, he at once fixed upon an old woman named Insh, as one of the persons engaged in making the figures. This woman stoutly denied all knowledge of the matter, and said she never saw her accuser before; but the magistrates now brought forward her own daughter, a girl only eight years old, who lived in Margaret Barclay's house as a servant, and who had been made by some means or other to declare that she had been a witness to the scene described by the juggler, and that her mother was one of the persons engaged in it. This little girl improved upon the details given by Stewart; she described other persons as being present, added a black man to the black dog, and said that the latter breathed flames from its jaws and nostrils, which illuminated the witches during the performance of the spell. She said that they had promised her a pair of new shoes to keep the secret, and that her mother Isobel Insh remained in the waste-house, and was not present when the images were thrown into the sea.

John Stewart now underwent a new examination, and added to his own story so as to make it agree with that of the child. When asked how he gained the knowledge of things to come, he told a strange story of his adventures with the fairies; it was probably a tale he had been accustomed to recount among the people where he visited in the exercise of his craft to give himself importance in their eyes, and which he now half unconsciously repeated before his judges. He stated that about twenty-six years before, as he was travelling on the night of All-hallow's Eve, between the towns of "Monygoif" and "Clary," in the county of Galway, (in Ireland,) he met with the king of the fairies and his company, and the king struck him over the forehead with a white rod, which deprived him of the power of speech and the use of one eye. After remaining in this condition during three years, his speech and eye-sight were restored to him by the king of the fairies and his company, whom he again met on a Hallowe'en night near Dublin, since which time he had been in the habit of joining these people every Saturday at seven o'clock in the evening, and remaining with them all that night. They likewise met every Hallowtide, sometimes on Lanark-hill, or, as Scott supposes, Tintock, and sometimes on Kilmaurs-hill, when he was taught by them.

Stewart pointed out the spot on his forehead where the king of the fairies struck him with a white rod, whereupon, after he had been blindfolded by order of the magistrates and ministers who were directing the examination, they pricked the spot with a large pin, of which he appeared to be quite insensible. He repeated the names of many persons whom he had seen at the court of faerie, and declared that all persons who were taken away by sudden death went thither.

After these confessions, Isobel Insh was more hardly pressed to "tell the truth," and at length she confessed that she was present at the making and drowning of the clay images, but declared that she took no part in the proceedings. She was at this moment in such a state of mind, that she evidently knew not what she was doing, and she supplicated her jailor, Bailie Dunlop, to let her go, promising him, for he also was a mariner, that if he did so, he should never make a bad voyage, but have success in all his dealings by sea and land, a promise that was easily construed into an acknowledgment that she possessed the powers attributed to her. Before she was conducted back to her prison in the belfry, she was made to promise that she would fully confess next day, but in the night she made a desperate attempt at escape. Although secured with iron bolts, locks, and fetters, she succeeded in getting out at a back window, and reached the roof of the church, for here she lost her footing and fell to the ground. She was so much hurt and bruised, that she survived but five days, during which time she resolutely persisted in asserting her innocence, and denied all that she had before admitted. In spite of the evident causes of her death, the inhabitants of Irvine attributed it to poison.

A commission was now granted for the trial of John Stewart and Margaret Barclay, and when the appointed day arrived, "my lord and earl of Eglintoune (who dwells within the space of one mile to the said burgh) having come to the said burgh at the earnest request of the said justices, for giving to them of his lordship's countenance, concurrence, and assistance, in trying of the foresaid devilish practices, conformable to the tenor of the foresaid commission, the said John Stewart, for his better preserving to the day of assize, was put in a sure lockfast booth, where no manner of person might have access to him till the down-sitting of the justice-court; and for avoiding of putting hands on himself, he was very strictly guarded, and fettered by the arms, as use is. And upon that same day of the assize, about half an hour before the down-sitting of the justice-court, Mr. David Dickson, minister at Irvine, and Mr. George Dunbar, minister of Ayr, having gone to him to exhort him to call on his God for mercy for his bygone wicked and evil life, and that God would of his infinite mercy loose him out of the bonds of the devil, whom he had served these many years bygone, he acquiesced in their prayer and godly exhortation, and uttered these words,—'I am so straitly guarded, that it lies not in my power to get my hand to take off my bonnet, nor to get bread to my mouth.' And immediately after the departure of the two ministers from him, the juggler being sent for, at the desire of my lord of Eglintoune, to be confronted with a woman of the burgh of Ayr called Janet Bous, who was apprehended by the magistrates of the burgh of Ayr for witchcraft, and sent to the burgh of Irvine purposely for that affair, he was found, by the burgh officers who went about him, strangled and hanged by the cruik of the door, with a *tait*, or string, of hemp, supposed to have been his garter or string of his bonnet, not above the length of two span long, his knees not being from the ground half a span, and was brought out of the house, his life not being totally expelled. But, notwithstanding of whatsoever means used in the contrary for remeid of his life, he revived not, but so ended his life miserably, by the help of the devil his master."

Margaret Barclay was the only one who now remained for trial, and it was determined to proceed with her at once, lest she should follow the example of the others. "Therefore, and for eschewing of the like in the person of the said Margaret, our sovereign lord's justice in that part, constituted by commission, after solemn deliberation and advice of the said noble lord, whose concurrence and advice was chiefly required and taken in this matter, concluded with all possible diligence, before the downsitting of the justice court, to put the said Margaret to torture; in respect the devil, by God's permission, had made her associates, who were the lights of the cause, to be their own 'burrioes' (*executioners*). They used the torture underwritten as being most safe and gentle (as the said noble lord assured the said justices,) by putting of her two bare legs in a pair of stocks, and thereafter by on-laying of certain iron gauds (*bars*) severally one by one, and then eking and augmenting the weight by laying on more gauds, and in easing of her by off-taking of the iron gauds one or more as occasion offered, which iron gauds were but little short gauds, and broke not the skin of her legs After using of the which kind of gentle torture, the said Margaret began, according to the increase of the pain, to cry and crave for God's cause to take off her shins the foresaid irons, and she would declare truly the whole matter. Which being removed, she began at her former denial; and being of new arrayed in torture as of before, she then uttered these words, 'Take off! take off! and before God I shall show you the whole form!' And the said irons being of new, upon her faithful promise, removed, she then desired my lord of Eglintoune, the said four justices, and the said Mr. David Dickson, minister at the burgh, Mr. George Dunbar, minister of Ayr, and Mr. Mitchell Wallace, minister of Kilmarnock, and Mr. John Cunninghame, minister of Dalry, and Hugh Kennedy, provost of Ayr, to come by themselves, and to remove all others, and she should declare truly as she should answer to God the whole matter. Whose desire in that being fulfilled, without any kind of demand, freely, without interrogation, God's name by earnest prayer being called upon for opening of her lips, and easing of her heart, that she by rendering of the truth, might glorify and magnify his holy name, and disappoint the enemy of her salvation."

Margaret Barclay's confession was a mere acknowledgment of the truth of what had been said by the others, but she declared that her purpose was to kill none but her brother-in-law and provost Tran. To make up the number of persons pretended to have been present at the making of the images, she introduced the name of another woman of Irvine, Isobel Crawford; who was thereupon arrested, and in great terror confessed it all. But when they proceeded with the trial, Alexander Dein, the husband of Margaret Barclay, appeared in court with a lawyer to act in her defence, and she was asked by the lawyer if she wished to be defended, to which she made answer, "As you please; but all I have confessed was in agony of torture, and, before God, all I have spoken is false and untrue;" adding pathetically, "Ye have been too long in coming." The jury were unmoved by this appeal; it was considered that as the iron bars were off her legs at the moment of her making the confession, it could not be said to be made under compulsion, and she was unanimously found guilty. After her sentence was passed, she returned to her confession, influenced, perhaps, by the hope in some way or other of better treatment. She was strangled at the stake, and then burnt to ashes.

Before her death, Margaret Barclay had entreated earnestly for Isobel Crawford, the woman implicated in her confession, that no injury should be done to her, but in vain. A new commission was obtained for her trial, and, as she was now obstinate in her denial, the same torture was applied to her, and with the same effect. She made a new confession acknowledged everything that was imputed to her. and avowed that she had lived in intercourse with the evil one for several years. But when her sentence was passed, she again denied all that she had confessed, and persisted in her denial to the last.

It appears to have been a mere quarrel among the wives of the burghers of Irvine which led to this tragical conclusion. The singularly detailed report of the proceedings of the trial, which was published by sir Walter Scott, furnishes a most remarkable illustration of the manner in which they were conducted. We now return to the registers published by Mr. Pitcairn for a few examples illustrative of the character of the Scottish witches of this period. They show us not only how generally these "weird" women were employed to cure diseases, but the particular character of their remedies.

Margaret Wallace, the wife of a burgess of Glasgow, was tried for sorcery on the 20th of March, 1622. The particular crime for which she was brought into court was the bewitching of a burgess of the same town named Cuthbert Greg, a cooper, who had excited her "deadly hatred," by publicly calling her a witch. It was deposed that she had been heard to threaten that she would make him within a few days unable to earn a cake of bread by his work. Shortly after this, he fell into sickness and extreme debility. His friends were convinced that Margaret Wallace was the cause of this visitation, and they went to her to beg her to restore him to his health. After many "malicious refusals," she yielded to their request, and went with them to his house, where she "took him by the shakel (*wrist bone*) with one hand, and laid the other hand upon his breast, and without one word speaking, save only by moving of her lips, passed from him at that instant; and upon the morn thereafter, returning back again to the said Cuthbert, she took him by the arm and bade him arise, who at that time and fifteen days before was not able to lift his legs without help; yet she, having urged him to rise, and taking him by the hand, as said is, brought him out of his bed, and thereafter led him about the house; who immediately thereafter, by her sorcery and charming practised upon him, walked up and down the floor, without help or support of any; and from that time quickly recovered and convalesced of the former grievous disease."

Margaret Wallace had formerly been intimate with a woman of Glasgow named Cristiane Grahame, who was burnt three years before as a notorious witch, and they seem to have been in the habit of assisting one another. On one occasion, when the child of one of her neighbours was taken ill, she recommended Grahame to be sent for, and, on an objection being made, she protested "Cristiane Grahame could do as mickle in that errand in curing of that disease, as if God himself would come out of heaven and cure her; and albeit the death-stroke were laid on, she could take it off again; and without her help there could be no remedy to the bairn." She further showed her confidence in the healing powers of this woman by sending for her when she was in want herself. A woman made the following deposition. It appeared that a man named Robert Stewart went with Margaret Wallace to an inn in Glasgow kept by one Alexander Vallange, where this deponent was servant, and, as she said, they there "called for a choppine of ale, which was brought by a boy to them, named James Symsone; and in drinking thereof, betwixt Robert Stewart his taking the cup and offering it to Margaret Wallace, the said Margaret took a sudden 'brasche' of sickness, unknown to the deponent what sickness it was, wherein the said Margaret was so extremely handled that she was likely to rive herself." In her convulsions she cried, "Bring me hither my dear bird!" Margaret Montgomerie, the "good-wife" of the house, who was present, and who imagined that she was calling for her husband, said, "What dear bird would you have? I believe he is not at home." "Na," answered Margaret Wallace, "bring me Cristiane Grahame, my dear bird!" "All this while Margaret Montgomerie was holding her by the one hand, and Cristiane M'Clauchlane by the other. Thereafter, at her desire, Robert Stewart past, and with great diligence brought Cristiane Grahame to her, at whose sudden coming Margaret Montgomerie said to Robert Stewart, 'Jesus save us! I believe thou has met her by the way!' And Cristiane Grahame answered, 'Faith, he met me not; but came and brought me out of my own chamber; and fra I heard that my bird was sa diseased, I sped me hither.' Says, thereafter, that Cristiane Grahame took Margaret Wallace by the shackel bone, and kist her; and in her arms carried her down the stairs, saying to her, nothing should ail her." Another witness, a "chirurgeon," named Andro Mure, who deposed relating to the cure of one Margaret Mure, reveals a little glimpse of Scottish character.

This man said, "He knows nothing of Margaret Mure's sickness, except that he himself coming down the bridge-gate, he saw Cristiane Grahame come forth of Marioun Mure's house; who thereafter came to the deponent, and desired him to gang in to the said Marioun; and the deponent, at her desire, having passed into the house, at his incoming a roasted hen was set down on the board; and the deponent, with David Scheirar and the said Marioun Mure, sat down at the the board together; and within a short space thereafter, Margaret Wallace came in to them; declares, at Margaret Wallace's incoming, a goose was set down on the board; and the deponent, perceiving that such entertainment would draw him to charges, he paid his choppine of wine and came his way, and left the rest of the company behind him; and further he knows not."

Some pains seem to have been taken in this woman's defence, and the worst accusation against her appears to have been her acquaintance with Cristiane Grahame; but the jury brought her in guilty, and she was strangled and burnt.

In the May of 1623, a woman named Isobel Haldane made a "voluntary" confession at the sessions at Perth, in which she described the manner in which she cured diseases, chiefly by the use of crosses and charms such as those found in the old medical manuscripts. Being asked if she had any conversation with the fairy folk, she said that ten years before, while she was lying in her bed, she was taken forth she knew not how, and was carried to a hill side, which opened, and she went in and remained there three days, from Thursday to Sunday at noon. She met a man with a grey beard, who brought her forth again. This man with the grey beard, resembling the Thome Reid of a former story, was the person from whom she received her knowledge of hidden things, and who imparted to her the art by which she worked her cures. She often delivered people from the witchcraft of others. One Patrick Ruthven acknowledged that he had been bewitched, and that Isobel had cured him. "She came into the bed, and stretched herself above him, her head to his head, her hands over him, and so forth, mumbling some words, he knew not what they were." Isobel seems to have been famous for curing "bairns." She confessed that, for this purpose, she made three several cakes, every one of them of nine handfuls of meal obtained from nine women that were married maidens, and that she made a hole in the crown of every one of them, and put a bairn through it three times, in the name of Father, Son, and Holy Ghost."

A man named Thomas Greave was burnt at the beginning of August, 1623. He was accused of causing sickness in some people, and curing it in others. His cures were performed with crosses and signs, and by washing the patient's sark, or shirt, in the water of a south-running stream, or with water from the holy well. He sometimes passed his patients through a hasp of yarn. He took one woman's sickness from her, and put it on a cow. "Item, about Martinmas, 1621, Elspeth Thomesone, sister to John Thomesone, portioner of Petwar, being visited with a grievous sickness, the said Thomas came to her house in Corachie, where, after sighing and 'gripping' of her, he promised to cure her thereof; and for this effect called for her sark, and desired two of her 'nearest friends' to go with him, like as John and William Thomesone, her brothers, being sent for, past with the said Thomas, in the night season, from Corachie towards Burley, by the space of twelve miles, and enjoyned the two brothers not to speak a word all the way; and whatever they heard or saw, no ways to be afraid, saying to them, it might be that they would hear great rumbling, and such uncouth and fearful apparitions, but nothing should annoy them. And at the ford by East Burley, in a south-running water, he there washed the sark; during the time of the which washing of the sark, there was a great noise made by fowls, or the 'lyll beasts,' that arose and flittered in the water. And coming home with the sark, put the same upon her, and cured her of her sickness."

As I have before intimated, there may be some affinity between this process and the modern cure by wet sheets; in the instance of Thomas Greave the cold-water cure was punished with death.

CHAPTER XXVIII.

CONFESSIONS OF ISOBEL GOWDIE.

THE extraordinary cases related in the last chapter give us but a faint notion of the immense number of prosecutions for the crime of sorcery which occurred in Scotland during the first half of the seventeenth century. The cases which came before the high court of justiciary were few indeed when compared with those which were disposed of no less summarily in the multitude of inferior courts throughout that kingdom. The superstitious feelings of the Scottish clergy assisted the popular imagination, and it is not surprising if the persecution against this miserable class of people was increased, rather than otherwise, when the presbyterians were in power. Matthew Hopkins had his reflection in a number of Scottish witch-finders, or, as they were called, prickers, who gained their living by going from town to town to search suspected women or men for their marks, and we have even seen that on the eve of the restoration they were sent for from Scotland to assist in witch prosecutions in the north of England. At this period, and in the years immediately following the accession of Charles II., the mania seems to have suddenly extended itself in Scotland, and the year 1661 was especially remarkable for the number of trials it witnessed. We are informed that on the 7th of November, in the year just mentioned, at one session of the superior court, no less than fourteen commissions were issued for trying witches in different parts of the country. A case which occurred in the spring of the year following, is deserving of particular notice for its peculiarities.

The district about the village of Auldearn, on the coast of the little county of Nairn, contained at this time so many witches, that Satan was obliged for convenience to divide them into companies named covines, each covine consisting of thirteen persons. This number was anciently called the devil's dozen, from which we understand why still, wherever the popular superstitions leave their traces, it is looked upon as an unlucky number for a party at table, but another more useful individual has since taken the place of the evil one in the name applied to it. To one of these covines, which seems to have belonged especially to the village of Auldearn, belonged a woman of that place named Isobel Gowdie, who during the months of April and May, in the year 1662, made, without compulsion of any kind, (as it is said in the document,) before the clergy and magistrates of the district, four several confessions, all agreeing together, though some of them were rather fuller in detail than others.

Isobel Gowdie said that once as she was going between the farms of Drumdevin and the Heads, she was accosted by Satan, who made her promise to meet him at night. For some reason or other, in Scotland Satan preferred churches for the place of meeting of the witches, and on this occasion the rendezvous was to be in the kirk of Auldearn. Thither Isobel went on the night appointed, and she found a number of individuals who were well known to her in the kirk; the evil one stood in the reader's desk, and held a black book in his hand. After being duly introduced to the company, the new convert was made to deny her baptism, and then, placing one hand on the crown of her head and the other under the sole of her foot, she gave everything between them to the fiend. Margaret Brodie, of Auldearn, acted as her foster-mother, and held her up to the devil to be baptized. He marked her on the shoulder, and sucked the blood, which "spouted" into his hand, and with this he sprinkled her on the head, re-baptizing her in his own name by the nickname of Janet. After this ceremony, the whole party separated. Shortly afterwards the devil met Isobel again, alone, at the "New Wards" of Inshoch, and there the bond between them was completed. She described her new lord as a "mickle, black, rough man," with forked and cloven feet, which he sometimes concealed by wearing boots or shoes. Sometimes he appeared in the shape of a deer, or roe, or other animal.

To each covine was one female of more consideration than the others, Satan's favourite, who was chosen as the best looking of the younger witches, and she was called the maiden of the covine; and there was a man, who was their officer. The witches had only power to do injuries of an inferior kind when the maiden was not with them. They met from time to time to dance at places which seem to have been under fairy influence, such as the hill of Earlseat, the mickle burn, and the Downie hills, generally one or two covines at a time, where they danced; but they had larger general meetings towards the end of each quarter of a year. Jane Martin, a young lass of Auldearn, was the maiden of the covine to which Isobel Gowdie belonged. We have seen that in her intercourse with the evil one, each witch was known by a new name. Thus Jane Martin was named "Over-the-dyke-with-it," because she used to sing these words when she was dancing with the devil. Her mother, Isobel Nicoll, went by the name of Bessie Rule; Margaret Wilson was named Pickle-nearest-the-wind; Bessie Wilson's name was Through-the-corn-yard; Elspet Nishie was named Bessie Bauld; and Bessie Hay rejoiced in the name of Able-and-stout. Their familiar spirits, who were distinguished by the colour of their liveries, had names equally singular. Isobel Gowdie's own familiar was called Saunders-the-red-reaver, and was clothed in black; one of them had a spirit called Thomas-a-fairie; Margaret Wilson's spirit had a grass-green dress, and was called Swein; Bessie Wilson's spirit was Rorie, dressed in yellow; that of Isobel Nicoll was

Roaring-lion, and his colour sea-green; that of Margaret Brodie was called Robert-the-rule, and dressed in a sad dress; Bessie Wilson's familiar had the strange name of Thief-of-hell-wait-upon-her; Elspet Nishie's was Hendrie Laing; the familiar of Bessie Hay (old Able-and-stout) was named Robert-the-Jakis, and was always "clothed in dun, and seems aged; he is ane glaiked gowked spirit." Jane Martin, the maiden of the covine, had a spirit named M'Hector, who was a "young-like" devil, and his colour grass-green. These spirits were much smaller than the devil who presided at their meetings.

Isobel said that they sometimes went into the Downie hills, where they found a fair and large "brawe" room, where it was daylight. There she got meat from the queen of faerie more than she could eat. The queen was "brawlie" clothed in white linen, and in white and brown clothes. The king of faerie was a "brawe" man, well favoured, and broad faced. "There," says Isobel, "was elf-bulls rowtting and skoylling up and down, and affrighted me." She alluded repeatedly to the fear which she always felt on seeing these elf-bulls. In the caverns of the Downie hills, Isobel Gowdie saw the "elf-boys" making the elf-arrowheads. These elf-boys were "little ones, hollow and boss-backed, (*hump-backed;*) they spoke gowstie-like." The devil shaped the arrow-heads with his own hand, and gave them to the elf-boys, who sharpened and "dighted" them with a sharp thing like a packing-needle. When they were finished, the devil delivered them to the witches, saying,—

Shoot these in my name,
And they shall not go heal hame (*whole home*),

And when the witch shot at anybody with them, she said,—

I shoot yon man in the devil's name,
He shall not win heal hame!
And this shall be all so true,
There shall not be one bit of him on liew! (*alive*)

When they shot the arrow-heads at their victims, they "spang" them from their thumb-nails; sometimes they missed their object, but if they touched they carried certain death, even if the victim were cased in armour.

The account of what passed at the sabbaths of these Scottish witches is very imperfect, and the little that is told will be better passed over. The arch-fiend seems to have taken great delight in beating his subjects cruelly with ropes and thongs, and he resented bitterly any act of disrespect. "Sometimes among ourselves,," says Isobel Gowdie, "we would be calling him Black John, or the like, and he would ken it, and hear us well enough; and he even then come to us and say, 'I ken wele eneugh what ye were saying of me' And then he would beat and buffet us very sore." They were often beaten for absence from the meetings, or for neglect when present; some bore their punishment quietly, but others would resist, and there were some beldames in the company who did not hesitate to exchange blows with Satan. Alexander Elder, of Earlseat, was often beaten; "he is but soft, and could never defend himself in the least, but 'greit' (*lament*) and cry when he would be scourging him; Margaret Wilson would defend herself finely, and cast up her hands to keep the strokes off her; and Bessie Wilson would speak crusty with her tongue, and would be belling again to him stoutly." On the whole, Satan appears to have been but an ill master, for he was easily offended, and "when he would be angry at us, he would grin at us like a dog, as if he would swallow us up." However, as a peace-offering at the end of the meeting, he sometimes gave them the "brawest like money that ever was coined," but if they had the misfortune to keep it more than twenty-four hours in their possession, they found it was nothing but horse-dung!

Isobel Gowdie stated that when they went to the meetings, they took a straw or a bean-stalk, placed it between their feet, and said,—

> Horse and hattock, horse and go,
> Horse and pellattis, ho! ho!

Then they were immediately carried into the air, "as straws would fly upon a highway." If it were at night, and the witch were afraid that her husband might miss her from his bed, she took a besom or three-legged stool, placed it beside him in bed, and said thrice,—

> I lay down this besom (*or stool*) in the devil's name,
> Let it not stir till I come again,

"and immediately it seems a woman beside our

husbands." They often travelled in this way by day, and then it was that they amused themselves by shooting people with the elf-arrowheads; and people who see straws flying about the air in a whirlwind on a fine day, are recommended to bless themselves devoutly, because if they omit that precaution they are liable to be shot by the witches who ride on them. "Any that are shot by us," Isobel informs us, "their souls will go to heaven, but their bodies remain with us, and will fly as horses to us, as small as straws." Isobel Gowdie confessed to having killed many people in this manner. The first time she went to her covine was to Ploughlands, where she shot a man between the "plough-stilts," and he presently fell on his face to the ground. The devil gave her an arrow to shoot at a woman in the fields, which she did, and the victim dropped down dead. As they were riding one day, Isobel by the side of Satan, and Margaret Brodie and Bessie Hay in close company with them, they met Mr. Harry Forbes, the minister of Auldearn, going to Moynes, on which the devil gave Margaret Brodie an arrow to shoot at him. Margaret shot and missed her mark, and the arrow was taken up again by Satan; but when she offered to shoot again he said, "No, we cannot have his life this time." Presently afterwards they saw the laird of Park, and the devil gave Isobel an arrow. She shot at him as he was crossing a burn, and, perhaps owing to this circumstance, missed him, for which Bessie Hay gave her "a great cuff."

The witches seem to have entertained an especial hostility towards these two gentlemen. In the winter of 1660, Mr. Forbes was sick, it appears, in consequence of a conspiracy of these enemies. They made a mixture of the galls, flesh, and entrails of toads, grains of barley, parings of finger and toe nails, the liver of a hare, and "bits of clouts." These ingredients were mixed together and seethed, or boiled, all night in water. Satan was with them during this process, and they repeated after him, thrice each time, the words—

He is lying in his bed, he is lying sick and sair,
Let him lie intill his bed two months and three days mair.

And then—

Let him lie in his bed, let him lie intill it sick and sair,
Let him lie intill his bed two months and three days mair.

And then finally—

He shall lie in his bed, he shall lie sick and sair,
He shall lie intill his bed two months and three days mair.

At night they went into Forbes's chamber to swing this mixture over him as he lay sick in bed, but for some reason or other they were not able to do it. They now chose one of their covine who was most intimate and familiar with the minister, which happened to be Bessie Hay, who, as they could not injure him by night, was to visit him by day, and swing the noxious mixture over him; but she failed, because there were some other "worthy persons" with him at the time, though she "swung" a little of the mixture on the bed where he lay.

Mr. Harry Forbes appears to have received no serious injury from the witches, as he was one of those who sat in court to hear Isobel's confession. The laird of Park was less fortunate in his family, if he escaped in his person. A meeting was held at the house of John Taylor of Auldearn, at which the devil was present with Isobel Gowdie, John Taylor and his wife, and one or two others, for the purpose of making a picture of clay, to destroy the laird of Park's male children. John Taylor brought home the clay in "his plaidnewk" (a corner of his plaid), and they broke it into fine powder, and passed it through a sieve. Then they poured water on it to make a paste, and "wrought it very sore like rye-bowt." As they threw the water in, they said, in the devil's name,—

> We pour in this water among this meal,
> For lang dwining (*languishing*) and ill heal;
> We put it into the fire,
> That it may be burnt with stick and stowre,
> It shall be burnt, with our will,
> As any stickle (*stubble*) upon a hill.

"The devil," says Isobel, "taught us these words, and when we had learnt them, we all fell down upon our bare knees, and our hair about our eyes, and our hands lifted up, looking stedfastly upon the devil, still saying the words thrice over, till it was made." They moulded the paste into the figure of a male child, having all its members complete, and its hands folded down by its sides; and they laid it with the face to the fire till it was almost dry, then in the devil's name they put it in the fire.

and let it remain till it was red like a coal, when it was drawn out with the same ceremony. This image was entrusted to the care of John Taylor and his wife; it was kept wrapped up in a "clout," in a cradle of clay, and hung up in a "knag" in their house. As often as they wanted to kill a male child of the laird of Park, they took it down, wet it, and roasted it every other day till the child died, and then put it away again; and as soon as another male child was born to him, they let it live six months, and then destroyed it by the same process. We are told in the confession that "till it be broken, it will be the death of all the male children that the laird of Park will ever get. Cast it over a kirk it will not break, till it be broken with an axe, or some such like thing, by a man's hand. If it be not broken, it will last a hundred years." This seems to be a remnant of the early belief which led the Teutonic invaders to destroy the Roman statuary; we continually find, on Roman sites, bronzes that have been intentionally mutilated with an axe, or some other sharp instrument.

These Scottish witches appear to have had no eating and drinking at their Sabbaths, but they went for this purpose into the houses of the lairds and gentlemen round about, to feast by night on the provisions which were always found there in plenty. They went thus into the house of the earl of Murray himself. On the Candlemas before this confession was made, they visited Grangehill, the house of Brodie of Lethin, where they got "meat and drink enough." On these occasions the devil always sat at the head of the table, and the maiden of the covine sat next to him, and was served first and best. The grace they said before meat was as follows :—

We eat this meat in the devil's name,
With sorrow, and "sych," (*sighing*) and mickle shame;
We shall destroy house and hold,
Both sheep and neat intill the fold.
Little good shall come to the fore
Of all the rest of the little store.

In these excursions the witches did not always go in their own semblances, for they had the power of transforming themselves into the shape of any animals except lambs or doves, which, as emblems of innocence, they might not assume. Isobel Gowdie describes minutely the process of transformation. When the witch would change herself into a hare, the form that appears to have been adopted most commonly, she said thrice,—

I shall go into a hare,
With sorrow, and sych, and mickle care;
I shall go in the devil's name,
Ay till I come home again.

"and instantly we start in a hare." When they wished to return to their own shape, they repeated thrice the words—

Hare, hare, God send the care!
I am in a hare's likeness just now,
But I shall be in a woman's likeness even now.

When they chose the likeness of a cat, which was the next favourite form, they said thrice—

I shall go intill a cat,
With sorrow, and sych, and a black shot;
And I shall go in the devil's name,
Ay till I come home again.

The formula was similarly varied for other animals. As thus transformed they passed by the houses of other witches, they called them out, and they came in similar shapes. Travelling in these assumed shapes was not always safe. Isobel Gowdie, who often went in the form of a hare, was sent one day, about day-break, in this shape, with one of Satan's messages to some of her neighbours, and on her way met with the servants of Patrick Pepley of Killhill, who happened to have his hounds with them. The latter immediately gave chase to the transformed witch, and ran after her a long course, until weary and hard pressed, she gained her own house, and ran behind a chest. The door being open, the hounds followed her, but they happening to go to the other side of the chest, she had just time to run out and enter the house of a neighbour, where she was able to say the disenchanting charm, and recovered her shape. She said that, while thus transformed, the hounds had not power to kill them, but if they chanced to be bitten, the wound remained after they had recovered their natural shape. "When we would be in the shape of cats, we did nothing but cry and 'wraw,' [a very expressive word for caterwauling,] and 'rywing' (*tearing*) and, as it were, worrying one another; and when we come to our own shapes again, we will find the scratches and 'rywes' on our skins *very sore!*" About the summer of 1659, "they went in the shape of rooks to the house of Mr. Robert Donaldson, where the devil, with John Taylor and his wife, went down the kitchen chimney, and perched on the crook, or iron on which the pot was suspended over the fire. The others seem not to have liked this mode of entry, and they waited till their friends opened a window, and then they all went into the house, and feasted on beef and drink, " but did no more harm."

Isobel Gowdie repeated in her confessions a great number of the verses which they used in their incantations, some of which are curious. Their method of raising a tempestuous wind was to take a rag of cloth, wet it in water, and then take a beetle (with which washerwomen beat their linen) and knock it on the stone, repeating thrice—

> I knock this rag npon this stane,
> To raise the wind in the devil's name!
> It shall not lie until I please again!

To appease the wind, they dried the rag, and said,—

> We lay the wind in the devil's name,
> It shall not rise till I like to raise it again!

If the wind, on this appeal, did not instantly abate, the witch called her spirit, and said to him, " Thief, thief, conjure the wind, and cause it to lie!" Isobel said that they had no power over rain. One of the witches, whose husband sold cattle, used to put a swallow's feather in the hide of the beast, and say thrice over it, before it went,—

"I put out this beef in the devil's name,
That mickle silver and good price come hame!"

They had many charms for curing diseases, as well as for sending them. It was common with them, by such charms, to appropriate to themselves the property or gain of others. When they wished to "take the fruit of fishes" from the fishermen, they went to the shore before the boat came in, and standing on the brink of the water, they said thrice,—

"The fishers are gone to the sea,
And they will bring home fish to me;
They will bring them hame intill the boat,
But they shall get of them but the smaller sort."

As soon as the boat arrived, they stole a fish, or bought or begged one, and with it came to them "all the fruit of the whole fishes in the boat, and the fishes that the fishermen themselves will have will be but froth."

At Lammas, (the first of August,) the witches usually appropriated to themselves, in a similar manner, the corn and other produce of the fields, though the particular ceremonies for this purpose varied. Isobel Gowdie told, in her confession, how, soon after her conversion to sorcery, she, with John Taylor and his wife, and some others, met in the kirk-yard of Nairn, and raised from its grave the corpse of an unchristened child. With this and some other ingredients, such as parings of finger and toe-nails, grains of different sorts, and leaves of cole-work, chopped very small, she formed a noxious mixture, and going to the end of the cornfields opposite the mill of Nairn, they threw some on the land. By this means, while the farmers reaped nothing but straw, all the grain was conveyed to the secret storehouse of the witches, who usually kept it there till the following Christmas or Easter, and then shared it among the covine. She further stated, that one night before the Candlemass of 1661, she went with the other witches to some fields 'be-east' Kinlos, where they yoked a plough of paddocks, or frogs; the braces were of quickens, (quick or dog-grass,) and a riglen's or ram's-horn was the coulter. The officer of their covine, one John Young, was driver, while the devil held the plough. Thus they went several times about, all they of the covine going up and down with it, praying Satan for the fruit of that land, "and that thistles and briers might grow there," i. e. that this might be the only fruit reserved to the owners of the land. When they wished to take a cow's milk, they took tow or hemp, and twined and plaited it the wrong way, in the devil's name. They then drew the rope thus made in between the cow's two hind feet, and out between the fore feet, always in the name of the arch-fiend, and milked the rope. To restore the cow its milk, they must cut the rope in two. They had similar methods of taking and transferring the strength of people's ale, and of abstracting various other things. Isobel Gowdie further stated, that when any one of them fell into the hands of justice, she lost all her power, which was thereupon shared amongst the rest of her covine, in addition to that which they already possessed.

We are not informed what became of Isobel

Gowdie, but her case must have been considered, at least in the district where it occurred, an important one, for the examinations were continued through two months. Her first confession is dated on the 13th of April, 1662, and her last bears date of the 27th of May. Her most intimate associates appear to have been John Taylor and his wife, the latter of whom made a confession corroborating in some important points, especially in the history of the conspiracy against the laird of Park, those of Isobel Gowdie. These confessions have been printed entire by Robert Pitcairn.

Such were the confessions of Isobel Gowdie of Auldearn. If, as we are assured, they were purely voluntary, we must imagine that this woman was labouring under some strange delusion of the mind, and that she really believed the story she told. From the circumstantial character of her narrative, we can hardly avoid supposing that there were persons so far influenced by the popular superstitions, that they joined together in practising such ceremonies as are above described, and that they really believed in their efficacy. That such delusion was possible on an extensive scale is shown by the celebrated example of major Weir and his sister, who were executed less than ten years after the date of Isobel's confessions. This man had distinguished himself by his extraordinary zeal in the cause of the covenant, and had been appointed, in 1649, with the rank of major, to command the city guard of Edinburgh. He lived in a retired manner with a maiden sister. Both professed in their utmost rigour the severe doctrines of the party whose cause they had espoused, and the major, who always appeared in his ordinary behaviour reserved and melancholy, was especially endowed with the gift of prayer, which made him a welcome visitor to the side of a sick-bed. After the restoration, the melancholy of the major and his sister appeared to have become more and more sombre, until it settled into a kind of lunacy, and they believed themselves guilty of the most revolting crimes which disgrace humanity. The major now began to make extraordinary confessions to his friends, declaring that his sins were of that character, that he had no hopes of salvation, unless he should be brought to a shameful end in this world. His presbyterian friends did their utmost to restrain him, alarmed at the scandal that Weir's conduct was likely to bring on their religion; but the affair soon reached the ears of the royalists, who were just as glad to seize upon any occasion of hurting the cause of their opponents. Major Weir and his sister were arrested, and both made what was called a full confession, involving crimes of a degrading character. As these were most of them vices which the king's party had long been in the habit of ascribing to their religious adversaries, we are perhaps justified in believing that they may have taken advantage of their state of mind to suggest to them some of these self-accusations. They found two or three witnesses to those parts of his story which were most improbable. His sister declared that he had a magical staff, which he always carried with him, and which gave him eloquence in prayer. She said, that once a person called upon them at noon-day with a fiery chariot, visible only to themselves, and took them to visit a friend at Dalkeith, where her brother received information, by supernatural means, of the event of the battle of Worcester, and that she herself had intercourse with the queen of the fairies, who assisted her in spinning an unusual quantity of yarn. There was a woman who lived in the West Bow, at no great distance from major Weir's house, who gave the following evidence. She was a substantial merchant's wife, and " being very desirous to hear him pray, for that end spoke to some of her neighbours, that when he came to their house she might be sent for. This was done, but he could never be persuaded to open his mouth before her, no, not to bless a cup of ale; he either remained mute, or up with his staff and away. Some few days before he discovered himself, this gentlewoman coming from the castle-hill, where her husband's niece was lying-in of a child, about midnight perceived about the Bow-head three women in the windows, shouting, laughing, and clapping their hands. The gentlewoman went forward, till just at major Weir's door, there arose, as from the street, a woman about the height of two ordinary females, and stepped forward. The gentlewoman, not as yet excessively feared, bid her maid step on, if by the lantern they could see what she was; but haste what they could, this long-legged spectre was still before them, moving her body with a vehement cachinnation, a great unmeasurable laughter. At this rate the two strove for place, till the giantess came to a narrow lane in the Bow, commonly called the Stinking-close, into which she turning, and the gentlewoman looking after her, perceived the close full of flaming torches, (she could give them no other name,) and as it had been a great multitude of people, stentoriously laughing, and gaping with tahees of laughter. This sight, at so dead a time of the night, no people being in the windows belonging to the close, made her and her servant haste home, declaring all what they saw to the rest of the family, but more passionately to her husband. And though sick with fear, yet she went the next morning with her maid to view the noted places of her former night's walk, and at the close inquired who lived there. It was answered, major Weir; the honest couple now rejoicing that to Weir's devotion they never said amen." When major Weir's sister was brought to the place of execution, and saw the multitude of spectators, she exclaimed, "Many weep and lament for a poor old wretch like me; but, alas! few are weeping for a broken covenant." A clear proof of the state of mind in which these miserable people suffered.

CHAPTER XXIX.

THE WITCHES OF MOHRA IN SWEDEN.

In general the countries of northern Europe appear to have been less subject to these extensive witch-prosecutions than the south, although there the ancient popular superstitions reigned in great force. Probably this latter circumstance contributed not a little to the extraordinary character assumed by a case of this nature, which, during the years 1669 and 1670, caused a great sensation throughout Sweden, and drew also the attention of other countries. It began in a district which would seem by its name of Elfdale to have been the peculiar domain of the fairies, and the chief actors in it were children, whom, according to the old popular belief, the fairies were always on the look out to carry away.

The villages of Mohra and Elfdale are situated in the dales of the mountainous districts of the central part of Sweden. In the first of the years above-mentioned, a strange report went abroad that the children of the neighbourhood were carried away nightly to a place they called Blockula, where they were received by Satan in person; and the children themselves, who were the authors of the report, pointed out to numerous women who they said were witches and carried them thither. We have no information as to the manner in which this affair arose, or how it was first made public, but within a short space of time nearly all the children of the district became compromised in it, and agreed in nearly the same story. They asserted in the strongest manner the fact of their being carried away in multitudes to the place of ghostly rendezvous, and we are told that the pale and emaciated appearance of these juvenile victims gave consistency to their statements, although there was the testimony of their own parents that during their pretended absence they had never been missed from home.

Some of the incidents in this singular and tragical case seem to have been borrowed from the witchcraft-cases in France and Germany, although it is not very easy to understand how this could have been the case in what was evidently a very retired part of the country. The minister seems to have shared largely in the delusion, and he may perhaps have been involuntarily the means of working the story of the children into its finished form. The alarm and terror in the district became so great, that a report was at last made to the king, who nominated commissioners, partly clergy and partly laymen, to inquire into the extraordinary circumstances which had been brought under his notice, and these commissioners arrived in Mohra and announced their intention of opening their proceedings on the 13th of August, 1670.

On the 12th of August, the commissioners met at the parsonage-house, and heard the complaints of the minister and several people of the better class, who told them of the miserable condition they were in, and prayed that by some means or other they might be delivered from the calamity. They gravely told the commissioners that by the help of witches some hundred of their children had been drawn to Satan, who had been seen to go in a visible shape through the country, and to appear daily to the people; the poorer sort of them, they said, he had seduced by feasting them with meat and drink. Prayers and humiliations, it appears, had been ordered by the church authorities, and were strictly observed, but the inhabitants of the village lamented before the commissioners that they had been of no avail, and that their children were carried away by the fiend in spite of their devotions. They therefore earnestly begged that the witches who had been the cause of the evil might be rooted out, and that they might thus regain their former rest and quietness, "the rather," they said, "because the children which used to be carried away in the country or district of Elfdale, since some witches had been burnt there, remained unmolested." This certainly was a cogent argument for persecution.

The 13th of August was the last day appointed for prayer and humiliation, and before opening their commission the commissioners went to church, "where there appeared a considerable assembly both of young and old. The children could read most of them, and sing psalms, and so could the women, though not with any great zeal and fervour. There were preached two sermons that day, in which the miserable case of those people that suffered themselves to be deluded by the devil was laid open; and these sermons were at last concluded with very fervent prayer. The public worship being over, all the people of the town were called together in the parson's house, near three thousand of them. Silence being commanded, the king's commission was read publicly in the hearing of them all, and they were charged, under very great penalties, to conceal nothing of what they knew, and to say nothing but the truth, those especially who were guilty, that the children might be delivered from the clutches of the devil; they all promised obedience; the guilty feignedly, but the guiltless weeping and crying bitterly."

The commissioners entered upon their duties on the next day with the utmost diligence, and the result of their misguided zeal formed one of the most remarkable examples of cruel and remorseless persecution that stain the annals of sorcery. No less than threescore and ten inhabitants of the village and district of Mohra, three-and-twenty of whom made confessions, were condemned and executed. One woman pleaded that she was with child, and the rest denied their guilt, and these were sent to Fahluna, where most of them were afterwards put to death. Fifteen children were among those who suffered death, and thirty-six more, of different ages between nine and sixteen, were forced to run the gauntlet, and be scourged on the hands at the church-door every Sunday for one year; while twenty more, who had been drawn into these practices more unwillingly, and were very young, were condemned to be scourged with rods upon their hands for three successive Sundays at the church-door. The number of the children accused was about three hundred.

It appears that the commissioners began by taking the confessions of the children, and then they confronted them with the witches whom the children accused as their seducers. The latter, to use the words of the authorized report, having "most of them children with them, which they had either seduced or attempted to seduce, some seven years of age, nay, from four to sixteen years," now appeared before the commissioners. "Some of the children complained lamentably of the misery and mischief they were forced sometimes to suffer of the devil and the witches." Being asked, whether they were sure, that they were at any time carried away by the devil? they all replied in the affirmative. "Hereupon the witches themselves were asked, whether the confessions of those children were true, and admonished to confess the truth, that they might turn away from the devil unto the living God. At first, most of them did very stiffly, and without shedding the least tear, deny it, though much against their will and inclination. After this the children were examined every one by themselves, to see whether their confessions did agree or no, and the commissioners found that all of them, except some very little ones, which could not tell all the circumstances, did punctually agree in their confessions of particulars. In the meanwhile, the commissioners that were of the clergy examined the witches, but could not bring them to any confession, all continuing stedfast in their denials, till at last some of them burst out into tears, and their confession agreed with what the children said; and these expressed their abhorrence of the fact, and begged pardon. Adding that the devil, whom they called Locyta, had stopped the mouths of some of them, so loath was he to part with his prey, and had stopped the ears of others. And being now gone from them, they could no longer conceal it; for they had now perceived his treachery."

The various confessions, not only of the witches and children in Mohra, but of those of Elfdale, presented a remarkable uniformity, even in their more minute details. They all asserted that they were carried to a place called Blockula, although they appear to have been ignorant where or at how great a distance it lay, and that they were there feasted by the arch-fiend. The confession of the witches of Elfdale ran thus:—"We of the province of Elfdale do confess, that we used to go to a gravel-pit, which lies hard by a cross-way, and there we put on a vest over our heads, and then danced round; and after this ran to the cross-way, and called the devil thrice, first with a still voice, the second time somewhat louder, and the third time very loud, with these words,—'Antecessor, come and carry us to Blockula.' Whereupon immediately he used to appear; but in different habits; but for the most part we saw him in a grey coat and red and blue stockings; he had a red beard, a high-crowned hat, with linen of divers colours wrapt about it, and long garters upon his stockings. (It is very remarkable,—says the report,—that the devil never appears to the witches with a sword by his side.) Then he asked us, whether we would serve him with soul and body. If we were content to do so, he set us on a beast which he had there ready, and carried us over churches and high walls, and after all we came to a green meadow where Blockula lies. We must procure some scrapings of altars, and filings of church clocks; and then he gave us a horn, with a salve in it, wherewith we do anoint ourselves, and a saddle, with a hammer and a wooden nail, thereby to fix the saddle; whereupon we call upon the devil, and away we go."

The witches of Mohra made similar statements; and being asked whether they were sure of a real personal transportation, and whether they were awake when it took place, they all answered in the affirmative; and they said that the devil sometimes laid something down in their place that was very like them; but one of them asserted that he did only take away "her strength," while her body lay still upon the ground, though sometimes he took away her body also. They were then asked, how they could go with their bodies through chimneys and unbroken panes of glass; to which they replied, that the devil did first remove all that might hinder them in their flight, and so they had room enough to go. Others, who were asked how they were able to carry so many children with them, said that they came into the chamber where the children lay asleep, and laid hold of them, upon which they awoke; they then asked them whether they would go to a feast with them. To which some answered, Yes; others, No, "yet they were all forced to go;" they only gave the children a shirt, and a coat and doublet, which was either red or blue, and so they set them upon a beast of the devil's providing, and then they rode away. The children confessed that this was true, and some of them added, that because they had very fine clothes put upon them, they were very willing to go. Some of the children said that they concealed it from their parents, while others made no secret of their visits to Blockula. "The witches declared, moreover, that till of late, they had never power to carry away children, but only this year and the last; and the devil did at that time force them to it; that heretofore it was sufficient to carry but one of their own children, or a stranger's child with them, which happened seldom; but now he did plague them and whip them, if they did not procure him many children, insomuch that they had no peace nor quiet for him. And whereas that formerly one journey a week would serve their turn from their own town to the place aforesaid, now they were forced to run to other towns and places for children, and that they brought with them some fifteen, some sixteen children every night."

The journey to Blockula was not always made with the same kind of conveyance; they commonly used men, beasts, even spits and posts, according as they had opportunity. They preferred, however, riding upon goats, and if they had more children with them than the animal could conveniently carry, they elongated its back by means of a spit anointed with their magical ointment. It was further stated, that if the children did at any time name the names of those, either man or woman, that had been with them, and had carried them away, they were again carried by force, either to Blockula or the cross-way, and there beaten, insomuch that some of them died of it; "and this some of the witches confessed, and added, that now they were exceedingly troubled and tortured in their minds for it." One thing was wanting to confirm this circumstance of their confession. The marks of the whip could not be found on the persons of the victims, except on one boy, who had some wounds and holes in his back, that were given him with thorns; but the witches said they would quickly vanish.

The confessions were very minute in regard to the effects of the journey on the children after their return. "They are," says the history, "exceedingly weak; and if any be carried over night, they cannot recover themselves the next day, and they often fall into fits; the coming of which they know by an extraordinary paleness that seizes on the children, and when a fit comes upon them, they lean upon their mother's arms, who sits up with them, sometimes all night, and when they observe the paleness, shake the children, but to no purpose. They observe, further, that their children's breasts grow cold at such times, and they take sometimes a burning candle and stick it in their hair, which yet is not burned by it. They swoon upon this paleness, which swoon lasteth sometimes half an hour, sometimes an hour, sometimes two hours, and when the children come to themselves again, they mourn and lament, and groan most miserably, and beg exceedingly to be eased. This the old men declared upon oath before the judges, and called the inhabitants of the town to witness, as persons that had most of them experience of the strong symptoms of their children."

One little girl in Elfdale confessed that, happening accidentally to utter the name of Jesus, as she was carried away, she fell suddenly upon the ground, and received a hurt in her side, which the devil presently healed, and away he carried her.

A boy of the same district said that one day he was carried away with his mistress; and to perform the journey he took his father's horse out of the meadow, where it was feeding, and upon his return, she let the horse go into her own ground. The next morning the boy's father sought for the horse, and not finding it in its place, imagined that it was lost, till the boy told him the whole story, and the father found the horse according to his child's statement.

The account they gave of Blockula was, that it was situated in a large meadow, like a plain sea, "wherein you can see no end." The house they met at had a great gate painted with many divers colours. Through this gate they went into a little meadow distinct from the other, and here they turned their animals to graze. When they had made use of men for their beasts of burthen, they set them up against the wall in a state of helpless slumber, and there they remained till wanted for the homeward flight. In a very large room of this house, stood a long table, at which the witches sat down; and adjoining to this room was another chamber, where there were "lovely and delicate beds."

As soon as they arrived at Blockula, the visitors were required to deny their baptism, and devote themselves body and soul to Satan, whom they promised to serve faithfully. Hereupon he cut their fingers, and they wrote their name with blood in his book. He then caused them to be baptized anew, by priests appointed for that purpose. Upon this the devil gave them a purse, wherein there were filings of clocks, with a big stone tied to it, which they threw into the water, and said, "As these filings of the clock do never return to the clock, from which they were taken, so may my soul never return to heaven!" Another difficulty arose in verifying this statement, that few of the children had any marks on their fingers to show where they had been cut. But here again the story was helped by a girl who had her finger much hurt, and who declared, that because she would not stretch out her finger, the devil in anger had thus wounded it.

When these ceremonies were completed, the witches sat down at the table, those whom the fiend esteemed most being placed nearest to him; but the children were made to stand at the door, where he himself gave them meat and drink. Perhaps we may look for the origin of this part of the story in the pages of Pierre de Lancre. The food with which the visitors to Blockula were regaled, consisted of broth, with coleworts and bacon in it; oatmeal bread spread with butter, milk, and cheese. Sometimes, they said, it tasted very well, and sometimes very ill. After meals they went to dancing, and it was one peculiarity of these northern witches' sabbaths, that the dance was usually followed by fighting. Those of Elfdale confessed that the devil used to play upon a harp before them. Another peculiarity of these northern witches was, that children resulted from their intercourse with Satan, and these children having married together, became the parents of toads and serpents. Satan loved to play tricks upon his subjects. One day he pretended to be dead, and, singularly enough, there was great lamentation among the witches at Blockula; but he soon showed signs of life. If he had a mind to be merry with them, he let them all ride upon spits before him, and finished by taking the spits and beating them black and blue, and then laughed at them. Then he told them that the day of judgment was at hand, and set them to build a great house of stone, promising that in this house he would preserve them from God's wrath, and cause them to enjoy the greatest delights and pleasures; but while they were hard at work, he caused a great part of the work to fall down upon them, and some of the witches were severely hurt, which made him laugh.

Some of the children spoke of a very great demon like a dragon, with fire round about him, and bound with an iron chain; and the devil told them that if they confessed anything, he would set that great devil loose upon them, whereby all Sweden should come into great danger. They said that the devil had a church there like that in the village of Mohra. When he heard that the commissioners were coming, he told the witches they should not fear them, for he would certainly kill them all. And they confessed some of them had attempted to murder the commissioners, but had not been successful. Some of the children improved upon these stories, and told of "a white angel, which used to forbid them what the devil had bid them do, and told that these things should not last long; what had been done had been permitted, because of the sin and wickedness of the people and their parents; and that the carrying away of the children should be made manifest. And they added, that this white angel would place himself sometimes at the door betwixt the witches and the children, and that when they came to Blockula he pulled the children back, but the witches went on."

The witches of Sweden appear to have been less noxious than those of most other countries, for, whatever they acknowledged themselves, there seems to have been no evidence of mischief done by them. They confessed that they were obliged to promise Satan that they would do all kind of mischief, and that the devil taught them to milk, which was after this manner. They used to stick a knife in the wall, and hang a kind of label on it, which they drew and stroaked; and as long as this lasted, the persons they had power over were miserably plagued, and the beasts were milked that way, till sometimes they died of it. A woman confessed that the devil gave her a wooden knife, wherewith, going into houses, she had power to kill anything she touched with it; yet there were few that would confess that they had hurt any man or woman. Being asked whether they had murdered any children, they confessed that they had indeed tormented many, but did not know whether any of them died of these plagues, although they said that the devil had showed them several places where he had power to do mischief. The minister of Elfdale declared, that one night these witches were, to his thinking, on the crown of his head, and that from thence he had a long continued pain of the head. And upon this one of the witches confessed that the devil had sent her to torment that minister, and that she was ordered to use a nail, and strike it into his head; but his skull was so hard that the nail would not penetrate it, and merely produced that headache. The hard-headed minister said further, that one night he felt a pain as if he were torn with an instrument used for combing flax, and when he awoke he heard somebody scratching and scraping at the window, but could see nobody; and one of the witches confessed, that she was the person that had thus disturbed him. The minister of Mohra declared also, that one night one of these witches came into his house, and did so violently take him by the throat, that he thought he should have been choaked, and awaking, he saw the person that did it, but could not know her; and that for some weeks he was not able to speak, or perform divine service. An old woman of Elfdale confessed, that the devil had helped her to make a nail, which she struck into a boy's knee, of which stroke the boy remained lame a long time. And she added, that, before she was burned or executed by the hand of justice, the boy would recover.

Another circumstance confessed by these witches was, that the devil gave them a beast, about the shape and bigness of a cat, which they called a carrier, and a bird as big as a raven, but white; and these they could send anywhere, and wherever they came they took away all sorts of victuals, such as butter, cheese, milk, bacon, and all sorts of seeds, and carried them to the witch. What the bird brought they kept for themselves, but what the carrier brought, they took to Blockula, where the arch-fiend gave them as much of it as he thought good. The carriers, they said, filled themselves so full oftentimes, that they were forced to disgorge it by the way, and what they thus rendered fell to the ground, and is found in several gardens where coleworts grow, and far from the houses of the witches. It was of a yellow colour like gold, and was called witches' butter.

"The lords commissioners," says the report, "were indeed very earnest, and took great pains to persuade them to show some of their tricks, but to no purpose; for they did all unanimously declare, that since they had confessed all, they found that all their witchcraft was gone; and the devil at this time appeared very terrible, with claws on his hands and feet, with horns on his head, and a long tail behind, and showed them a pit burning, with a hand out; but the devil did thrust the person down again with an iron fork, and suggested to the witches that if they continued in their confession, he would deal with them in the same manner."

Such are the details, as far as they can now be obtained, of this extraordinary delusion, the only one of a similar kind that we know to have occurred in the northern part of Europe during the "age of witchcraft." In other countries we can generally trace some particular cause which gave rise to great persecutions of this kind, but here, as the story is told, we see none, for it is hardly likely that such a strange series of accusations should have been the mere involuntary creation of a party of little children. Suspicion is excited by the peculiar part which the two clergymen of Elfdale and Mohra acted in it, that they were not altogether strangers to the fabrication. They seem to have been weak superstitious men, and perhaps they had been reading the witchcraft books of the south till they imagined the country round them to be overrun with these noxious beings. The proceedings at Mohra caused so much alarm throughout Sweden, that prayers were ordered in all the churches for delivery from the snares of Satan, who was believed to have been let loose in that kingdom. On a sudden a new edict of the king put a stop to the whole process, and the matter was brought to a close rather mysteriously. It is said that the witch prosecution was increasing so much in intensity, that accusations began to be made against people of higher class in society, and then a complaint was made to the king, and they were stopped. Perhaps the two clergymen themselves became alarmed, but one thing seems certain, that the moment the commission was revoked, and the persecution ceased, no more witches were heard of. It was thus in most countries; as long as the poor alone were the victims, their sufferings excited little commiseration, but the moment the persecution began to reach the rich, it excited their alarm, and means were found to put a stop to it, except when it had some ulterior object which it was the interest of those in power to pursue.

CHAPTER XXX.

SIR MATTHEW HALE AND CHIEF JUSTICE HOLT.

On the tenth of March, 1664, there was a remarkable trial of witches at Bury St. Edmunds, in Suffolk, the scene of the labours of Matthew Hopkins nearly twenty years before. The victims were two poor widows of Lowestoff, who appear to have obtained a living by performing a number of menial offices for their neighbours. One of the chief witnesses was a woman of the same town, named Dorothy Durent, who deposed that, about five or six years before, she had employed Amy Duny, one of the prisoners, to nurse her infant child while she went out of the house about her affairs, and that on her return she quarrelled with her for having acted contrary to her directions, upon which Amy Duny went away in anger, uttering "many high expressions and threatening speeches." The same night her child was seized with strange and dangerous fits. "And the said examinant further said, that she being exceedingly troubled at her child's distemper, did go to a certain person named doctor Job Jacob, who lived at Yarmouth, who had the reputation in the country to help children that were bewitched; who advised her to hang up the child's blanket in the chimney-corner all day, and at night, when she put the child to bed, to put it into the said blanket; and if she found anything in it she should not be afraid, but to throw it into the fire. And this deponent did according to his direction, and at night, when she took down the blanket with an intent to put her child therein, there fell out of the same a great toad, which ran up and down the hearth, and she having a young youth only with her in the house, desired him to catch the toad and throw it into the fire, which the youth did accordingly, and held it there with the tongs; and as soon as it was in the fire, it made a great and horrible noise, and after a space there was a flashing in the fire like gun-powder, making a noise like the discharge of a pistol, and thereupon the toad was no more seen nor heard. It was asked by the court, if that after the noise and flashing there was not the substance of the toad to be seen to consume in the fire; and it was answered by the said Dorothy Durent, that after the flashing and noise, there was no more seen than if there had been none there. The next day there came a young woman, a kinswoman of the said Amy, and a neighbour of this deponent, and told this deponent that her aunt (meaning the said Amy) was in a most lamentable condition, having her face all scorched with fire, and that she was sitting alone in her house, in her smock, without any fire. And thereupon this deponent went into the house of the said Amy Duny to see her, and found her in the same condition as was related to her, for her face, her legs, and thighs, which this deponent saw, seemed very much scorched and burnt with fire, at which this deponent seemed much to wonder, and asked the said Amy how she came into that sad condition; and the said Amy replied that she might thank her for it, for that she, this deponent, was the cause thereof, but that she should live to see some of her children dead, and she upon crutches. And this deponent further saith, that after the burning of the said toad her child recovered, and was well again, and was living at the time of the assizes."

Subsequent to these new threats, another child of Dorothy Durent's was taken ill and died, and she herself was seized with a lameness in her legs, in consequence of which she had remained a cripple ever since.

The next offence laid to the charge of Amy Duny was the bewitching of the children of Samuel Pacy, a merchant of Lowestoff, who "carried himself with much soberness during the trial." This man deposed "that his younger daughter, Deborah, upon Thursday the tenth of October last, was suddenly taken with a lameness in her leggs, so that she could not stand, neither had she any strength in her limbs to support her, and so she continued until the seventeenth day of the same month, which day being fair and sunshiny, the child desired to be carried on the east part of the house, to be set upon the bank which looketh upon the sea; and whilst she was sitting there, Amy Duny came to this deponent's house to buy some herrings, but being denied, she went away discontented, and presently returned again, and was denied, and likewise the third time, and was denied as at first; and at her last going away, she went away grumbling, but what she said was not perfectly understood. But at the very same instant of time the said child was taken with most violent fits, feeling most extreme pain in her stomach, like the pricking of pins, and shrieking out in a most dreadful manner, like unto a whelp, and not like unto a sensible creature. And in this extremity the child continued, to the great grief of the parents, until the thirtieth of the same month. During this time this deponent sent for one Dr. Feavor, a doctor of physick, to take his advice concerning his child's distemper. The doctor being come, he saw the child in those fits, but could not conjecture (as he then told this deponent, and afterwards he affirmed in open court at this trial) what might be the cause of the child's affliction. And this deponent further saith, that by reason of the circumstances aforesaid, and in regard Amy Duny is a woman of an ill fame, and commonly reported to be a witch and a sorceress, and for that the said child in her fits would cry out of Amy Duny as the cause of her malady, and that she did affright her with apparitions of her person (as the child in the interval of her fits related), he, this deponent, did suspect the said Amy Duny for a witch, and charged her with the injury and wrong to his child, and caused her to be set in the stocks on the twenty-eighth of the same October; and during the time of her continuance there, one Alice Letteridge and Jane Buxton demanded of her (as they also affirmed in court upon their oaths) what should be the reason of Mr. Pacy's child's distemper, telling her that she was suspected to be the cause thereof. She replied, 'Mr. Pacy keeps a great stir about his child, but let him stay until he hath done as much by his children as I have done by mine.' And being further examined what she had done to her children, she answered that she had been fain to open her child's mouth with a tap to give it victuals. And the said deponent further deposeth, that within two days after speaking of the said words, being the thirtieth of October, his eldest daughter Elizabeth fell into extreme fits, inasmuch that they could not open her mouth to give her broth to preserve her life without the help of a tap, which they were enforced to use; and the younger child was in like manner afflicted, so that they used the same also for her relief."

The children were now continually visited with fits, similar to other supposed sufferers from witchcraft, including the vomiting of crooked pins, nails, &c., and the spasmodic trances, in the latter of which they were in the habit of crying out against various women of ill-repute in the town, who, they said, were present tormenting them, but more especially against Amy Duny and the other prisoner, whose name was Rose Cullender. The children declared that these two women appeared to them sometimes in the act of spinning, and at other times in a variety of postures, threatening and mocking them. A friend of the family appeared in court as an independent witness, and deposed, that in her presence "the children would in their fits cry out against Rose Cullender and Amy Duny, affirming that they saw them; and they threatened to torment them ten times more if they complained of them. At some times the children (only) would see things run up and down the house in the appearance of mice; and one of them suddenly snapt one with the tongs, and threw it into the fire, and it screeched out like a bat. At another time, the younger child being out of her fits, went out of doors to take a little fresh air, and presently a little thing like a bee flew upon her face, and would have gone into her mouth, whereupon the child ran in all haste to the door to get into the house again, shrieking out in a most terrible manner; whereupon this deponent made haste to come to her, but before she could get to her, the child fell into her swooning fit, and at last, with much pain and straining herself, she vomited up a twopenny nail with a broad head; and after that the child had raised up the nail she came to her understanding, and being demanded by this deponent how she came by this nail, she answered that the bee brought this nail and forced it into her mouth. And at other times the elder child declared unto this deponent that during the time of her fits, she saw flies come unto her, and bring with them in their mouths crooked pins; and after the child had thus declared the same, she fell again into violent fits, and afterwards raised several pins. At another time the said elder child declared unto this deponent, and sitting by the fire suddenly started up and said she saw a mouse, and she crept under the table looking after it, and at length she put something in her apron, saying she had caught it; and immediately she ran to the fire and threw it in, and there did appear upon it to this deponent, like the flashing of gunpowder, though she confessed she saw nothing in the child's hands."

Another person bewitched was a servant girl named Susan Chandler, whose mother, besides deposing to the discovery of Satan's marks on the body of one of the witches, said, "that her said daughter being of the age of eighteen years, was then in service in the said town, and rising up early the next morning to wash, this Rose Cullender appeared to her, and took her by the hand, whereat she was much affrighted, and went forthwith to her mother, (being in the same town,) and acquainted her with what she had seen; but being extremely terrified, she fell extreme sick, much grieved at her stomach, and that night, after being in bed with another young woman, she suddenly shrieked out, and fell into such extreme fits as if she were distracted, crying against Rose Cullender, saying she would come to bed to her. She continued in this manner beating and wearing herself, insomuch that this deponent was glad to get help to attend her. In her intervals she would declare that sometimes she saw Rose Cullender alone, at another time with a great dog with her; she also vomited up divers crooked pins; and sometimes she was stricken with blindness, and at another time she was dumb, and so she appeared to be in court when the trial of the prisoners was, for she was not able to speak her knowledge; but being brought into court at the trial, she suddenly fell into her fits, and being carried out of the court again, within the space of half an hour she came to herself and recovered her speech, and thereupon was immediately brought into the court, and asked by the court whether she was in condition to take an oath, and to give evidence. She said she could. But when she was sworn, and asked what she could say against either of the prisoners, before she could make any answer she fell into her fits, shrieking out in a miserable manner, crying, 'Burn her, burn her!' which was all the words she could speak."

Such was the evidence against the two miserable women dragged before the court as prisoners; and the barrister who advocated their cause earnestly pleaded its insufficiency as the mere effect of the imaginations of the persons aggrieved, which was supported by no direct and substantial evidence fixing the crime on the two persons accused, even supposing that the accusers had really been bewitched. The celebrated Sir Thomas Brown was next brought forwards in court, and on being asked what he thought of the case, declared that "he was clearly of opinion that the persons were bewitched," with some further remarks, which appear strange as coming from the mouth of the great exposer of "vulgar errors."

Doubts still existed among some of those who were present in court, and they attempted to dispel these by a practical experiment. "At first, during the time of the trial, there were some experiments made with the persons afflicted, by bringing the persons to touch them; and it was observed, that when they were in the midst of their fits, to all men's apprehension wholly deprived of all sense and understanding, closing their fists in such a manner as that the strongest man in the court could not force them open, yet by the least touch of one of those supposed witches, Rose Cullender by name, they would suddenly shriek out, opening their hands, which accident would not happen by the touch of any other person. And lest they might privately see when they were touched by the said Rose Cullender, they were blinded with their own aprons, and the touching took the same effect as before. There was an ingenious person that objected there might be a great fallacy in this experiment, and there ought not to be any stress put upon this to convict the parties, for the children might counterfeit this their distemper, and perceiving what was done to them, they might in such manner suddenly alter the motion and gesture of their bodies, on purpose to induce persons to believe that they were not natural, but wrought strangely by the touch of the prisoners. Wherefore to avoid this scruple, it was privately desired by the judge that the lord Cornwallis, sir Edmund Bacon, and Mr. Serjeant Keeling, and some other gentlemen there in court, would attend one of the distempered persons in the farthest part of the hall, whilst she was in her fits, and then to send for one of the witches, to try what would then happen, which they did accordingly; and Amy Duny was conveyed from the bar and brought to the maid;

they put an apron before her eyes, and then one other person touched her hand, which produced the same effect as the touch of the witch did in the court. Whereupon the gentleman returned, openly protesting that they did believe the whole transaction of this business was a mere imposture. This put the court and all persons into a stand; but at length Mr. Pacy did declare, that possibly the maid might be deceived by a suspicion that the witch touched her when she did not. For he had observed divers times, that although they could not speak, but were deprived of the use of their tongues and limbs, that their understandings were perfect, for that they have related divers things which have been when they were in their fits, after they were recovered out of them."

Disappointed in this experiment, the accusers now brought forward some other evidence to prove the character of the prisoners, the principal of which was "one John Soam of Lowestoff, yeoman, a sufficient person," who deposed, "That not long since, in harvest time, he had three carts which brought home his harvest, and as they were going into the field to load, one of the carts wrenched the window of Rose Cullender's house, whereupon she came out in a great rage and threatened this deponent for doing that wrong, and so they passed along into the fields and loaded all the three carts, the other two carts returned safe home, and back again, twice loaded that day afterwards; but as to this cart which touched Rose Cullender's house, after it was loaded it was overturned twice or thrice that day; and after that they had loaded it again this second or third time, as they brought it through the gate which leadeth out of the field into the town, the cart stuck so fast in the gate-stead, that they could not possibly get it through, but were enforced to cut down the post of the gate to make the cart pass through, although they could not perceive that the cart did of either side touch the gate-post. And this deponent further said, that after they had got it through the gateway, they did with much difficulty get it home into the yard; but for all that they could do, they could not get the cart near into the place where they should unload the corn, but were fain to unload it at a great distance from the place; and when they began to unload, they found much difficulty therein, it being so hard a labour that they were tired that first came; and when others came to assist them, their noses burst forth a bleeding; so they were fain to desist, and leave it until the next morning, and then they unloaded it without any difficulty at all. Robert Sherringham also deposeth against Rose Cullender, that about two years since, passing along the street with his cart and horses, the axle-tree of his cart touched her house, and broke down some part of it, at which she was very much displeased, threatening him that his horses should suffer for it, and so it happened, for all those horses, being four in number, died within a short time after; since that time he hath had great losses by sudden dying of his other cattle; so soon as his sows pigged, the pigs would leap and caper, and immediately fall down and die. Also, not long after, he was taken with a lameness in his limbs that he could neither go nor stand for some days. After all this, he was very much vexed with a great number of lice of an extraordinary bigness, and although he many times shifted himself, yet he was not anything the better, but would swarm again with them; so that in the conclusion he was forced to burn all his clothes, being two suits of apparel, and then was clean from them."

This was the kind of evidence brought forward in a public court of justice in the year 1664, in a trial which has obtained especial celebrity from the circumstance that the lord chief baron who presided over it was the great lawyer, sir Matthew Hale. Yet even he was not exempt from the superstitious feeling of his own age, and the cautiously-worded declaration in his charge to the jury,—"that there were such creatures as witches he made no doubt at all; for first the Scriptures had affirmed so much; secondly, the wisdom of all nations had provided laws against such persons, which is an argument of their confidence of such a crime, and such hath been the judgment of this kingdom, as appears by that act of parliament which hath provided punishments proportionable to the quality of the offence"—was considered as a public declaration of the judge's opinion in favour of the witchcraft prosecutions. The jury retired, passed half an hour in deliberation, and returned with an unanimous verdict against the prisoners. Sir Matthew Hale interfered no further, but proceeded on his circuit; and the two poor widows of

Lowestoff were hanged on the following Monday. They persisted to the last in asserting their innocence.

The trial before sir Matthew Hale had a great influence in increasing the number of trials for the crime of sorcery under the restoration, although the return of the Stuarts seemed from the first to have brought back some of the spirit which had been spread in England by the first of their race who came to the throne. Among other rather ridiculous cases, it will be sufficient to instance that of Julian Coxe, a wretched old woman, who, in the preceding year, had been convicted and hanged at Taunton in Somersetshire, on the evidence of a huntsman, who declared that, having given chase to a hare, it was lost in a bush, and that on examining the spot, he found on the other side of the bush this woman in such an attitude and condition as convinced him that he had been hunting a witch who had taken the opportunity of the shelter afforded by the bush to regain her own shape. In the same year that witnessed the trial before sir Matthew Hale at Bury, a justice of the peace in Somersetshire, named Hunt, was ambitious of becoming another witch-finder-general, and had already put twelve persons under arrest, when a stop was put on his proceedings by the interference of a higher authority. In 1679, a witch condemned at Ely was saved by a reprieve from the king, and her accuser is said to have subsequently avowed his imposture, yet three years afterwards the city of Exeter witnessed the execution of three witches under circumstances well calculated to expose the absurdity of such charges.

Seaport towns appear to have been rather frequently the haunts of witches, and the scenes of some of their more extraordinary operations. At the town of Biddeford on the coast of Devon dwelt three women, named Temperance Lloyd, Mary Trembles, and Susanna Edwards, who seem to have enjoyed a character similar to that of Amy Duny and Rose Cullender at Lowestoff, and they were arrested and carried prisoners to Exeter in the summer of 1682. One of the persons who accused them was a mariner's wife named Dorcas Coleman, who said that in the year 1680 she had been taken with "tormenting pains by prickling in her arms, stomach, and heart, in such a manner as she was never taken so before." She applied to one doctor Beare, a professed physician, who told her it was past his skill to save her, inasmuch as she was bewitched. We thus see, what has indeed occurred often before, how unskilful physicians, in the attempt to conceal their own ignorance, added to and strengthened the prejudices of the vulgar. Dorcas Coleman had no suspicion of the person that had bewitched her, until Susanna Edwards was thrown into prison, and then she went to her to ask if she were her persecutor, and received an answer in the affirmative. Another woman of Biddeford, named Grace Thomas, was attacked somewhat in the same manner, and declared that as soon as Temperance Lloyd was committed to prison, she "immediately felt her pricking and sticking pains to cease and abate." Upon this one of the friends of Grace Thomas "did demand of the said Temperance Lloyd whether she had any wax or clay in the form of a picture whereby she had pricked and tormented the said Grace Thomas; unto which the said Temperance made answer, that she had no wax nor clay, but confessed that she had only a piece of leather which she had pricked nine times." Temperance Lloyd was searched, and they found on her body two "teats," which she confessed had been sucked by "the black man;" and one of the searchers, who was an acquaintance of the accused, declared that on the morning of the preceding Thursday, "she, this informant, did see something in the shape of a magpie to come at the chamber window where the said Grace Thomas did lodge. Upon which this informant did demand of the said Temperance Lloyd whether she did know of any bird to come and flutter at the said window; unto which question the said Temperance did then say that it was the black man in the shape of the bird." Having obtained thus much of foundation to build upon, the account of the black man was soon amplified, and "being demanded of what stature the said black man was," she was prevailed upon to describe him as being "about the length of her arm; and that his eyes were very big; and that he hopped or leaped in the way before her." The very picture, in fact, of a "puck" or hobgoblin.

It is hardly necessary to enter further into the rather numerous depositions made on this occasion. A piece of leather was found, in which the prosecutors and judges "conceived there might be some enchantment;" a child's doll was also produced, which it was further imagined might have been pricked with pins; it was deposed that Temperance Lloyd had appeared in the form of a red pig to a woman while she was brewing; and upon this evidence, and more of the same description, the three women were convicted by the jury, and they were all hanged at Exeter. When these wretched women were on the scaffold, they were again tormented with questions, and returned such answers as might be expected from persons in a condition that they hardly knew what they were asked or what they said in reply. Among other things, Temperance Lloyd was asked, "How did you come in to hurt Mrs. Grace Thomas? did you pass through the keyhole of the door, or was the door open?

"*Temp.* The devil did lead me up-stairs, and the door was open: and this is all the hurt I did.

"*Q.* How do you know it was the devil?

"*Temp.* I knew it by his eyes.

"*Q.* Had you no discourse or treaty with him?

"*Temp.* No; he said I should go along with him to destroy a woman, and I told him I would not; he said he would make me; and then the devil beat me about the head.

"*Q.* Why had you not called upon God?

"*Temp.* He would not let me do it.

"*Q.* You say you never hurt ships nor boats—did you never ride over an arm of the sea on a cow?

"*Temp.* No, no, master, 'twas she (*meaning Susan*)."

Another interrogator, equally unfeeling, closed the scene with asking the victim if she had never seen the devil but once.

"*Temp.* Yes, once before; I was going for brooms, and he came to me and said, 'that poor woman has a great burthen,' and would help and ease me of my burthen; and I said, 'The Lord had enabled me to carry it so far, and I hope I shall be able to carry it further.'

"*Q.* Did the devil never promise you anything?

"*Temp.* No, never.

"*Q.* Then you have served a very bad master, who gave you nothing. Well, consider you are just departing from this world; do you believe there is a God?

"*Temp.* Yes.

"*Q.* Do you believe in Jesus Christ?

"*Temp.* Yes; and I pray Jesus Christ to pardon all my sins. *And so was executed.*"

These three women are said to have been the last persons who were executed in England for the crime of witchcraft. A great change in opinion on this subject was now taking place in the minds of reflecting people. The vice of the court of Charles II. was scepticism rather than credulity, and although bigotry and superstition again appeared under the influence of his brother, their reign was of short duration. Two books were published during this period which certainly had some influence in breaking the strength of the popular prejudice on the subject. The first of these was a small volume by a gentleman of education named John Wagstaffe, which appeared in 1669, under the title of "The Question of Witchcraft Debated." In the opening of this work Wagstaffe expresses in strong terms his horror at the multitudes of human beings who had been during so many ages sacrificed to "this idol, Opinion;" and he protests against the "evil and base custom of torturing people to confess themselves witches, and burning them after extorted confessions. Surely the blood of men ought not to be so cheap, nor so easily to be shed by those who, under the name of God, do gratify exorbitant passions and selfish ends; for without question, under this side heaven, there is nothing so sacred as the life of man, for the preservation whereof all policies and forms of government, all laws and magistrates are most especially ordained." Wagstaffe's book was replied to in a tone of flippant self-sufficiency by Meric Casaubon, in a treatise published in the following year under the title of, "Of Credulity and In credulity in Things Divine and Spiritual."

A still greater champion soon afterwards stepped into the field of controversy thus opened. This was John Webster, a native of Lancashire, the same whom we have already seen in his youth opposing in vain the imposture of the boy of Pendle. Webster had lived, a careful observer, throughout the whole period of the great witchcraft mania in England, and now in his old age he published his matured judgment on the subject which had so long agitated men's minds, under the title which at once indicated the view he took of it, of "The Displaying of supposed Witchcraft." This stately folio appeared in the year 1677, and there can be little doubt of its having made a strong impression on the succeeding generation. Webster attacked with all the force of argument and wit the superstition to which so many victims had been sacrificed, and he exposed the fallacies by which it had been sustained. He made no concessions to public opinion, like most of those who preceded him on the same side of the question, and who were afraid to push too far the reasons on which they rested their cause; but he boldly published the opinion that witchcraft was nothing but a vulgar error, and that all the instances which had occurred and which had led to such a fearful destruction of human life, were founded only in deliberate imposture, in statements made under fear of torture, in mental delusion, or in natural phenomena which were easily explained by science and reason without the necessity of calling in supernatural causes.

Books like these were chiefly calculated to influence the educated part of society, and we soon perceive their effects in the courts of justice. After the revolution of eighty-eight, there seems to have been a strong tendency to renew the persecution against witches, but sir Matthew Hale had been succeeded by a judge of no less weight and talent, who was in this respect at least more enlightened—the lord chief justice Holt. Three women were thrown into prison in 1691 for bewitching a person near Frome, in Somersetshire, of whom one died before she was brought to trial; but the other two, having chief justice Holt for their judge, were acquitted. This case seems to have been the first check put upon the courts of law; and the populace, disappointed of what they called justice, had recourse, without appealing to the law, to the old popular trial of swimming the persons suspected, of which there were numerous instances during this and the following year in the counties of Essex, Suffolk, Cambridge, and Northampton. Some of the patients died under the infliction. The scene of the labours of Matthew Hopkins seems to have retained its witch-persecuting celebrity. In 1693, one widow Chambers of Upaston in Suffolk, who is described by Dr. Hutchinson as "a diligent industrious poor woman," died in Beccles jail in consequence of the treatment she had experienced. She had been walked between two men, according to the celebrated plan of the witch-finder Hopkins, and was thus drawn to confess a number of absurdities, such as the bewitching to death of persons who were then living and in good health. In the year following, another poor woman named mother Munnings, of Hartis in Suffolk, was tried before the lord chief justice Holt at Bury St. Edmunds; many things were deposed concerning her, such as spoiling of wort, and hurting cattle, and it was stated that several persons upon their death-beds had complained that she killed them. It was further deposed, that her landlord, Thomas Pennel, wishing to force her out of a house she had of him, took away the door, and left her without one. Some time after, she said to him as he passed by the door, "Go thy way, thy nose shall lie upward in the church-yard before Saturday next." On the Monday following we are assured he sickened, and died on Tuesday, and was buried within the week, according to her word. To confirm this, it was added by another witness, that a doctor whom they had consulted about an afflicted person, when mother Munnings was mentioned, said she was a dangerous woman, for she could "touch the line of life." In her indictment, she was charged with having an imp like a pole-cat; and one witness deposed, that coming from the alehouse about nine at night, he looked in at her window, and saw her take out of her basket two imps, one black the other white. It was also deposed, that one Sarah Wager, after a quarrel with this woman, was taken dumb and lame, and was in that condition at home at the time of the trial. Many other such things were sworn, but in consequence of the charge from the judge, the jury brought her in not guilty. Dr. Hutchinson, who obtained the notes of this trial through chief justice Holt himself, adds on this statement, "Upon particular inquiry of several in or near the town, I find most are satisfied that it was a very right judgment. She lived about two years after, without doing any known harm to anybody, and died declaring her innocence. Her landlord was a consumptive spent man, and the words not exactly as they swore them, and the whole thing seventeen years before. For by a certificate from the register, I find he was buried June 20, 1667. The white imp is believed to have been a lock of wool, taken out of her basket to spin, and its shadow it is supposed was the black one."

The same year, a woman of the name of Margaret Elmore was tried at Ipswich before the lord chief justice Holt. She was accused of having bewitched one Mrs. Rudge of that town, who was three years in a languishing condition, because, as it was alleged, Mr. Rudge, the husband of the afflicted person, had refused to let her a house. Some witnesses said that Mrs. Rudge was better upon the confinement of the woman, and worse again when her chains were off. Other witnesses gave an account, that her grandmother and her aunt had formerly been hanged for witches, and that her grandmother had said she had eight or nine imps, and that she had given two or three imps a-piece to her children. This grave accusation was considered to be fully confirmed, when a midwife who had searched Margaret Elmor's grandmother, who had been hanged, said, this woman had plainer marks than she. Others deposed to their being covered with lice after quarrels with her. But notwithstanding these depositions, the jury brought her in not guilty, "and," says Dr. Hutchinson, "though I have made particular inquiry, I do not hear of any ill consequence."

In 1695, Mary Guy was tried before the lord chief jnstice Holt at Launceston in Cornwall, for supposed witchcraft upon a girl named Philadelphia Row. It was deposed, that the aqpearance of the said Mary Guy was often seen by the girl, and that she vomited pins, straws, and feathers ; but notwithstanding such depositions, the prisoner was acquitted. One Elizabeth Horner was tried before the same intelligent judge at Exeter, in 1696, for bewitching three children of William Bovet, one of whom was dead. It was deposed, that another had her legs twisted, and yet from her hands and knees she would spring five feet high. The children vomited pins, and were bitten, (if the depositions were true,) and pricked, and pinched, the marks appearing; the children said, Bess Horner's head would come off from her body, and go into their bellies; the mother of the children deposed, that one of them walked up a smooth plastered wall, to the height of nine feet, her head standing off from it; this, she said, she did five or six times, and laughed and said, Bess Horner held her up. This poor woman had something like a nipple on her shoulder, which the children said was sucked by a toad. Many other strange things were asserted by different witnesses; but the jury brought her in not guilty, "and no inconvenience hath followed from her acquittal."

CHAPTER XXXI.

THE DOINGS OF SATAN IN NEW ENGLAND.

As Satan found that, beaten by the force of public opinion, he was losing his hold on the mother country, he seemed resolved to fix a firmer grasp upon her distant colonies, and the new world presented at this moment a scene which exemplifies the horrors and the absurdities of the witchcraft persecutions more than anything that had occurred in the old world.

New England, or, as it has been since called, Massachusetts, was essentially a religious—a puritanical settlement. One of the congregations of the English presbyterians who sought refuge in Holland from the intolerance of James I., finding their position there uneasy, came to the resolution of establishing themselves in the wilds of north America, where they could worship the Almighty after their own convictions, unseen and untroubled by those who differed from them. They made arrangements for settling in the English colony of Virginia, and set sail for America in 1618, but carried out of their course by stress of weather and other causes, they arrived on a coast more to the north, on which no settlement had hitherto been made. In the last days of the year they laid the foundations of the first town in New England, to which they gave the name of Plymouth. They formed an alliance with an Indian chief by whom this territory had been previously occupied, a great part of whose tribe had been carried off by the small-pox, and who was glad of their support against the hostile tribes of Narraghansetts. Several other settlements were subsequently attempted on this coast, but the settlers were ill-fitted for amalgamating with the puritans of New Plymouth or to struggle with the difficulties they had encountered, and they therefore soon abandoned their enterprize. Under Charles I. the religious emigration from England was greatly increased, and the old settlers on these distant shores were soon joined by multitudes of friends who shared in their principles and feelings. Some of these founded, in 1628, the town of Salem. Soon afterwards Boston was founded, which became at once the principal town of Massachusetts bay. From the peculiar constitution of this singular colony, it became as intolerant as it was religious, and its earlier history presents us with frequent instances of persecution for the sake of conscientious convictions. Religious discussions here took the place of political disputes, and disturbed from time to time the peace of the infant colony. A school having been founded at a small town called Newtown, it was erected into a university in 1638, and named Haward College, from a pious minister who left a legacy for its endowment, and the name of Newtown was changed for that of Cambridge, in memory of the celebrated scholastic establishment in the mother country. One of the most distinguished of the New England ministers, Elliott, laboured to convert the Indians, and to establish more intimate and friendly relations with them, with great success, and his example having been followed by many others, there were, in 1687, no less than four-and-twenty Indians who were preachers of the gospel among their countrymen. During the period of the protectorate, the intolerant spirit of the colony was shown in the persecution of several Anabaptists who had settled there. This was followed by a much more severe persecution of the Quakers. The reign of Charles II. was a period of trouble for the colonists. Many perished in a fierce war with the Indians, although the latter were entirely defeated and reduced. This was followed by vexatious proceedings on the part of the government of the mother country, which ended in the seizure of their charter. In 1689, after the accession of the prince of Orange to the English throne, the charter was restored, or rather a new one was given to them, and sir William Phipps was appointed their governor. It was during the forfeiture of the charter that the following events commenced.

It is not to be wondered at if the planters of New England carried with them all the superstitious feelings which had been shown by their brethren in England. It was the general belief of those times that the gods or idols worshipped by the heathens—

and especially by the Indians—were demons, and that they were constantly waging war with the Christian professors through the instrumentality of sorcery. Some of the old doctors in demonology were of opinion that the devil was unable to work evil against the persons or property of Christians unless he could obtain Christians to be his willing agents, and in this way they accounted for his eagerness to make and multiply witches. It was natural enough for men placed like the colonists of New England, and with their feelings, to believe that the demon who had previously held undisturbed possession of this district should be angered at the plantation of the gospel in it, and that he should be hostile to the puritanical settlers; but they were a select body—select in faith and select in personal attachment—and they had no enemies among themselves who were likely to sell themselves to Satan and to become his instruments of persecution. It is not surprising, therefore, if during the first half-century after the foundation of the colony the idea of suspecting any one of witchcraft hardly occurred to their minds. It was only when there were more people of a miscellaneous character in the settlement, and after the fiend had failed in destroying it by an insurrection of the Indians, that he formed the more insidious design of overthrowing it by a confederation of witches.

Four persons had indeed been charged with witchcraft in 1645, and had been executed; but this single case made no great sensation, and the crime was not heard of again for many years. At length, in the year 1688, a case occurred at Boston, which struck the colonists with no little dismay A mason of that town, named John Goodwin, who had six children, was in the habit of employing as a washerwoman one of his neighbours named Glover, an Irishwoman and a papist, neither of them any great recommendation in the state of New England. About the midsummer of the year last-mentioned, some linen having been missed, Goodwin's wife accused the woman of theft, on which she became angry and abusive, and used cross language to one of the children, a little girl. Immediately afterwards, this girl was seized with fits and strange afflictions, which soon communicated themselves to three of her sisters. The Irishwoman fell under suspicion, and was arrested, and in her examination she answered so incoherently, and with such a strange mixture of Irish and broken English, that she was soon brought in guilty, and the solemnity of the examination and execution made a deep impression on the minds of the people of Boston.

There were in that town two ministers, (father and son,) who, for many reasons, held a distinguished place among the clergy of New England, and their opinions were looked up to with the utmost respect. These were Increase and Cotton Mather, the first principal, and the second a fellow of Haward College. These men seem to have studied deeply the doctrines on the subject of witchcraft which had so long been held in Europe, and to have been fully convinced of their truth. Cotton Mather was called in to witness the afflictions with which Goodwin's children were visited, and not content with what he saw there, he took the girl whose visitations seemed most extraordinary to his own home, that he might examine her more leisurely, and he has left us a printed account of his observations. It appears that some of the stories of European witchcraft had been impressed on her mind, for when in her fits she believed that the witches came for her with a horse on which she rode to their meetings. Sometimes, in the presence of a number of persons, she would suddenly fall into a sort of trance, and then she would jump into a chair, and placing herself in a riding posture, move as if she were successively ambling, trotting, and gallopping. At the same time she would talk with invisible company, that seemed to go with her, and she would listen to their answers. After continuing in this way two or three minutes, she seemed to think herself at a meeting of the witches, a great distance from the house where she was sitting; then she would return again on her imaginary horse, and come to herself again; and on one occasion she told Cotton Mather of three persons she had seen at the meeting. Dr. Mather's simplicity, to say the least, was shown by the sort of experiments he made on this fantastical patient. When she was in her fits, and therefore under the influence of Satan, she read or listened to bad books with pleasure, but good books threw her into convulsions. He tried her with the Bible, the Assembly's Catechism, his grandfather Cotton Mather's "Milk for Babes," and his father Increase's "Remarkable Providences," with a treatise written to prove the reality of witchcraft, and the existence of witches. These good books, Cotton Mather tells us, "were mortal to her," they threw her into trances and convulsions. Next he tried her with books of a different character, such as quakers' books, (the quakers were looked upon with a very evil eye in New England,) popish books, the Cambridge and Oxford Jests, a Prayer-book, (against which the puritans always professed the greatest hostility,) and a book written to prove that there were no witches. These the devil let her read as long as she liked, and he showed particular respect to the Prayer-book, even allowing her to read the passages of scripture in it, although he threw her into the most dreadful sufferings if she attempted to read the same texts in the Bible.

Dr. Cotton Mather gave the world a full account of this case in a little book entitled, "Late memorable Providences relating to Witchcraft and Possession," in which he also collected together a few other cases of witchcraft in New England, which show that there was already a strong excitement abroad on the subject. This he increased by repeating to the colonists the details of the trial before Matthew Hale and other cases which had occurred in England; and further, by dispersing among them in the following year, with a warm recommendation of its merits, Baxter's "Certainty of the World of Spirits," a work well calculated to spread the terror of witchcraft.

There can be little doubt that Cotton Mather's zeal in spreading abroad the doctrines of the old world on this subject contributed to the catastrophe which followed in the new.

A Mr. Paris had been for some years minister of Salem village. He appears to have been on indifferent terms with his parishioners, on account of some disputes relating to the house and land he occupied as their minister, of which he had obtained a gift in fee simple. Towards the end of February of 1692, some young persons in his family, and some others of their neighbours, began to act after a strange manner, creeping into holes and under chairs and stools, using antic gestures, uttering ridiculous speeches, and falling into fits. The physicians were consulted, but they were unable to discover the nature of the disorder, or to effect a cure, and they declared their belief that they were bewitched. Mr. Paris had an Indian man and woman —the latter named Tituba—as servants in his house, and they, with Mr. Paris's consent, made an enchanted cake, according to the custom of their tribes, and this being given to a dog belonging to the family, was to enable the persons afflicted to declare who had bewitched them. The result was that they accused the two Indians, and the woman confessed herself guilty, and was thrown into prison: she was subsequently sold to pay the prison fees. Several private fasts were now held in the house of Mr. Paris, and a public fast was directed throughout the colony, to avert God's wrath.

Bing visited and noticed, the children and others afflicted proceeded to other denunciations, and other persons exhibited similar fits and contortions. At first they ventured only on accusing poor women, who were of ill-repute in the place, and they talked of a black man who urged them to sign a book, which they said was red, very thick, and about a cubit long. They were gradually encouraged to accuse persons of a more respectable position in life, and among the first of these were goodwife Cory and goodwife Nurse, members of the churches at Salem village and Salem town. On the 21st of March goodwife Cory was subjected to a solemn examination in the meeting-house of the village. Ten afflicted persons accused her of tormenting them. They said that in their fits they saw her likeness coming with a book for them to sign. She earnestly asserted her innocence, and represented that they were poor distracted creatures, who knew not what they were saying. Upon this they declared, "that the black man whispered to her in her ear now, (while she was upon examination,) and that she had a yellow bird, that did use to suck between her fingers, and that the said bird did suck now in the assembly.* Order being given to look in that place to see if there were any sign, the girl that pretended to see it said that it was too late now, for she had removed a pin, and put it on her head. It was upon search found that a pin was there stick-

* These yellow birds—perhaps canaries—form a peculiar feature of witchcraft in New England. "In sermon time, when goodwife C. was present in the meeting-house, Abigail Williams called out, 'look where goodwife C. sits on the beam suckling her yellow bird betwixt her fingers!' Anne Pitman, another girl afflicted, said, 'there was a yellow bird sat on my hat as it hung on the pin in the pulpit;' but those that were by restrainad her from speaking loud about it." INCREASE MATHER'S "FURTHER ACCOUNT OF THE NEW ENGLAND WITCHES," p, 2

ing upright. When the accused had any motion of her body, hands, or mouth, the accusers would cry out; as when she bit her lip, they would cry out of being bitten; if she grasped one hand with the other, they would cry out of being pinched by her, and would produce marks; so of the other motions of her body, as complaining of being pressed, when she leaned to the seat next her; if she stirred her feet, they would stamp and cry out of pain there. After the hearing, the said Cory was committed to Salem prison, and then their crying out of her abated."

On the 24th of March goodwife Nurse was suddenly examined before the ministers and magistrates in the meeting-house, with the same result. A child between four and five years old was now also committed. The accusers said that this child came invisibly, and bit them, and they would show the marks of small teeth on their arms to corroborate the statement; and when the child cast its eye upon them, they immediately cried out that they were in torment.

The number of accusers and accused now increased fast, and some of the latter, as the only means of saving themselves, made confessions, and accused others. They all spoke of a black man, and some described him as resembling an Indian, a circumstance we can easily understand. We are told by one of the historians of these events of a converted Indian, who was a zealous preacher of the Gospel among his countrymen; "being a little before he died at work in the wood making of tar, there appeared unto him a black man, of a terrible aspect and more than human dimensions, threatening bitterly to kill him, if he would not promise to leave off preaching to his countrymen." This is said to have occurred just before the events I am now relating; the black man of the confessions was of ordinary stature, but he made no secret of his design to destroy the Christian settlement, and he held meetings of his converts — those who had signed his book—where they had mock ceremonies and participated in a mock sacrament. One of the accused, who saved himself by confessing, told how the devil appeared "in the shape of a black man, in the evening, to set my name to his book, as I have owned to my shame; he told me that I should not want, so doing. At Salem village, there being, a little off the meeting-house, about a hundred fine blades, some with rapiers by their sides, ... and the trumpet sounded, and bread and wine, which they called the sacrament; but I had none, being carried over all on a stick, and never was present at any other meeting."—"The design was to destroy Salem village, and to begin at the minister's house, and to destroy the churches of God, and to set up Satan's kingdom, and then all will be well."

The ministers and magistrates went on with their fastings and examinings, as the number of persons accused increased, until, on the 11th of April, there was a grand public hearing at Salem before six magistrates and several ministers. One goodwife Procter was among the persons accused on this occasion. Her husband attended to assist and advise her, and when he took her part, the accusers "cried out on him," and both were accordingly committed.

On the 14th of May, 1692, sir William Phipps arrived, bringing with him the new charter of the colony. Instead of being the harbinger of peace by importing the liberal principles which were now gaining ground in England, the new governor either shared in the prejudices of the colonists, or wished to gain popularity among them by appearing to do so, and he ordered all the prisoners who were charged with witchcraft to be thrown into chains. Upon this the afflicted persons are said to have been in general relieved from their tortures. The accusations were now multiplied, and people of the greatest respectability in society became subject to the denunciations of the afflicted. On the 24th of May, a Mrs. Cary of Charlestown, having been accused by some of the girls and an Indian, was arrested and brought before the ministers and magistrates for examination. Her husband went with her, to support her in her trials, and we have his account of the manner in which the examination was carried on. "Being brought before the justices," he says, "her chief accusers were two girls. My wife declared to the justices that she never had any knowledge of them before that day. She was forced to stand with her arms stretched out. I did request that I might hold one of her hands, but it was denied me. Then she desired me to wipe the tears from her eyes and the sweat from her face, which I did. Then she desired she might lean herself on me, saying she should faint. Justice Hathorn replied, she had strength enough to torment those persons, and she should have strength enough to stand. I speaking something against their cruel proceedings, they commanded me to be silent, or else I should be turned out of the room. The Indian before mentioned was also brought in to be one of her accusers; being come in, he now (when before the justices) fell down and tumbled about like a hog, but said nothing. The justices asked the girls, who afflicted the Indian. They answered, 'she,' (meaning my wife,) and now lay upon him; the justices ordered her to touch him, in order to his cure, but her head must be turned another way, lest instead of curing she should make him worse by her looking on him, her hand being guided to take hold of his; but the Indian took hold on her hand, and pulled her down on the floor, in a barbarous manner; then his hand was taken off, and her hand put on his, and the cure was quickly wrought."

When this man proceeded to expostulate in favour of his wife, he only provoked the court by his interference, and the afflicted were ready to "cry out" against him. Both, however, succeeded in making their escape; and they proceeded to Rhode Island, and thence to New York. The prosecutors now adopted some of the modes of trial which they learnt from the printed books that had been imported from England, such as making the accused say the Lord's Prayer, and searching for teats. One of the latter was said to have been found on the person of goodwife Bishop. On the 31st of May the accusers struck a step higher, and "cried out" upon a sea-captain of Boston named John

Aldin, who was brought to Salem for examination. He asked his accusers, "Why they should think that he should come to that village to afflict those persons that he never knew or saw before?" But he found expostulation vain, and he was committed to prison in Boston. The jailor, however, began to treat his prisoners with less rudeness, and after a long imprisonment, captain Aldin escaped, perhaps with the jailor's connivance.

On the 2nd of June a special commission was opened at Salem for the trial of the offenders. The depositions were many of them of such an extraordinary character, that we cannot be surprised at being told that on the fifteenth of the same month governor Phipps found it necessary to consult with the ministers of Boston, and that he was advised by them to proceed with caution. Five days before, Bridget Bishop had been hanged, which was the first of this series of executions.

The actors in this tragedy began, as I have already intimated, by accusing persons who were already despised and disliked by their neighbours, whose ears therefore were open to any charges against them. Bridget Bishop, the first woman executed, and Susanna Martin, who was condemned about the same time, belonged to this class, and, to judge by the extraordinary depositions on their trials, both had been for some time regarded as dangerous individuals. One of the "afflicted" stated that "the shape" of the prisoner appeared to her frequently, and bit, pricked, and otherwise tormented her. Another testified, "that it was the shape of this prisoner (Bishop) with another, which one day took her from her wheel, and carried her to the river side, threatening there to drown her if she did not sign the book." It is added, " one Deliverance Hobbes, who had confessed her being a witch, was now tormented by the spectres for her confession. And she now testified, that this Bishop tempted her to sign the book again, and to deny what she had confessed. She affirmed that it was the shape of this prisoner which whipped her with iron rods to compel her thereunto. And she affirmed that this Bishop was at a general meeting of the witches, in a field at Salem village, and there partook of a diabolical sacrament in bread and wine there administered." Several persons stated that they had been disturbed in their beds by nocturnal visits of the "shape" of Bishop; and one man complained of her for bewitching his sow.

Other witnesses accused Bridget Bishop of still more extraordinary pranks, such, for example, as that recounted by one John Louder, who deposed, " that upon some little controversy with Bishop about her fowls going well to bed, he did awake in the night by moonlight, and did see clearly the likeness of this woman grievously oppressing him; in which miserable condition she held him, unable to help himself, till near day. He told Bishop of this; but she denied it, and threatened him very much. Quickly after this, being at home on a Lord's day, with the doors shut about him, he saw a black pig approach him; at which he going to kick, it vanished away. Immediately after, sitting down, he saw a black thing jump in at the window, and come and stand before him. The body was like that of a monkey, the feet like a cock's, but the face much like that of a man's. He being so extremely affrighted that he could not speak, this monster spoke to him, and said, 'I am a messenger sent unto you, for I understand that you are in some trouble of mind, and if you will be ruled by me, you shall want for nothing in this world.' Whereupon he endeavoured to clap his hands upon it; but he could feel no substance; and it jumped out of the window again; but immediately came in by the porch, though the doors were shut, and said, 'You had better take my counsel!' He then struck at it with a stick, but struck only the groundsel, and broke the stick. The arm with which he struck was presently disenabled, and it vanished away. He presently went out at the back door, and spied this Bishop in her orchard going towards her house, but he had no power to set one foot forward unto her. Whereupon, returning into the house, he was immediately accosted by the monster he had seen before; which goblin was now going to fly at him; whereat he cried out, 'The whole armour of God be between me and you.' So it sprang back, and flew over the apple-tree, shaking many apples of the tree in its flying over. At its leap it flung dirt with its feet against the stomach of the man; whereupon he was then struck dumb, and so continued for three days together."

As to Susanna Martin, who was also accused of paying visits to people through their chamber windows, a man named Bernard Peache deposed in court, "that being in bed, on the Lord's day at night, he heard a scrabbling at the window, whereat he then saw Susanna Martin come in and jump down upon the floor. She took hold of this deponent's foot, and drawing his body into a heap, she lay upon him near two hours, in all which time he could neither speak nor stir. At length, when he could begin to move, he laid hold on her hand, and pulling it up to his mouth, he bit some of her fingers, as he judged, unto the bone. Whereupon she went from the chamber, down stairs, out at the door. This deponent thereupon called out to the people of the house, to advise them of what had passed; and he himself did follow her. The people saw her not, but there being a bucket at the left hand of the door, there was a drop of blood found upon it, and several more drops of blood upon the snow newly fallen abroad. There was likewise the print of her two feet just without the threshold, but no more sign of any footing further on. At another time this deponent was desired by the prisoner to come unto a husking of corn at her house, and she said if he did not come it were better that he did. He went not; but the night following Susanna Martin, as he judged, and another came towards him. One of then said, 'Here he is,' but he having a quarter-staff, made a blow at them. The roof of the barn broke his blow, but following them to the window, he made another blow at them, and struck them down; yet they got up and got out, and he saw no more of them. About this time there was a rumour about the town that Martin had a broken head, but the deponent could say nothing to that." Another neighbour, whose name was John Kembal, stated that, "being desirous to furnish himself with a dog, he applied himself to buy one of this Martin, who had a bitch with whelps in her house. But she not letting him have his choice, he said he would apply himself then at one Blezdel's. Having marked a puppy which he liked at Blezdel's, he met George Martin, the husband of the prisoner, going by, who asked him whether he would not have one of his wife's puppies, and he answered no. The same day, one Edward Elliot, being at Martin's house, heard George Martin relate where this Kembal had been, and what he had said. Whereupon Susanna Martin replied, 'If I live I'll give him puppies enough.' Within a few days after this, Kembal coming out of the woods, there arose a little black cloud in the north-west, and Kembal immediately felt a force upon him, which made him not able to avoid running upon stumps of trees that were before him, albeit he had a broad plain cart way before him; but though he had his axe also on his shoulder to endanger him in his falls, he could not forbear going out of his way to tumble over them. When he came below the meeting-house, there appeared to him a little thing like a puppy, of a darkish colour, and it shot backwards and forwards between his legs. He had the courage to use all possible endeavours of cutting it with his axe, but he could not hit it; the puppy gave a jump from him, and went, as to him it seemed, into the ground. Going a little further, there appeared unto him a black puppy, somewhat bigger than the first, but as black as a cole. Its motions were quicker than those of his axe; it flew at his belly, and away; then at his throat; so over his shoulder one way, and then over his shoulder another way. His heart now began to fail him, and he thought the dog would have tore his throat out; but he recovered himself, and called upon God in his distress, and naming the name of Jesus Christ, it vanished away at once." Another witness, John Pressy, declared "that being one evening very unaccountably bewildered, near a field of Martin's, and several times, as one under an enchantment, returning to the place he had left, at length he saw a marvellous light, about the bigness of a half-bushel, near two rods out of the way. He gave it near forty blows, and felt it a palpable substance. But going from it, his heels were struck up, and he was laid with his back on the ground, sliding, as he thought, into a pit, from whence he recovered by taking hold on the bush; although afterward he could find no such pit in the place. Having, after his recovery, gone five or six rods, he saw Susanna Martin standing on his left hand, as the light had done before; but they changed no words with one another. The next day it was upon inquiry understood that Martin was in a miserable condition by pains and hurts that were upon her."

These tales have somewhat of novelty, but others were decidedly adopted from the witches' trials in Europe, and they even went so far as to make the pretended sufferers, when under the influence of the "spirit," talk languages which they had never learnt, such as Latin, and Greek, and even Hebrew, although it appeared that even Satan himself would not condescend to talk the barbarous jargon of the

Indians.* It was the "shapes," or spectral appearances of the witches who tormented the sufferers, and performed all these mischievous pranks, and the strange perversion of justice which allowed the presumed acts of these spectres to be considered as the crimes of the individuals they represented, rendered the only possible defence, the plea of *alibi*, inadmissible. The statement regarding these

* Dr. Cotton Mather gives the following humourous description of the difficulty of acquiring the Indian language: "Behold new difficulties to be surmounted by our indefatigable Elliot! He hires a native to teach him this exotic language, and, with a laborious care and skill, reduces it into a grammar, which afterwards he published. There is a letter or two of our alphabet which the Indians never had in theirs; but if their alphabet be short, I am sure the words composed of it are long enough to tire the patience of any scholar in the world; they are *sesquipedalia verba*, of which their lingo is composed; one would think they had been growing ever since Babel unto the dimensions to which they are now extended. For instance, if my reader will count how many letters there are in this one word, *Nummatchekodtantamoongaunnonash*, when he has done, for his reward, I'll tell him it signifies no more in English than 'our lusts;' and if I were to translate 'our loves,' it must be nothing shorter than *Noowomantammononkanunonnash*, Or, to give my reader a longer word than either of these, *Kummogkodonattoottummooetiteaongannunnonash*, is, in English, 'our question;' but I pray, sir, count the letters! Nor do we find in all this language the least affinity to, or derivation from, any European speech that we are acquainted with." He then adds, "I know not what thoughts it will produce in my reader when I inform him, that once finding that the dæmons in a possessed young woman understood the Latin and Greek and Hebrew languages, my curiosity led me to make trial of this Indian language, and the dæmons *did seem as if they did not understand it*."—MATHER'S MAGNALIA, book iii. p. 193.

spectral appearances were often as bold as they were extraordinary, and they found corroborative witnesses to support them. "It is well known," says Cotton Mather, in a subsequent history of the colony, "that these wicked spectres did proceed so far as to steal several quantities of money from divers people, part of which individual money was dropt sometimes out of the air, before sufficient spectators, into the hands of the afflicted, while the spectres were urging them to subscribe their covenant with death. Moreover, poisons, to the standers by wholly invisibly, were sometimes forced upon the afflicted; which, when they have with much reluctancy swallowed, they have swoln presently, so that the common medicines for poisons have been found necessary to relieve them. Yea, sometimes the spectres in the struggle have so dropt the poisons, that the standers by have smelt them, and viewed them, and beheld the pillows of the miserable stained with them. Yet more, the miserable have complained bitterly of burning rags run into their forcibly distended mouths; and though nobody could see any such cloths, or, indeed, any fires in the chambers, yet presently the scalds were seen plainly by everybody on the mouths of the complainers, and not only the smell, but the smoke, of the burning sensibly filled the chambers. Once more, the miserable exclaimed extremely of branding irons heating at the fire on the hearth to mark them; now, though the standers by could see no irons, yet they could see distinctly the print of them in the ashes, and smell them too as they were carried by the unseen furies unto the poor creatures for whom they were intended; and those poor creatures were thereupon so stigmatised with them, that they will bear the marks of them to their dying day. Nor are these the tenth part of the prodigies that fell out among the inhabitants of New England.—Flashy people may burlesque these things, but when hundreds of the most sober people in a country, where they have as much mother-wit certainly as the rest of mankind, know them to be true, nothing but the absurd and froward spirit of Sadducism can question them. I have not yet mentioned so much as one thing that will not be justified, if it be required, by the oaths of more considerate persons than any that can ridicule these odd phenomena."

The moment the executions commenced, the evil, instead of stopping, spread wider and wider. The accused were multiplied in proportion to the accusers, and no one was for one moment sure that the next moment he might not be denounced and ordered for trial, which was almost equivalent to being convicted. For so fully convinced were magistrates and ministers that Satan was in the midst of them, using human instruments to effect his purposes, that the slightest evidence was received with the utmost eagerness. The court met again on the 30th of June, and five more were condemned, who were all executed on the 19th of July. Among these were Sarah Good and Rebecca Nurse, the two "good-wives" above mentioned. "On the trial of Sarah Good, one of the afflicted fell in a fit, and after coming out of it, she cried out of the prisoner for stabbing her in the hand with a knife, and that she had broken the knife in stabbing of her; accordingly a piece of the blade of a knife was found about her. Immediately information being given to the court, a young man was called, who produced a haft and part of the blade, which the court having viewed and compared, saw it to be the same. And upon inquiry, the young man affirmed that yesterday he happened to break that knife, and that he cast away the upper part, this afflicted person being then present, The young man was dismissed, and she was bidden by the court not to tell lies; and was improved after (as she had been before) to give evidence against the prisoner." As to goodwife Nurse, the jury at first brought her in not guilty; on which the accusers and the afflicted suddenly raised a hideous outcry, pretending that she was tormenting them again, and it being represented to the jury that they had not given due consideration to one expression of hers, they returned to reconsider their verdict, and sent her to the gallows. Like her companions in suffering, she persisted in declaring her innocence.

At another court, on the 5th of August, six were condemned, who were all executed on the 19th, except Procter's wife, who pleaded pregnancy. Among these was Mr. George Burroughs, a minister of the gospel, who provoked his judge by resting his defence on the bold argument, "that there neither are, nor ever were witches that, having made a compact with the devil, can send a devil to torment other people at a distance." When brought to the place of execution, he addressed the multitude assembled around him with so much feeling, that many of the spectators were in tears, and all seemed to relent. The accusers cried out upon him, and said the black man was standing by him and dictating his discourse; and Dr. Cotton Mather, who was present on horseback, came forward to address the crowd, assuring them that he was not a minister regularly ordained, intimating that his piety was all deception, and telling them "that the devil has often been transformed into an angel of light." Thus was the rising sympathy of the people checked, and the executioner suffered to go through with his duties.

Some persons began now to feel alarmed at the manner in which these proceedings multiplied, or were disgusted at the injustice which they exhibited, though for some time it was dangerous to express such sentiments. One John Willard, who had been employed to arrest those accused, refused to perform the office any longer, and he was immediately cried out upon by the accusers. He sought safety in flight, but he was pursued and overtaken, and he was one of those executed with Burroughs. Giles Cory was brought up for trial on the 16th of September, but indignant at the injustice which was shown to others, he refused to plead, and he was pressed to death. In the infliction of this punishment his tongue was forced out of his mouth, and the unfeeling sheriff forced it in again with his cane as the victim lay in the agonies of death. On the 22nd of September, eight more were executed; on their way to the place of execution the cart which conveyed them was upset, and the "afflicted" declared that the devil accompanied the cart, and that he overthrew it in order to retard their punishment.

Nineteen individuals had now been hanged, in addition to the man who was pressed to death, and the magistrates themselves seem to have been anxious to find some justification for their conduct. Thereupon Cotton Mather, at the express desire of the governor, prepared for the press reports of seven of the trials, and justified them by examples taken from the similar trials in England and by the doctrines of the English writers in favour of the prosecutions for this crime. His book, entitled, "More Wonders of the Invisible World," was published in the month of October. The persecution received a check at this time from another circumstance. Mr. Hale, minister of Beverley, had been one of the warmest promoters of these prosecutions; but in the month of October the accusers, who were now aiming at more respectable people than at first, cried out upon this minister's wife. As he and his friends were fully convinced of her purity and innocence, this charge was treated as absurd, but it convinced Mr. Hale and others of the injustice of the whole proceedings. Still the leaders of the persecution persisted in their course, and to get over this serious difficulty, they raised the question whether the devil could assume the "shape" or spectre of a good person to afflict his victims. Increase Mather, the principal of Haward College, was requested to treat this question, which he did very learnedly, in a book entitled, "Cases of Conscience concerning witchcraft and Evil Spirits personating Men," resolving it in the affirmative. People's faith, however, was so far shaken by these latter occurrences, that though the accusations continued, and new arrests were made daily, there were no more executions. The persecutors, disappointed in their thirst after the blood of their own species, now vented their rage upon inferior animals. A dog was strangely afflicted at Salem, upon which those who had the spectral sight declared that a brother of one of the justices afflicted the poor animal, by riding upon it invisibly. The man made his escape, but the dog was very unjustly hanged. Another dog was accused of afflicting others, who fell into fits the moment it looked upon them, and it also was killed!

The infection was now communicated from Salem to other places. "About this time," says one of the writers of these events, "a new scene began. One Joseph Ballard, of Andover, whose wife was ill, sent to Salem for some of those accusers, to tell him who afflicted his wife; others did the like. Horse and man were sent from several places to fetch those accusers who had the spectral sight, that they might thereby tell who afflicted those that were any way ill. When these came into any place where such were, usually they fell into a fit; after which, being asked who it was that afflicted the person. they would for the most part name one who they said sat on the head and another that sat on the lower part of the afflicted. More than fifty people of Andover were thus complained of for afflicting their neighbours. Here it was that many accused themselves of riding upon poles through the air; many parents believed their children to be witches, and many husbands their wives."

At Andover the accusations multiplied so rapidly, that a justice of the peace of that place named Dudley Bradstreet, after committing thirty or forty, became alarmed, and refused to grant any more warrants. The afflicted now cried upon the justice and his wife ; they said that he had killed nine persons by witchcraft, and they declared that they saw the ghosts of the murdered people hovering about him. Justice Bradstreet saw how things were going, and judged it advisable to make his escape. Soon after this, they cried out against a gentleman of Boston, who immediately obtained a writ of arrest against his accusers on a charge of defamation, and laid his damages at a thousand pounds. This bold proceeding did more than anything else to stop the accusations, which from that time began to fall into discredit. Some of those who had confessed, retracted their confessions. On the 3rd of January, 1693, in the superior court of Salem, of fifty-six bills of indictment containing charges of this kind, thirty were ignored, and of the other six-and-twenty, when they were put on their trial, three only were found guilty. At the end of January, seven who lay under condemnation were reprieved.

About the month of April governor Phipps was recalled, and he signalised his departure by setting at liberty all the prisoners charged with witchcraft. They amounted at this time to about a hundred and fifty, of whom fifty had confessed themselves witches. About two hundred more had been accused, who were not yet placed under arrest. The people of Salem expected the worse consequences from this, as they considered it, mistaken leniency, and they were astonished to find that the moment the accusations were discountenanced, there were no more afflicted—the witchcraft ceased. People in general now began to reflect, were convinced of their error, and lamented it. Seized with remorse, their resentment fell first and principally on Mr. Paris, the minister of Salem village, with whom the accusations commenced; many of his congregation withdrew from his communion, and they drew up articles against him. The disputes between the minister and his people lasted two or three years, and although he acknowledged his mistakes and professed that he should be far from acting again upon the same principles, they were not satisfied till he left them. In a strong remonstrance against him they enumerated the setting afloat of these accusations as his principal crime, and declared their opinion that, "by these practices and principles, he had been the beginner and precursor of the sorest afflictions, not to this village only, but to this whole country, that did ever befall them."

Some persons persisted in believing in the witchcraft, and in Satan's active agency in this affair, though they acknowledged that the accusations had been carried too far; and among these were the two Mathers. Before the conclusion of the year an opportunity occurred for reviving the subject. On the 10th of September, 1693, a girl at Boston, named Margaret Rule, was seized with convulsions, and stated that she was visited by eight spectres, some of which she recognized as being those of persons she knew. Cotton Mather visited her, professed himself convinced of the truth of her statement, and would soon have raised up a new flame. But there was an influential and intelligent merchant of Boston, named Robert Calef, who also visited Margaret Rule, and who formed a totally different opinion to that expressed by Cotton Mather, whose doctrine of witchcraft he controverted, and he gained the better in the argument. From a book published by Calef, published at Boston under the title of "More Wonders of the Invisible World," we obtain the best and most intelligible account of the extraordinary proceedings at Salem and Andover.

From this time we hear no more of witches in New England. Ashamed of their weakness, the people of Salem seem to have brooded over their past folly for several years. On the 17th of December, 1696, a fast was proclaimed, one of the reasons for which was, "That God would show us what we knew not, and help us wherein we have done amiss to do so no more; and especially that whatever mistakes on either hand had been fallen into, either by the body of this people, or any orders of men, referring to the late tragedy raised among us by Satan and his instruments through the awful judgment of God, he would humble us therefore, and pardon all the errors of his servants." At this fast one of the judges stood up to declare publicly his remorse for the part he had taken in these lamented transactions. The jurors signed a paper also proclaiming their repentance, and ending with the declaration, "that we justly fear that we were sadly deluded and mistaken, for which we are much disquieted and distressed in our minds; and do therefore humbly beg forgiveness, first of God, for Christ's sake, for this our error; and pray that God would not impute the guilt of it to ourselves or others; and we also pray that we may be considered candidly, and aright, by the living sufferers, as being then under the power of a strong and general delusion, utterly unacquainted with, and not experienced in, matters of that nature." The delusion was further exposed by voluntary confessions of those who had previously confessed themselves witches, which they declared they had done only to save their lives. The following declaration, signed by several of the women who had acted as accusers, no doubt acquaints us with the secret of many of the witch-delusions in England. "Joseph Ballard of Andover's wife being sick," say they, "he either from himself, or the advice of others, fetched two of the persons called the afflicted persons from Salem village to Andover, which was the cause of that dreadful calamity which befel us at Andover. We were blindfolded, and our hands were laid on the afflicted persons, they being in their fits, and falling into these fits at our coming into their presence, and then they said that we were guilty of afflicting them, whereupon we were all seized as prisoners by a warrant from the justice of peace, and forthwith carried to Salem; and by reason of that sudden surprisal, we knowing ourselves altogether innocent of that crime, we were all exceedingly astonished, and amazed, and consternated, and affrighted out of our reason; and our dearest relations seeing us in that dreadful condition, and knowing our great danger, they, out of tender love and pity, persuaded us to confess what we did confess; and, indeed, that confession was no other than what was suggested to us by some gentlemen, they telling us that we were witches, and they knew it, and we knew it, and they knew that we knew it, which made us think that we were so, and our understanding, and our reason, and our faculties being almost gone, we were not capable of judging of our condition; as also the hard measures they used with us rendered us incapable of making any defence, but we said anything and everything they desired, and most of what we said was, in fact, but a consenting to what they said."

CHAPTER XXXII.

CONCLUSION.

The narrative of Satan's doings in New England may be looked upon as an appropriate conclusion to a historical sketch of the prosecutions for witchcraft. We see here combined in one short act the sudden force exercised by the superstition over the popular mind, the disasters to which it led, and the final triumph of good sense and honest feelings in dispelling the illusion. It was that good sense which was now overcoming popular ignorance in most of the countries of Europe.

In France, where in the earlier period the persecution of witches was most intense, the same circumstances had not existed to keep it up as in England and Scotland. With the exception of several cases of pretended possession, intrigues of the Catholic priesthood, who thus practised on the credulity of the populace, which occurred at this time, we hear little of witchcraft in France during the latter half of the seventeenth century. The belief still existed among the peasantry, who, when blights and diseases fell upon their produce or stock unexpectedly, were too apt to ascribe it to such agency, but they were discountenanced by the better classes of society. In 1672, a great number of shepherds were arrested in Normandy, on a charge of witchcraft, and prosecuted before the parliament of Rouen; but when the king was informed of it, he at once put a stop to the process by an order of council, directing the prisoners to be set at liberty. This proceeding on the part of the king had the immediate effect *de faire taire le demon!* Yet a similar accusation was brought against the shepherds of Brie in 1691.

Still the belief existed in sufficient force to admit of its being used as an instrument for indulging personal animosity, and that between a minister of the crown and one of the most distinguished and celebrated of the maréchals of Louis XIV. There lived at Paris four men who professed to be magicians, and pretended to be able to raise the devil at will; they told people's fortunes, helped them to recover things stolen or lost, and sold powders and unguents. Their names were Lavoisin, Lavigoureux and his brother, the latter a priest, and another priest named Lesage. In the year 1680 these men were arrested, and as the crimes in which they and many others were involved had usually been punished by burning, a tribunal was appointed to sit at the Arsenal, under the title of a *chambre ardente*. Although few fires were eventually lit by the judgments of this court, a great number of persons were more or less compromised, and many of them belonging to the highest classes of society. Among them were two nieces of cardinal Mazarin; the countess of Soissons, who was cited before this tribunal, was so far implicated, that she was obliged to leave Paris and retire to Brussels. Most of these personages were probably led to consult the conjurers more by curiosity than from any other motive, and the whole matter was made a subject of ridicule and raillerie in the fashionable world. When the duchess of Bouillon, who was one of the ladies implicated in this affair, was examined before the *chambre ardente*, one of the judges, la Reynie, who was not remarkable for beauty or politeness, asked her if she had seen the devil, and what he was like; she replied, "Yes, I see him now; he is *fort laid et fort vilain*, and appears in the disguise of a conseiller d'état!"

It appears that the maréchal de Luxembourg had employed Lesage to draw his horoscope, and thus the name of this great man was introduced into the process. Louvois was at that time prime minister of France, and having some cause of hostility against the maréchal, he determined to make this an opportunity for indulging his animosity, and the maréchal de Luxembourg was thrown into the Bastille. It appears that one of the maréchal's agents named Bonard had lost some papers of consequence belonging to his employer, and that, unable to discoved any traces of them, he had consulted the priest Lesage, who instructed him how he was to visit the churches, recite psalms, and make confessions. Bonard did all this, but still he was as far from recovering his papers as ever. Then Lesage told him that a girl named Dupin knew something about them, and, under his directions, Bonard performed a conjuration to force her to bring them back, but without effect. Upon this it appears that Bonard had obtained the maréchal's signature to a paper which turned out to be a compact with Satan, and which was produced at the trial. It would seem that the maréchal had been concerned in some intrigue with the girl Dupin. Lesage deposed that the maréchal had addressed himself to him, and through him to the devil, to effect the death of this girl, who perhaps had been murdered, for men were brought forward who confessed themselves the assassins, and who declared that, by order of the maréchal de Luxembourg, they had cut her in pieces and thrown the fragments into the river. The maréchal was confronted with Lesage, and with another priest and conjurer named Davaux, with whom he was accused of practising sorcery, for the purpose of killing more than one person. But he rebutted all these and other charges with indignation, and, instead of bringing him to a trial, Louvois caused him to be kept in close confinement, and took care that the process should be carried on as slowly as possible. It was only after fourteen months of imprisonment that he was set at liberty; the accusations were dropped without any judgment, and he was restored to favour and to the high offices he had previously held. The four magicians were less fortunate, for they had all been burnt.

France had, however, the honour of leading the way in discouraging prosecutions of this kind. The irreligion and scepticism of the court of Charles II. contributed no doubt towards producing the same effect in England, where many, who before ventured only to doubt, now hesitated not to treat the subject with ridicule. Although works like those of Baxter and Glanvill had still their weight with many people, yet, in the controversy which was now carried on upon this subject through the instrumentality of the press, those who wrote against the popular creed had certainly the best of the argument. Still it happened from their form and character that the books written to expose the absurdity of the belief in sorcery, were restricted in their circulation to the more educated classes, while popular tracts in defence of witchcraft, and collections of cases, were printed in a cheaper form, and widely distributed among that class in society where the belief was most firmly rooted. The effect of these popular publications has continued in some districts down to the present day Thus the press, the natural tendency of which was to enlighten mankind, was made to increase ignorance by pandering to the superstitions of the multitude.

An instance of the continuance of the belief which had in former times produced the sacrifice of so much human life, occurred at the beginning of the year 1712, in the village of Walkern, in the north of the county of Hertford. There was a poor woman in that town named Jane Wenham, who, it appears, had for some time been looked upon by the more ignorant of her neighbours as a witch. When the horses or cattle of the farmers of that parish died, they usually ascribed their losses to this woman's sorcery. This was particularly the case with a farmer named John Chapman, one of whose labourers, named Matthew Gilson, examined on the fourteenth of February, declared "that on New Year's day last past, he carrying straw upon a fork from Mrs. Gardiner's barn, met Jane Wenham, who asked him for some straw, which he refused to give her; then she said she would take some, and accordingly took some away from this informant. And further this informant saith, that on the 29th of January last, when this informant was threshing in the barn of his master John Chapman, an old woman in a riding-hood or cloak, he knows not which, came to the barn door, and asked him for a pennyworth of straw; he told her he could give her none, and she went away muttering. And this informant saith, that after the woman was gone he was not able to work, but ran out of the barn as far as a place called Munder's-hill, (which was above three miles from Walkern,) and asked at a house there for a pennyworth of straw, and they refused to give him any; he went further to some dung-heaps, and took some straw from thence, and pulled off his shirt, and brought it home in his shirt; he knows not what moved him to this, but says he was forced to it he knows not how." Another witness declared that he saw Matthew Gilson returning with the straw in his shirt; that he moved along at a great pace, and that instead of passing over a bridge, he walked straight through the water.

John Chapman conceived now that his suspicions were fully verified, and meeting Jane Wenham soon afterwards, he applied to her in anger several offensive epithets, of which that of "witch" was the least opprobrious. On the 9th of February, Jane Wenham made her complaint to sir Henry Chauncy, who was a magistrate, and obtained a warrant against Chapman for defamation. In the sequel, at the recommendation of this magistrate, the quarrel between Jane Wenham and the farmer was referred to the decision of the minister of Walkern, the Rev. Mr. Gardiner, who appears to have spoken somewhat harshly to the woman, advising her to live more peaceably with her neighbours, and condemned Chapman to pay her one shilling.

As far as we can see, Jane Wenham took the most sensible course to retrieve herself from the imputation of being a witch; but Mr. Gardiner, although a clergyman of the church of England, was as firm a believer in witchcraft as farmer Chapman, and he fancied that he had provoked the poor woman by not giving her the justice she expected. His judgment was delivered in the kitchen of the parsonage-house, where a maid-servant, between sixteen and seventeen years of age, named Anne Thorn, was sitting by the fire-side, who had put her knee out the evening before, and had just had it set. It appears that the supposed witch resolved to take vengeance on this poor girl for the offence committed by her master. Jane Wenham and Chapman were gone, and Mr. Gardiner had entered the parlour to his wife, accompanied by a neighbour named Bragge. These three persons deposed at the subsequent trial, that "Mr. Gardiner had not been in the parlour with his wife and Mr. Bragge above six or seven minutes at most since he left Anne Thorn sitting by the fire, when he heard a strange yelling noise in the kitchen, and when he went out and found this Anne Thorn stripped to her shirt sleeves, howling and wringing her hands in a dismal manner, and speechless, he calling out, Mrs. Gardiner and Mr. Bragge came immediately to him. Mrs. Gardiner seeing her servant in that sad condition, asked her what was the matter with her. She not being able to speak, pointed earnestly at a bundle which lay at her feet, which Mrs. Gardiner took up and unpinned, and found it to be the girl's gown and apron, and a parcel of oaken twigs with dead leaves wrapt up therein. As soon as this bundle was opened, Anne Thorn began to speak, crying out, 'I'm ruined and undone;' and after she had a little recovered herself, gave the following relation of what had befallen her. She said when she was left alone she found a strange roaming in her hand (I use her own expressions); her mind ran upon Jane Wenham, and she thought she must run some whither; that accordingly she ran up the close, but looked back several times at the house, thinking she should never see it more; that she climbed over a five-bar gate, and ran along the highway up à hill; that there she met two of John Chapman's men, one of whom took hold of her hand, saying, she should go with them; but she was forced away from them, not being able to speak, either to them, or to one Daniel Chapman, whom, she said, she met on horseback, and would fain have spoken to him, but could not; then she made her way towards Cromer, as far as a place called

Hockney-lane, where she looked behind her, and saw a little old woman muffled in a riding-hood, who asked her whither she was going. She answered, to Cromer to fetch some sticks to make her a fire; the old woman told her there were now no sticks at Cromer, and bade her go to that oak-tree, and pluck some from thence, which she did, and laid them upon the ground. The old woman bade her pull off her gown and apron, and wrap the sticks in them, and asked her whether she had e'er a pin. Upon her answering she had none, the old woman gave her a large crooked pin, bade her pin up her bundle, and then vanished away; after which she ran home with her bundle of sticks, and sat down in the kitchen stript, as Mr. Gardiner found her. This is the substance of what she related, upon which Mrs. Gardiner cried out, 'The girl has been in the same condition with Chapman's man; but we will burn the witch;' alluding to a received notion, that when the thing bewitched is burned the witch is forced to come in; accordingly she took the sticks, together with the pin, and threw them into the fire. Immediately, in the instant that the sticks were flaming, Jane Wenham came into the room, and inquired for Elizabeth, the mother of Anne Thorn, saying she had an errand to do to her from Ardley Bury, (sir Henry Chauncy's house,) to wit, that she must go thither to wash the next day. Now this mother Thorn had been in the house all the time that Jane Wenham was there with John Chapman, and heard nothing of it, and was then gone home. Mrs. Gardiner bad Jane Wenham go to Elizabeth Thorn, and tell her there was work enough for her there; on which she departed. And upon inquiry made afterwards, it was found that she never was ordered to deliver any such errand from Ardley Bury."

Here was an excellent groundwork for an accusation of witchcraft. Chapman's two men, and the horseman, deposed to meeting Anne Thorne on the road, as she described; and others of Jane Wenham's enemies testified that other people had been bewitched by her. All received encouragement from the readiness of the clergyman to promote the prosecution, and a warrant was obtained from sir Henry Chauncy to arrest the supposed witch. The examinations were taken before sir Henry at Ardley Bury, and he directed four women to search Jane Wenham's body for marks, but none were found. Next day the examination was continued, and the evidence of the Gardiners was taken. Jane Wenham expressed her horror of being sent to jail, earnestly protested her innocence, entreating Mrs. Gardiner not to swear against her, and offering to submit to trial by swimming in the water. Sir Henry, who seems to have yielded to the prejudices of the prosecutors in most things, refused to allow of this mode of trial. But the vicar of Ardley, no less superstitious than the rector of Walkern, tried her with the Lord's Prayer, which she repeated incorrectly, and he subsequently induced her, by fright and torment, to confess that she was a witch and had intercourse with Satan, and to accuse three women of Walkern as her confederates, who were also put under arrest.

Jane Wenham was now committed, and her trial came on on the 4th of March before justice Powell, when no less than sixteen witnesses, among whom were three clergymen, were heard against the prisoner. The lawyers refused to draw up the indictment for any other charge than that of "conversing with the devil in the form of a cat," which, to the great anger of the prosecutors, threw an air of ridicule over the whole proceeding. Yet upon this indictment, in spite of her declarations of innocence, the Hertfordshire jury found her guilty. The judge was obliged to pronounce sentence of death, as a matter of form; but he subsequently obtained her pardon, and a gentleman of more enlightened mind than the people of Walkern, Colonel Plummer, of Gilston in the same county, took her under his protection, and placed her in a cottage near his own house, where she passed the rest of her life in a quiet inoffensive manner.

Few events of this kind have caused a greater sensation than the case of Jane Wenham. The report of the trial passed through several editions in a few days, and gave rise to a very bitter controversy, in which several clergymen joined in the cry against the innocent victim. The dispute seems to have become in some degree identified with the bitter animosities then existing between the church and the dissenters—it was just the time when the intolerant party, with their hero Sacheverell, had gained the upper hand, and they seemed not unwilling to recall into force even the old degrading belief in witchcraft if they could make it an instrument for effecting their purposes. But the most important result of this trial, and the controversy to which it gave rise, was the publication, two or three years afterwards, of the "Historical Essay concerning Witchcraft," by the king's chaplain in ordinary, Dr. Francis Hutchinson. This book may be considered as the last blow at witchcraft, which from this time found credit only among the most ignorant part of the population.

The case of Jane Wenham is the last instance of a witch being condemed by the verdict of an English jury. When the prosecutors were no longer listened to in courts of justice, they either ceased to find objects of pursuit, or they appealed for judgment to the passions of the uneducated peasantry. An occurrence of this kind, no less brutal than tragical, is said to have led to the final repeal of the witchcraft act. The scene is again laid in Hertfordshire. In the middle of the last century, there lived at Tring in that county a poor man and his wife of the name of Osborne, each about seventy years of age. During the rebellion of forty-five, mother Osborne, as she was popularly called, went to one Butterfield, who kept a dairy at Gubblecot, to beg for some butter-milk, but he told her with great brutality that he had not enough for his hogs. The old woman, provoked by this treatment, went away, telling him that the pretender would soon have him and his hogs too. The connexion with what followed perhaps arose from the popular outcry which had long coupled the pretender with Satan. Some time afterwards, some of Butterfield's calves became distempered, and the ignorant people of the neighbourhood, who had heard the story of the buttermilk, declared that they were bewitched by mother Osborne. In course of time Butterfield left his dairy, and took a public-house in the same village, where, about the beginning of the year 1751, he was troubled with fits, and, although he had been subject to similar fits in former times, these also were now ascribed to mother Osborne. He was persuaded that the doctors could do him no good, and was advised to send for an old woman out of Northamptonshire, a white witch, who had the reputation of being skilful in counteracting the effects of sorcery. This woman confirmed the opinion already afloat of the cause of Butterfield's disorder, and she directed that six men should watch his house day and night, with staves, pitchforks, and other weapons, at the same time hanging something about their necks, which she said was a charm to secure them from being bewitched themselves. This produced, as might be expected, no effect, and the accusation might have dropped; but some persons, desirous of collecting together a large number of persons with a lucrative object, caused notice to be given at several of the market-towns around that witches were to be tried by ducking at Longmarston on the 22nd of April. The consequence was that a vast concourse of people assembled at Tring on the day announced. The parish officers had removed the old couple from the workhouse into the church, for security; upon which the mob, after searching in vain the workhouse, and even looking into the salt-box to see if the witch had transformed herself into any diminutive form that could be concealed there, exhibited their disappointment in breaking the windows, pulling down the pales, and demolishing a part of the house. They then seized upon the governor, and collecting together a quantity of straw, threatened to drown him and set fire to the town unless the unfortunate couple were delivered up to them. Fear at length induced the parish officers to yield, and the two wretches were stripped stark naked by the mob, their thumbs tied to their toes, and thus, each wrapped in a loose sheet, they were dragged two miles and thrown into a muddy stream. A chimney-sweeper named Colley, one of the ringleaders, seeing that the poor woman did not sink, went into the pond and turned her over several times with a stick, by which her body slipped out of the sheet and was exposed naked. In this condition, and half choaked with mud, she was thrown on the bank, and there kicked and beaten till she expired. Her husband died also of the injuries he had received. The man who had superintended these brutal proceedings went round to the crowd collecting money for the amusement he had afforded them! The coroner's inquest brought a verdict of wilful murder against several persons by name, but the only one brought to justice was the sweep Colley, who was executed, and afterwards hung in chains, for the murder of Ruth Osborne.

From this time witchcraft has attracted no attention in England, except as a vulgar superstition in some rude localities where the schoolmaster had not yet penetrated. In Scotland the struggle between superstition and common sense continued longer and was more obstinate. A few of the later cases of Scottish sorcery were collected by George Sinclair, in a little book published in the beginning of the last century, under the title of "Satan's Invisible World Discovered." One or two of these will serve to show the form which witchcraft assumed in Scotland at the time when it was falling into discredit among men of education.

There was a man named Sandie Hunter who called himself Sandie Hamilton, but was better known by the nickname of Hattaraick, given him, it seems, by the devil. He was first a "noltherd" in East Lothian, but he had assumed the character of a conjuror, curing men and beasts by spells and charms. "His charms sometimes succeeded, sometimes not." However, the extent of Hattaraick's practice seems to have raised the jealousy of Satan. "On a day herding his kine upon a hill-side in the summer-time, the devil came to him in the form of a medeciner, and said, 'Sandie, you have too long followed my trade, and never acknowledged me for your master; you must now take with me, and be my servant, and I will make you more perfect in your calling.' Whereupon the man gave up himself to the devil, and received his mark, with this new name. After this he grew very famous through the country, for his charming, and curing of diseases in men and beasts, and turned a vagrant fellow, like a jockey, gaining meal and flesh and money by his charms; such was the ignorance of many at the time, whatever house he came to, none durst refuse Hattaraick an alms, rather for his ill than his good. One day he came to the yait (*gate*) of Samuelston, when some friends after dinner were going to horse, a young gentleman, brother to the lady, seeing him, switched him about the ears, saying, 'You warlock cairle, what have you to do here?' Whereupon the fellow goes away grumbling, and was overheard say, 'You shall dear buy this ere it be long.' This was *damnum minatum*. The young gentleman conveyed his friends a way off, and came home that way again, where he supped. After supper, taking his horse, and crossing Tyne water to go home, he rode through a shady piece of haugh, commonly called Cotters, and the evening being somewhat dark, he met with some persons there that begat a dreadful consternation in him, which, for the most part, he would never reveal. This was *malum secutum*. When he came home, the servants observed terror and fear in his countenance. The next day he became distracted, and was bound for several days. His sister, the lady Samuelston, hearing of it, was heard say, 'Surely that knave Hattaraick is the cause of his trouble, call for him in all haste.' When he had come to her, 'Sandie,' said she, 'what is this you have done to my brother William?' 'I told him,' says he, 'I should make him repent his striking of me at the yait lately.' She giving the rogue fair words, and promising him his pock full of meal, with beef and cheese, persuaded the fellow to cure him again. He undertook the business, 'but I must first,' says he, 'have one of his sarks;' which was soon gotten. What pranks he played with it cannot be known; but within a short while the gentleman recovered his health.

When Hattaraick came to receive his wages, he told the lady, 'Your brother William shall quickly go off the country, but shall never return.' She knowing the fellow's prophecies to hold true, caused her brother to make a disposition to her of all his patrimony, to the defrauding of his younger brother George. After that this warlock had abused the country for a long time, he was at last apprehended at Dunbar, and brought into Edinburgh, and burnt upon the castle hill."

Another extraordinary case occurred about the end of August, 1696. One Christian Shaw, the daughter of John Shaw of Bargarran, in the shire of Renfrew, about eleven years of age, perceiving one of the maids of the house, named Catharine Campbell, to steal and drink some milk, she told her mother of it. Whereupon the maid, "being of a proud and revengeful humour, and a great curser and swearer, did, in a great rage, thrice imprecate the curse of God upon the child, and utter these words, 'the devil harle your soul through hell!' On Friday following, one Agnes Nasmith came to Bargarran's house, where she asked the said Christian, how the lady and young child was? and how old the young child was? To which Christian replied, 'What do I know?' Then Agnes asked, how herself did, and how old she was? To which she answered that she was well, and in the eleventh year of age. On Saturday night thereafter, the child went to bed in good health; but so soon as she was asleep, she began to cry, 'Help, help;' and did fly over the resting-bed where she was lying, with such violence, that her brains had been dashed out, if a woman had not broken the force of the child's motion, and remained as if she had been dead, for the space of half an hour. After this she was troubled with sore pains, except in some short intervals, and when any of the people present touched any part of her body, she did cry and screech with such vehemence, as if they had been killing her, but would not speak. Some days thereafter she fell a crying that Catharine Campbell and Agnes Nasmith were cutting her side and other parts of her body. In this condition she continued a month, with some variation, both as to the fits and intervals. She did thrust out of her mouth parcels of hair, some curled, some plaited, some knotted, of different colours, and in large quantities, and likewise coal cinders, which were so hot that they could scarcely be handled. One of which Dr. Brisbane, being by her when she took it out of her mouth, felt to be hotter than any one's body could make it. The girl continued a long time in this condition, till the government began to take notice of it, and gave commission to some honourable gentlemen for the trials of those two, and several others concerned in these practices; and being brought before the judges, two of their accomplices confessed the crime; whereupon they were condemned and executed."

Somewhere about the same time an equally strange affair occurred at the town of Pittenweem in Fife, which may also be told in the words of Sinclair. "Peter Morton, a smith at Pittenweem, being desired by one Beatie Laing to do some work for her, which he refused, excusing himself in respect he had been pre-engaged to serve a ship with nails, within a certain time; so that till he had finished that work, he could not engage in any other; that notwithstanding the said Beatie Laing declared herself dissatisfied, and vowed revenge. The said Peter Morton afterwards being indisposed, coming by the door, saw a small vessel full of water, and a coal of fire 'slockened' in the water; so perceiving an alteration in his health, and remembering Beatie Laing's threatenings, he presently suspects devilry in the matter, and quarels the thing. Thereafter, finding his indisposition growing worse and worse, being tormented and pricked as with bodkins and pins, he openly lays the blame upon witchcraft, and accused Beatie Laing. He continued to be tormented, and she was, by warrant, apprehended, with others in Pittenweem. No natural reason could be given for his distemper, his face and neck being dreadfully distorted, his back prodigiously rising and falling, his belly swelling and falling on a sudden, his joints pliable, and constantly so stiff as no human power could bow them. Beatie Laing and her hellish companions being in custody, were brought to the room where he was, and his face covered, he told his tormentors were in the room, naming them. And though formerly no confession had been made, Beatie Laing confessed her crime, and accused several others as accessories. The said Beatie having confessed her compact with the devil, and using of spells, and particularly her 'slockening' the coal in water, she named her associates in revenge against Peter Morton, viz., Janet Cornfoot, Lillie Wallace, and Lawson, who had framed a picture of wax, and every one of the forenamed persons having put their pin in the picture for torture. They could not tell what had become of the image, but thought the devil had stolen it, whom they had seen in the prison. Beatie Laing likewise said, that one Isobel Adams, a young lass, was also in compact with the devil. This woman was desired to see with Beatie, which she refused; and Beatie let her see a man at the other end of the table, who appeared as a gentleman, and promised her all prosperity in the world; she promised her service to him, and he put his mark on her flesh, which was very painful. She was shortly after ordered to attend the company, to go to one Mac Grigor's house to murder him; he awaking when they were there, and recommending himself to God, they were forced to withdraw. This Isobel Adams appeared ingenuous, and very penitent in her confessions; she said, he who forgave Manasseh's witchcrafts might forgive hers also; and died very penitent, and *to the satisfaction of many.* This Beatie Laing was suspected by her husband, long before she was laid in prison by warrant of the magistrates. The occasion was thus: she said, that she had packs of very good wool, which she instantly sold, and coming home with a black horse which she had with her, they drinking till it was late in the night ere they came home, that man said, "What shall I do with the horse?" She replied, "Cast the bridle on his neck, and you will be quit of him;" and, as her husband thought, the horse flew with a great noise away in the air. They were, by a complaint to the privy council, prosecuted by her majesty's advocate, in 1704, but all set at liberty save one who died in Pittenweem. Beattie Laing died undesired, in her bed, in St. Andrews; all the rest died miserable and violent deaths."

So says Mr. George Sinclair, who has, however, omitted to inform us of the most frightful part of this story. Janet Cornfoot, one of the persons accused, made her escape from prison, but she was recaptured, and brought back to Pittenweem, where, falling into the hands of a ferocious mob, they pelted her with stones, swung her on a rope extended from a ship to the shore, and at length put an end to her sufferings by throwing a door over her as she lay exhausted on the beach, and heaping stones on it till she was pressed to death. This was the woman who, according to Sinclair, "died in Pittenweem." The magistrates had made no attempt to rescue the miserable woman from the hands of her tormentors, and they were now violently attacked in print for their conduct, and were as warmly defended by some advocates. The agitation on the subject of the union with England contributed to the impunity with which the murderers escaped. But the controversy it occasioned, joined with the horror which such a barbarous outrage excited, tended more than anything else to open people's eyes in Scotland to the absurdity and wickedness of the prosecutions for witchcraft. It required, however, a few more instances, remarkable chiefly for their absurdity, to bring them entirely into discredit. In 1718, a carpenter in the shire of Caithness, named William

Montgomery, was infested at night with cats, which, according to the evidence of his servant-maid, " spoke among themselves," and in a violent attack upon them with every weapon within his reach, he inflicted personal injury to a very considerable extent. Two women were believed to have died in consequence of these injuries, and a third, in a weak state, was imprisoned and compelled to confess not only that she was one of the offending cats, but to declare against a number of her confederates in witchcraft. A century earlier, no doubt this confession would have been fatal to most of the old women in the neighbourhood; but times were changed, and the lord advocate, on being applied to, put a stop to all further proceedings. In 1720, some old women of Calder were imprisoned for certain pretended sorceries exercised on a boy, the son of James lord Torphichen, but the officers of the crown would not proceed to a trial. Yet two years later, a poor woman was burnt as a witch in the county of Sutherland, by order of the sheriff, captain David Ross, of Littledean. This was the last sentence of death for witchcraft that was ever passed in Scotland.

It appears that in Ireland the law against witchcraft has never been repealed, a circumstance that can only be explained on the supposition that since witchcraft began to fall into discredit it has never, or very rarely, been appealed to. In 1711, there occurred a case of witchcraft among the Scottish presbyterians of the island Magee, in Ulster, which excited so much interest, at least among the people of that persuasion, that it has been printed over and over again, the edition I have before me bearing date in 1822, upwards of a hundred years after that of the event it commemorates. There is something peculiarly Irish in the story—it is a house, or rather a family, haunted by a spirit sent by witches. Mrs. Anne Hattridge was the widow of the presbyterian minister of the district just mentioned, and was living with her son James Hattridge. At the beginning of September, 1710, the house began to be disturbed by an invisible visitor, who threw stones and turf about, pulled the pillows and bedclothes off the bed, and played a variety of other disagreeable pranks. Once it appeared in the shape of a cat, which they killed and threw into the yard, but when they looked for the body it had disappeared. "There was little remarkable for several days after, unless it were that her cane would be taken away, and be missing several days together: until the 11th of December, 1710, when the aforesaid Mrs. Hattridge was sitting at the kitchen-fire, in the evening, before daylight-going, a little boy (as she and the servants supposed) came in and sat down beside her, having an old black bonnet on his head, with short black hair, a half-worn blanket about him, trailing on the ground behind him, and a torn black vest under it. He seemed to be about ten or twelve years old, but he still covered his face, holding his arm with a piece of the blanket before it. She desired to see his face, but he took no notice of her. Then she asked him several questions; viz. if he was cold or hungry? if he would have any meat? where he came from, and whither he was going? To which he made no answer, but getting up, danced very nimbly, leaping higher than usual, and then ran out of the house as far as the end of the garden, and sometimes into the cow-house, the servants running after him to see where he would go, but soon lost sight of him; but when they returned, he would be close after them in the house, which he did above a dozen times. At last, the little girl seeing her master's dog coming in, said, 'Now my master is coming, he will take a course with this troublesome creature;' upon which he immediately went away, and troubled them no more till the month of February, 1711."

On the 11th of February, a volume of sermons that Mrs. Hattridge was reading suddenly disappeared in an unaccountable manner. "Next day, the apparition formerly mentioned, came to the house, and after having broken a quarry of glass in the kitchen-window, on the side of the house next the garden, he thrust in his arm with the book in his hand open, and entered into a conference with a girl of the house, called Margaret Spear, the particulars of which are as follows:—

"*Apparition.* Do you want a book?

"*Girl.* No.

"*Appar.* How come you to lie? for this is the book which the old gentlewoman wanted (*lost*) yesterday.

"*Girl.* How came you by it?

"*Appar.* I went down quietly to the parlour, when you were all in the kitchen, and found it lying upon a shelf, with a Bible and a pair of spectacles.

"*Girl.* How came it that you did not take the Bible too?

"*Appar.* It was too heavy to carry.

"*Girl.* Will you give it back? for my mistress can't want it any longer.

"*Appar.* No, she shall never get it again.

"*Girl.* Can you read on it?

"*Appar.* Yes.

"*Girl.* Who taught you?

"*Appar.* The devil taught me.

"*Girl.* The Lord bless me from thee! thou hast got ill lear (*learning*).

"*Appar.* Aye, bless yourself twenty times, but that shall not save you.

"*Girl.* What will you do to us? (Mr. Hattridge's son, about eight years of age, was with her at the time.)

"Upon which it pulled out a sword and thrust it in at the window, and said it would kill all in the house with that sword; at which the child said, 'Meg, let us go into the room and bar the door, for fear it should kill us;' which they did; then it jeered them, saying, 'Now you think you are safe enough, but I'll get in yet.'

"*Girl.* What way? for we have the street-door shut.

"*Appar.* I can come in by the least hole in the house, like a cat or mouse, for the devil can make me anything I please.

"*Girl.* God bless me from thee, for thou art no earthly creature if you can do that.

"Upon which it took up a stone of considerable bigness, and threw it in at the parlour-window, which upon trial could not be put out at the same place, and then went away for a little time A little after, the girl and one of the children came out of the parlour to the kitchen, and looking out of the window, saw the apparition catching a turkey-cock, which he threw over his shoulder, holding him by the tail; and the cock making a great sputter with his feet, the book before-mentioned was, as they thought, spurred out of the loop of the blanket he had about him: but he, taking no notice, run along the side of the house, and leapt, with the cock on his back, over a wall at the west-end of the garden, leaping a great deal higher than the wall. The girl, thinking this a good opportunity to get the book, told Mrs. Hattridge; upon which she, with the girl and a little boy, went to the garden, and got the book, without any harm done to it. At the same time they looked about the garden and fields adjoining, but could see nobody. There was no other person about the house at that time except children. A little after, the girl went to the window in the parlour, and looking out of the casement, saw the apparition again, with the turkey-cock lying on its back before him, he endeavouring to get his sword drawn to kill it, as she apprehended, but the cock got away. It then looked for the book in the loop of the blanket, and missing it, as she apprehended, threw away the blanket, and ran nimbly up and down upon the search for it. A little after, it came back with a club, and broke the glass of the side window in the parlour, and then went to the end window, through which the girl was looking, and pulled off the casement glass, (not leaving one whole quarry in it,) and left it lying on the south side of the garden. A little after, the girl ventured to look out of the broken window, and saw it as it were digging near the end of the house with the sword. She asked what he was doing? He answered, 'Making a grave.'

"*Girl.* For whom?

"*Appar.* For a corpse which will come out of this house very soon.

"*Girl.* Who will it be?

"*Appar.* I'll not tell you that yet. Is your master at home?

"*Girl.* Yes.

"*Appar.* How can you lie? he is abroad, and is dead fourteen days ago.

"*Girl.* Of what sickness did he die?

"*Appar.* I'll not tell you that.

"After this it went over the hedge, as if it had been a bird flying. Some persons of the neighbourhood came in immediately after, and being told, made a diligent search, but nothing could be seen. Thus it continued from eight in the morning till two or three in the afternoon, throwing a great many stones, turf, etc., in at the windows, to the great terror of those in the house."

Not long after this old Mrs. Hattridge was taken ill, and died. But the spirit still haunted the house, and tormented a young lady, a relative of the family, who had come to live there. Mary Dunbar, for this was her name, was seized with a strange disease on the 28th of February, accompanied with fits, in the course of which she had the spectral vision, as it was called, of certain women of the neighbourhood, who she said, had sent thither the tormenting spirit. All the other symptoms usually exhibited by persons bewitched followed in due course, and several persons whom she accused in her trances were taken into custody and imprisoned at Carrickfergus to await their trial. The jury brought them in guilty, but they appear not to have been executed.

From this time, in Europe at least, sorcery and magic hold no longer a place in the history of mankind. The magician disappeared more rapidly than the witch, because he belonged to the class of society in which the progress of intelligence was more decided; but we have seen that, as the agitation which brought it into importance subsided, and it could no longer be made a useful instrument in political or religious warfare, sorcery became more trivial and ridiculous in its details, until it was discarded even among the vulgar.

THE END.

835167

Printed in Great Britain by
Amazon.co.uk, Ltd.,
Marston Gate.